I0836877

THE

LAYMAN'S BREVIARY,

OR

MEDITATIONS FOR EVERY DAY IN THE YEAR.

FROM THE GERMAN OF LEOPOLD SCHEFER.

BY C. T. BROOKS.

BOSTON:
ROBERTS BROTHERS.
1867.

UNIVERSITY PRESS: WELCH, BIGELOW, & CO.,
CAMBRIDGE.

PREFACE.

Gottlieb Leopold Immanuel Schefer, the son of a physician, was born at Muskau, in Germany, in 1784, and at an early age, by his musical and poetic talents, attracted the notice of the celebrated Prince Pückler-Muskau, to whom, in 1813, he became private Secretary, and with whom he travelled through Italy and the Greek Islands, and acquired the stimulus, the subjects, and the plans for many of his voluminous works of fiction in prose and verse. From 1825 to 1829 he published five volumes of "novels"; from 1831 to 1835, four more; and five volumes of "little romances" from 1837 to 1839. "The Layman's Breviary" appeared in 1834, and the "World-Priest" in 1846. His novels number in all seventy-three. A great portion of them turn upon Oriental legends and musical experiences.

Of "The Layman's Breviary," his biographer says: "Returning home from distant travels, full of the poetic picture-wealth of the East, and buried again in German limitations, Schefer found in marriage and home the kernel, the pivot, and centre of gravity of his poetry. The wife, the mother, the child, — the human feeling answering to this triad, formed the point of return and departure for his poetic thought. The title of this collection of poems — standing alone in our literature — was chosen with uncommon felicity. These blooming pictures of Nature, praising the love, goodness, wisdom of the Creator and his work, form in truth a poetical book of devotion for the *Layman* whom the dogma does not satisfy, — a *Breviary* for man."

The edition of the "Breviary" from which this translation was made is the twelfth. For the headings of the several meditations the Translator is responsible.

Such a book as this ought not to be longer unknown among us. The author of the biography prefixed to it says, "Who can doubt that the 'Layman's Breviary' has helped more souls to the understanding of themselves than any other book of German poesy?"

With the hope that many a reader will find such help in this book, and in the belief that it will prove to more and more souls a *Vade Mecum*, the Translator commends his work of love and reverence to the thoughtful, poetic, and pious spirit.

NEWPORT, Sept. 30, 1867.

THE LAYMAN'S BREVIARY.

JANUARY.

JANUARY.

THE LAYMAN'S BREVIARY.

JANUARY.

I.

Harmony of the Universe.

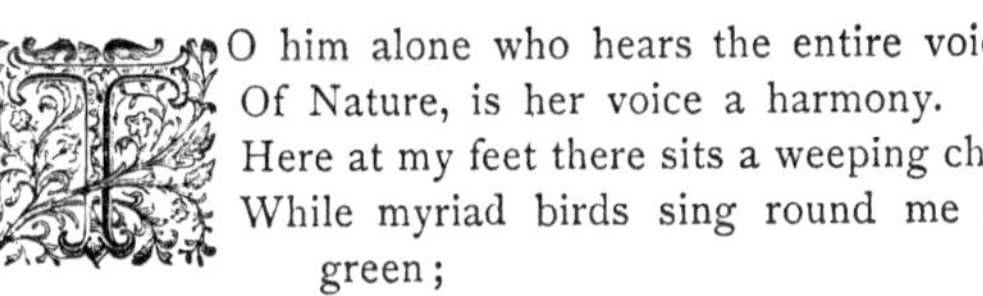

O him alone who hears the entire voice
Of Nature, is her voice a harmony.
Here at my feet there sits a weeping child,
While myriad birds sing round me in the
green;
There, crumbling, stands an old, decrepit oak,
And underneath, young blossom-laden trees
Exchange their friendly nods; here, dirges sound,
Borne from the sleeping chamber of the dead,
And from yon woodland winds a wedding train;
Through the half-open coffin now I see
The dead man's form, — and lo there, through the chink
Two little blooming children wondering gaze;
While overhead, heedless of all below,
The clouds move on their everlasting way.
How in the heart the various feelings blend
In modulation sweet, divine repose!
The soul of the fair Whole is born in me;
From joy and woe alike remote I stand,
Ready to take aright what life may bring.

II.

Contentment with Human Lot.

Whate'er a human lot brings with it will
At last content thee, art thou but content
To be a Man! Thy bliss is possible,
While thou know'st how to seek it. Then take note!
Be a whole man, no more and yet no less,—
So shalt thou live in gladness while thou liv'st,
So shalt thou die in peace, though called in youth,—
For Nature teaches thee, e'en blossoms fall;
So shalt thou die content in late old age,—
For to grow old is likewise laid on us,—
Knowing that thou shalt once be quite forgot,
For of the dead none thinketh in the days
We leave behind,—this too is human lot.
Yet if the fate of mortals touch thy heart,
Then weep! For tears, too, ay, and bitter tears,
And sorrows unassuaged, belong to men.—
Whate'er a human lot brings with it will
At last content thee, art thou but content
To be a man. And therefore, be a Man!

III.

Man the Part and the Whole.

Think not thou dost humiliate thyself,
When thou dost sink into the swarm of men,
And seemest to thyself so small, and say'st:
What have I then of the great universe
That I have left behind? If thou *art* not

The universe, thou canst enjoy it still,
Canst fill with it the chalice of thy breast,
As thine eye takes in all the stars. Behold,
Thou art a man, yea, all that thou canst be;
Thy wishes sought to cheat thee of thyself.
Then hence, thy dreams! Whatever thou canst think,
That thing thou art thyself, or hast, thyself,
Created it, though 't were the beauteous Gods.

IV.

The Past is secure.

Hold thou the past as what has won itself!
That, when thy dear ones die, when thou thyself
Art called to die, and naught is left of thee,
Thou shalt not say, — For what, then, have I lived?
'T is gone! I am as I had ne'er been born!
Think'st thou that all the dead have lived in vain,
Who once were walking on the holy earth?
That Heaven in vain moved round before their eyes?
That Earth in vain put on her loveliness?
Because they are not, have they never been?
Art *thou* not, then? Wilt thou, one day, not be?
Then are the dead in truth as good as thou,
And rich as thou will be one day the unborn,
Just as to them thou wast one time unborn,
Whom thou, thyself, now living, callest dead.

V.

Stand in thy Lot.

Hard is it to be joyous on the earth!
Now thou art told: A sick man here lies low;

And now in silence one is borne out dead.
Who should not feel, himself, another's woe?
Who will not one day meet another's fate?
Thou too wilt meet it. But it comes to each
In his appointed time; for, one by one,
As they appear, do men receive their gifts
From the bestowing Gods. To-day brings death
To this one, and to that one his first day;
This one still smiles, while in the other's eyes
Tears are already standing. Let not then
That which befalleth others trouble so
Thy mind, — but calmly stand in thine own lot!

VI.

Hope, the great Physician.

Does any grief prey on thee, first remove
Its cause, then will thy grief, too, disappear.
Only the past admits no longer help.
But for the present evil there is still,
And always, a physician; then, so long
As sorrow lasts, let hope last! mortal man
Can know no higher bliss than Hope, sweet Hope!

VII.

Hope gives Courage and Victory.

When one draws near to thee bowed down, and says:
"Friend, dry thy tears and cease thy sad lament!
Thou wilt one day in fields of light above,
Where falls no tear, forever live in bliss!" —
And at the word thou wip'st thy weeping eyes,

Liftest thy head and look'st on him with love,—
I pray, what has the man then given thee?
Is thy misfortune, therefore, less? No whit!
Must thou not therefore die? 'T is plain thou must!
See then, he gave thee nothing, only Hope,
And lo, Hope gives thee Courage, nothing more.
Courage to suffer death and misery
All craven dreamers teacheth thee to scorn,
Uplifts thee to the proper sphere of man,
And crowneth thee with manhood's noble worth.

VIII.

Loneliness on the Death of a Friend.

No joy of life knows he who still fears death;
And yet it is not human not to shun it.
Here dies a mortal;—What has Nature lost?
Her thousand children still can comfort her,
And her eternal stars. And lo, the heavens
Still sparkle gayly as before! The moon
Has met no loss! She, too, shines on and smiles.
But ah, the man who died, he was my friend!
Poor I find no such friend on earth again.
And therefore do I weep to the bright heavens,
And to the moon who smiles there,—without friend!

IX.

Nature teaches calm Views of Death.

That which is common, that which every day
And in all places silently goes on,
Cannot be much, though it were death itself.

Then entertain not too great hope of death;
It is a common link in Nature's chain.
Yet what is natural is never mean;
It is a something holy and divine;
Then cherish not too slight a hope of death,
To whom e'en Nature calmly offers up,
Perhaps e'en joyfully, her fairest things —
Even as Nature ever joys and mourns —
In silence. So be thou in silence glad.

X.

Regenerating Influence of Sorrow.

And this too I myself have learned of man!
When Sorrow lays on him her wintry hand,
Man takes the semblance of a chrysalis;
He shrinks and quivers at the slightest touch,
And hovers, through long moons, in still suspense;
And only a thin thread attaches him
To earthly life! But lo! at length his grief
Has grown by slow degrees a coat of mail,
Fast woven round him, and so cased about,
He nourishes and fashions to himself
From the materials of his earlier state,
Of all their earthly grossness purified,
His silently transfigured soul, renews
His youth and ripens toward a higher nature,
And soars, with pinions never known before,
A fair new creature, into a new world.

XI.

Whom God loveth He chasteneth.

This thing mine eyes see clearly, — this the world
In all its course irrefragably shows:
What trouble is, and what it means! It is
The darksome labyrinth whereinto a God
Doth graciously lead men, that every one
May prove his life; that the bad man may know
His wickedness and learn to cease from it, —
And that the good may by experience
Know his good spirit and enjoy it! For
We see the bad come forth from sorrow's cloud
A better, and the good a kindlier man.
And is there one whom God has never tried?
For what one of the children he has made
Loves he not? Child of sorrow, think of this!

XII.

Time and Nature heal Grief.

'T is ever best to grieve with him that grieves,
To loose the pent-up sorrows in his breast,
And to give words* to his mute wilderment,
That he may soon run through the round of woe.
For nothing measureless is meted out,
Nothing immortal, here, to mortal man.
Joy has its limit; pain too has its goal.
And were he fain to weep forever, — still

* "Give sorrow words, &c."
MACB. iv. 3.

His tears dry up at last; though he life-long
Would wake and watch his grief, yet faithful sleep
At last will loose his members, in sweet dreams
Wipe dry his tears and breathe into his soul
By slow degrees Hope's red and life's fresh zest,
With such a mild procession of fair dawns,
Which, unobtrusive, yet so fair and true,
Step daily to his bed* and softly ask,—
Wilt thou not, living man, return to life?
For they who live must gird their loins to work,
And when we 're dead, 't is time enough to rest.

XIII.

Preparation for Death.

Consider! thou canst not do otherwise
Than as earth's order wills, and all thy wails
Only torment thyself. So live thou, then,
Resigned and glad through all thy well-spent days,
That fate may be to thee no punishment,
But come to thee a calmly-looked-for thing,
As gently as the evening heaven comes down,
Softly as children who go home ere night.
For nothing ill can e'er befall the good!
Though like the autumn swallow youth departs,
Though pleasures pass away like summer flowers,
Though tears come to thine eyes like evening dew,
Though age comes, and though death at last must come,
As the year's seasons come to us in turn,
Thou know'st that Destiny means well with man.

* "Night,
Wrapt in her sable robe, with silent step,
Comes to our bed, and breathes it in our ears."
DANA.

XIV.

Greatness tested by little Things.

That is not greatness, calmness, strength of soul,
When, once for all, thou dost experience
Some sudden, terrible calamity,
Some last, decisive, heavy blow of fate,
The loss of reputation, of estate,
Of those thou lov'st, of health, of happiness,
And still remainest patient and composed, —
That is necessity laid on thy soul;
The suffering of violence humbles thee.
But if thou bearest all the lesser cares,
Burdens, and torments of each passing day,
Nor feel'st them bitter, — if, serene and strong,
Thou bearest little trials, blessing God,
That, only that, dear soul, is greatness, strength,
Collectedness of spirit, godly walk.
For little griefs thou *mightest* not endure,
But scorn them, prove thyself inferior
Ev'n to thy destiny. Then use, O heart,
Courage and strength, mildness and cheerfulness,
Where only thou canst do it, — in little things.

XV.

Learn of Nature to work calmly.

The stars move on along their giant path
Mysteriously up, across, and down,
And on their silver disks, meantime, God works
His holy wonders so mysteriously!
For lo! in blossom-laden twigs, the while,

The bird sleeps undisturbed; him wakeneth not
That mighty sweep of vast activity;
No sound brings tidings of it down to earth:
No echo hear'st thou in the silent groves!
That murmur is the brook's own rushing sound,
That sough is but the whisper of the leaves!
And thou, O man, desirest idle fame?
Thou dost whate'er thou dost so noisily,
And childishly wouldst write it on the stars!
But let that gentle spirit enter thee,
Which from the sun's noiselessly mighty work,
From earth and spring, from moon and starry night,
Speaks to thy soul,—then thou too art at rest,
Doing thy good things and creating fair,
And going so still along thy earthly way,
As if thy soul were woven of moonlight,
Or thou wert one with that calm spirit above.

XVI.

Thy Strength is as thy Day.

Let no misfortune ever master thee!
For only strong endurance leads thee to
The day of bliss. Whate'er can chance to man,
That he has strength to meet; what he has strength for,
That it behooveth him to bear, dear soul!

XVII.

No Man liveth to himself.

How seldom is the life we live our own!
Half would we follow in the old world's track,

Half would we break the after-world a path!
Life's date-tree we should never have enjoyed,
If others, thinking just as we do now,
Had not, long since, planted for us the tree!

XVIII.

Goodness a Law to itself.

The rich man or the bad man, — let him hold
Fast to the law. That only shelters him,
And hardly. Laws are only for the bad.
The freedom of the good man's action knows
No power within his breast but godly will,
And what he wills, that thing, despite the world,
He almost always executes; or if
He fails on earth, still he belongs to Heaven.
Whoso e'er wrought a great and glorious work
Was in his time a scandal, a destroyer,
An outcast, worthy of the hemlock cup,
Reprobate, fitted for the cross, and then
For divine honors in the after-age.

XIX.

Smiling Love conquers Evil.

'Gainst destiny and death, beloved soul,
Nor tears, nor sword, nor harness can prevail;
Not hosts, were they encamped about thy house!
To thee and thine will happen in its course
Whate'er must happen: this consider then:
Only by mildness canst thou conquer fate.
A smile suffices to smile death away,

And love defends thee e'en from wrath divine!
Then let what may befall thee, — still smile on!
And howe'er Death may rob thee, — still smile on!
Love never has to meet a bitter thing;
A Paradise blooms around him who smiles.
These weapons wear thou on the road of life,
For these a gracious God has given mankind
To fight with against death and destiny.

XX.

Earth transfigured as seen from another Planet.

High in the holy heavens thou seest how still,
Sweetly serene, the constellations move
In their appointed round, night after night;
And yet the moon, too, has her day and night!
And on the stars pale autumn comes and spring,
And death and life alternate even there,
Upon their still and beauteous silver disks;
And thou, O soul, so tranquil lookest on,
So blissful, aye, as blissful as they seem!
And dost thou tremble, here on earth alone,
To look on spring and autumn, death and life?
Her day enchants, her night appalleth thee?
O spread thy spirit's pinions, soar aloft
Up to that nearest planet's silver disk;
From there look out upon the earth, and let
This globe and all thou knowest hereupon
By distance be transfigured to a star, —
Cities and mountains and old monuments,
All the dear forms of men and every child!
Then see thyself, too, as a pilgrim here

Who, sojourning awhile upon the earth,
Bides in her valleys with the nightingales,
Dwells in her springs and autumns, days and nights.
So will sweet peace sink down into thy soul,
As when thou lookest at the evening star.

XXI.

The Stream of Love flows downward.

Life's nobler goods are not inherited
Like common goods. What once a mother's love
Did for each one of us, a helpless child,
That to our mother we can ne'er repay;
She is already great and self-sustained;
No more in need, and scarcely capable,
Henceforward of our help, she dies to us!
Yet God, that gratitude may be secured
To the kind sex, gives us in turn a child,
Which bears our mother's likeness more than ours!
So sweetly does He give her back to us!
And loving, cherishing our child, we love
Our mother! Grateful and most blest at once,
While in our grandchild we *our* thanks make sure,
Who us in turn resembles and requites.
Who but a God could so divinely twine
The gratitude and love and bliss of man
With his great world's bliss and continuance!

XXII.

Act as in God's Sight.

Whene'er thou purposest to do a deed,
First lift thine eyes to that blue heaven above,
And say: "This will I do! Behold it Thou,
And bless it, Thou in silence throned on high!"
And canst thou not say *that*, do not the act
From sheer presumption, idle human might,
Because He, silent, lets thee do thy will.
For know, whate'er thou dost, thou doest it
To be a part of memory all thy life;
The good deed sends a clear peal up to heaven,
Clear as a bell; ay, 't is a looking-glass
In which thou blissfully canst see thyself;
Then shalt thou seem to dwell in the blue heaven,
Or thou shalt feel, come down to dwell in thee,
The still and tranquil soul of Heaven itself!

XXIII.

Criticism on Men's Ingratitude criticised.

"Why is there shown so little gratitude?"
Who thanks the cloud that pours its rain on one,
And slays another with its lightning? He
Whose *will* claims no respect, must forfeit thanks.
The good man mankind ever loves to thank,
Not the good *thing* a bad man does to them,
Who has done many others ill, and does.
Thus is cleared up ingratitude towards men
Who one day do the right, and fail the next;

So God, who sends us many a bitter pain,
Is still to us the Ineffable Adored,
For that He bears good will to all, and us
Ev'n in that bitter pain. Then wait, O man,
For gratitude, till thou, by a long course
Of kindly deeds hast proved how pure thy will, —
Then shall men thank thee e'en for what is ill!
But thou, rewarded by the good thou dost,
Wilt then desire no thanks, and be like God.

XXIV.

We own only what we use.

What we possess and use alone makes rich, —
We do not own that which we do not use.
And thus would most men verily be rich
Did they not covet what they cannot use,
And what e'en he who has possesses not.

XXV.

Learn Patience with Patience.

Patience, of all the virtues blessedest,
Is not a gift! *Endurance* only buys it,
And not at once as other goods are bought;
But it is thine by calm continuance
In bearing, loving, hoping, and forgiving.
The good man only can be patient, for
As he grows patient, so too he grows good.
Would'st thou be so, then learn to bear a little,
Forgive, and love and hope; then more and more,
And with a growing pleasure, till at last

Thou doest this one thing gladliest, only this;
And so becomest good, and winnest thus
Patience, of all the virtues blessedest,
A thousand treasures for a single one.

XXVI.

The Heavenly Father's Children all great.

Let every task be easy to a man,
And all alike! For each one gives him power
To be a man! That is the thing. Who e'er
Has lived, that man has done much, has been much,
Much in the mansion of this beauteous world!
Therefore think worthily of human life,
Worthily of yourselves, ye living men!
Holy is whatsoever thing that breathes
This Ether! Underneath these golden stars
Is no one great or small; all is divine!
And none is mean who recognizes this;
In presence of this endless wealth of earth
No one is rich; and yet in view of Heaven
No one is poor! and no one is despised,
Whom the Eternal Father owns as child,
Who dares to call him Father; and that name
He loves to hear from all. Let all then love
To name Him by this high and tender name!

XXVII.

Anger punishes itself.

One way I know, by which thou canst revenge
Upon thyself the wrong men do to thee:

Thou must be angry! Or if life itself
Becomes a burden, and it lays on thee
Sickness and wretchedness and poverty,
And manifold discomfort and disgrace, —
Thou must afflict thyself! Or if the world
Bring change and death, ingratitude and hate, —
Thou must be vexed, if thou wilt be a fool!
For so thou visitest upon thyself
What others' sins deserve! — But art thou wise,
Thou then wilt bear in silence all that comes,
Rejoicing in thine own contented soul,
Which gives thee all things and takes from thee naught!
And griev'st thou for the fate of them thou lov'st,
Then think: They suffer nothing, like thyself,
If they have pious souls. And if thy tears
Still flow, consider, this thy seeming grief
Is only love! And then, then be as blest
As love makes every one in whom it dwells.

XXVIII.

God.

Thou hearest of a God, thou speak'st of Him,
The world is full of Him, — yet no one knows
Whence comes the name of God! The whole fair world
Teaches thee not that name, — no, not in all
Its order or continuance or change!
And yet thy soul assures thee that that name
Is not an empty sound, but shadows forth
The primal source of beings numberless.
Yea, thou hast rightly guessed, O pious heart;
Within the heart doth God declare himself

In still, low, confidential spirit-tones, —
He gently leads thee on in virtue's ways,
Opens the inner eye and by degrees
Upon thy actions prints his character;
Becomes within thee thought, becomes the essence
Of all the good and true and beautiful
Which like a seed-corn, all in secrecy,
Has now sprung up within thee, and of all
The good and fair and true this great world shows,
And all that nobly stirs the race of men.
And when thou long hast practised what is good,
Then hast thou felt the God that dwells in thee,
And by experience found the holy law
That rules the mighty all as well as thee,
That works unceasing in the human race,
Howe'er material, mortal shapings change.
Thou carriest the Father's image, then,
That shines in thee, high up above the stars,
Forward thou carriest it beyond all times;
Backward through all past times thou carriest it,
Bindest thyself and the fair world to Him,
Derivest all from Him, and piously
Leadest all nature back to Him again.
Yes, He it was who found Himself in thee;
And only he who never practised good,
Yearned for the true nor blessed the beautiful,
Were without God, and God were without him.

XXIX.

The Transitory is the Highest.

Short lived is man, and short lived is his work,
All he designs or executes or feels.

Of all the love he bears his human kind,
His mother country and his very gods,
No trace remains at last on earth; his death
Leaves not a trace, not ev'n his grave remains,
And all that once he reverenced, yea, adored,
His gods and temples, sink one day to dust,
Like him, his people, and his memory.
And yet does that then make him like the earth?
Or less, perchance, than dust?—O no, not so!
For that he came and wrought and loved and lived,
Ev'n that he went again, that is a sign
Of his descent from the blue heights of heaven,
While earth abides and evermore abides.
For that is highest which is transitory,
It is a thing of life divine! whate'er
Passes not by lived not and never shall.

XXX.

Equanimity amidst Change.

From all things, whether foreign or his own,
E'en from himself, doth changeful man receive
Pleasure to-day, to-morrow pain! All change
No less than he; Change comes o'er friend and foe!
Who smiles on him to-day, to-morrow will
Afflict him! The same heaven that yesterday
Affrighted, laughs on him to-day! The earth
That lately gave him flowers, now makes a grave
For some one of his darlings!—Naught abides
Constant to what it was and is,—nor ever
Will it or can it, more than man himself.
Musing this truth by long experience taught,

Beseems him with a sense of mastery,
With mild, sustained serenity of soul,
Neither, by joy and sorrow, friend and foe,
Too closely held, building on outward things,
To praise the world, — nor yet to blame that God
Who made him and made all things mutable,
That he might gain the even, godlike mind.

XXXI.

Emblems of a Pure Life.

Purely live my child, the life of beauty,
Free from every stain and evil conscience,
As in guileless stillness lives the lily,
As the dove within the leafy covert.
So that when the Father looketh downward,
Thou may'st be on earth his fairest eye-mark,
As involuntarily the traveller
Gazes on the beauteous star of evening;
So that when the sun one day dissolves thee,
Thou a pure and lucid pearl may'st show him,
That thy thought may be like scent of roses,
That thy love may be like to a sunbeam,
And thy life like evening song of herdsman,
Like a tone from his soft flute out-welling.

THE LAYMAN'S BREVIARY.

FEBRUARY.

FEBRUARY.

FEBRUARY.

I.

Miracles, to-day, yesterday, and forever.

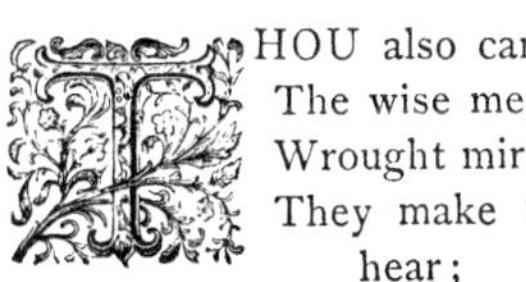

HOU also canst do miracles, beloved;
The wise men of all times have in their day
Wrought miracles and work them evermore.
They make the blind to see, the deaf to hear;
They heal the sick, and break the bondsman's chain,
And by their Gospel open to the poor
The heavenly kingdom. Mind alone does this.
The might of truth constrains the hearts of men.
How many generations heard the word!
How many nations have received their sight!
How many legions of the Cherubim
Are ministering this hour, to the Son
Of Paradise! How many devils now
Enter the swine and plunge into the sea
Of madness and of lies! — Only believe!
"Ye shall do greater miracles than I!"

II.

Duty the Way of Peace.

No duty leave undone, nor undertake
A new one, till to all outstanding ones
Thou hast done justice! Whatsoe'er with these

Consists not, turn away from; else shall thorns
Entangle thee, which thou no more canst loose.
Say not: I must get on in life, I must
Keep pace with all my fellow-travellers!—
Believe me, what thou seest, as thou thus
Lookest on men, is but the outer form,
Just where and as time's tide has driven them,
Dropped like the fig, where'er the tree impelled;
But where and how is each one's real soul?
Even as the fig, that duly in its time
Bears fruit?—the inner man thou seest not!
Yonder old man, with one foot in the grave,
Is still a child,—cannot with all his might
Be clear of childhood's grove,—"He once gave pain
To his dear mother's heart!" That widow there
Is not yet bride,—"A father's counsel once
She wickedly despised." Yet lo, the youth
Who turns the acres yonder with his plough,
Faithfully paying his poor father's debts,
He is already old,—as filial love
And virtue are! As blessed as the saints!
And a great fortune he has earned himself:
Namely, to covet nothing,—which would be
But debt; and naught to dread, which lets him rest
In peaceful slumber on his bed. My child,
Wisdom alone has eyes; all fools are blind:
Then see that thou no duty leave undone!

III.

Earth an Inn.

Though one should look upon the earth as only
A hostelry, what must he deem the host!

What fare was served! What joyous hours were spent!
What beauteous maidens handed him the wine!
What brilliant lustres sparkled through the hall!
And at the end, — the host has paid the score!
— Who lightly thinks of life and mirthsomely,
Well, for him too, 't is made and perfected.

IV.

True Riches.

Men — even rich men — have not, after all,
Such very lofty thoughts. Let come what will,
Let them do ill, or leave the good undone, —
Still they will house themselves, will eat and drink.
They will exist! *This* comfort riches bring,
This is the greatness of the great and high.
Yet hast thou mind and knowledge, love and works,
Thou hast then in thyself and in the world
Whatever gold can give thee; only that
The finer sense and the nobility,
The fill of beauty, and capacity
For joy the great heart has, the rich man — wants.
Be soul, then hast thou soul! — have peace of soul,
And in thee is a treasury of true wealth.

V.

Bereaved Parental Love consoled.

How else would God care for himself on earth,
If he appeared as child, to live there, than
By simply putting love into the hearts
Of mother and of father? If the child

Dies, now, how can, on the instant, love, too, die,
Or in the heart's blood lose itself again?
Does not the vine, when cut, still weep and bleed?
Then weep, O stricken mother, for thy child!
Bewail his loss! Thou mourn'st a heavenly thing,
Yet this know clearly in thy sorrows: this
Know surely in thy tears: Thou lovest still!
Still lov'st! Still doest what thou didst before!
And this, too, think, I pray thee: *who it was*
Thou heldest on thy bosom, in thy arms,
And who it was that loved thee so, and looked
So childlike on thee out of those true eyes!
And canst thou guess, weep not disconsolately:
For he thou weepest for needs not thy tears.
For thine own comfort only wail and weep;
And lov'st thou God, who loves thee, love thyself,—
And let it dry thy tears to think thou liv'st!
And see'st the All-present, not a child alone!

VI.

How to conquer and cure the Ill-tempered.

Treat every bad man gently, tenderly!
Meet him with help! For thou canst hardly think
How poor his being is, what strength he spends
To hold himself upright amidst the throng
Of nobler natures. Be right mild to him,
The bitter and morose! Thou knowest not
What heavy, year-long sufferings, in the form
Of low-voiced mutterings, gather on his lips,
How his whole heavy future takes the shape
Of a dark visage to thine eyes; and thou

Wouldst be more harsh to him than he to thee?
Meet thou the ugly-tempered lovingly,
For Love is what he thinks to do without;
And if he noticed thy forbearance, — still
Press not his hand! nor weep, not inwardly,
Else will he too burst into tears aloud!
No, sighing say: what dear ones thou hast lost!
What dear ones he may lose! Then shall he feel,
He lives! he loves! Be hard to him, — from love.

VII.

How soon we lose our Children.

Hold diligent converse with thy children! have them
Morning and evening round thee, love thou them
And win their love in these rare, beauteous years;
For only while the short-lived dream of childhood
Lasts, are they thine, — no longer! When youth comes
Much passes through their thoughts, — which is not thou,
And much allures their hearts, — which thou hast not.
They gain the knowledge of an older world
Which fills their souls; and floats before them now
The Future. And the Present thus is lost.
Then, with his little travelling pocket full
Of indispensables, the boy goes forth.
Weeping thou watchest till he disappears,
And never after is he thine again!
He comes back home, — he loves, — he wins a maid, —
He lives! They live, and others spring to life
From him, — and now thou hast a man in him, —
A human being, — but no more a child!
Thy daughter, wedded, takes a frequent joy

In bringing thee her children to thy house!
Thou hast the mother, — but the child no more! —
Hold diligent converse with thy children! have them
Morning and evening round thee, love thou them,
And win their love in the rare, beauteous years!

VIII.

Living in those we Love.

Whoever cannot live in those he loves,
In days when they are far from him, yea, dead,
Full often must have lost them. He alone
Possesses his beloved, his heart's friends,
In blessed, bright, uninterrupted presence,
Who in their spirit and peculiar being
Lives all his days and loves to look on all
Events, and smile on all, as they would do.
So have I oft; and when the silent friends
Smiled from my eyes upon a word, a work,
Or spoke aloud together with my might,
Or graciously showed forth their joy from me, —
Then have I wept alone! their tranquil life
In me, has awed me like a miracle,
And deeply have I felt: "So shall they still
Dwell with me all my days until the end."

IX.

Envy.

The violet, enviest thou its drop of dew?
The dew-drop, enviest thou its morning-sun,
Whose prism is imaged in its globe? The Bee,

Her sweet and purple-velvet thistle-top
O'er which she floats with busy art and toil?—
That dost thou not!—Well, then, deal so with man;
Begrudge him nothing! nothing envy him!
For he too has his thistle-top,—the earth!
O'er which he floats with busy art and toil;
His spirit is the drop of dew, wherein
The world is pictured for a few short days:
And dearer than the tender violet
Pays for her dew-drop, pays he for each hour
Of gladness with its loss and thousand tears,
Which he for others weeps, and others soon
Will weep for him! For to poor mortal man
The very goodness of the good, and even
Their very being, casts before itself
The shadow of a still and noble woe!

X.

Beauty.

Beauty the offspring is of a free soul
And vigorous healthiness. Free tribes of men
Who have thought nobly, greatly,—simply lived,—
Have in the mass been fair. Would'st thou have beauty,
Then give the people freedom, noble aims,
Busy them with great work. Humanity,
—Even on the way to freedom, as its thought
Grows freer, nobler, and it sees and lives
More truly, is already on the way
Into that realm of beauty which one day
Shall bloom on earth; for beauty of the form
Does but express a beauty of the soul;

A noble fruit grows from a noble stem.
O what good things Humanity one day
Shall win together and enjoy together!

XI.

Influence of Faith in the Eternal Life on the Present.

Say not: "I make no great account of life;
I could not choose but take it, as it is,
It was a gift,—and finding fault with gifts
Is not polite!"—O what mistake is thine!
Not as a gift hast thou received thy life!
Before *thou* could'st receive it, *thou* must be!*
Thou hast, then, an old right divine herein,
Thou canst, as Spirit, ask the Spirit of Spirits:
"What does it mean? How stands it in our house?
What weighs on us? What needs to be set right?
Who is 't would hold us down? Who lifts us up
And decks for us this isthmus-time of earth?"
And were this time to us the only time,
It were invaluable; then the bad
Were doubly bad, the good man heavenly good.
Because thou art an heir of endless life,—
Fly to the succor of the miserable!
Help every sufferer; not thy bread alone,
Thy garment, but thy very body give,
A joyful sacrifice, to save a child,
Much more thy race, from tyranny and woe!
For what is death itself? no more to thee
Than lightly through the flame to pass thy hand.

* "At the birth of my life if I wished it or no,
No question was asked me,—it could not be so!"
COLERIDGE.

XII.

A large View of Man begets Patience.

In all things act with a large oversight,
Appreciating each whole nature's worth,
Then wilt thou meet each one with gentleness!
The mother, pleased a moment since to watch
Her darling's smile, behold, she smites him now,
Vexed at some momentary naughtiness;
She bundles up the playthings of the child,
Threatening to send him to the colliers' huts!
So wives do, and ev'n mothers do the same.
But do thou rather imitate the child:
For now, when comes the hour to part from her,
He sees ev'n in his mother's angry form
All those soft tokens of a mother's love
That have been with him from the cradle up,
And lent a charm to all the days and nights!
He thinks of all the apples and the pears
That he must miss forever, evermore,—
Now he kneels down before her, and the mother
Relents, exiles him not,—but punishes;
And lo, the child kisses his mother's hands!

XIII.

Woman.

O not unsearchable is woman's mind.
Clearly it stood revealed in the long stream
Of lapsing ages in the days of old;
Only unhappier far is she than man,

Who, like the earth, displays in open bloom
His deepest mysteries, while the tender heart
Of woman, like the fig, blooms inwardly.
To know, then, whom her earthly love desires,
How strong, how rich Heaven's dowry is in her,
How noble, virtuous, steadfast each one is,—
There is the riddle! Often dark to *her;*
For where she loves, herself is only love.
She is, she has naught else,—not even herself;
She is as her beloved,—good or bad;
She is as is the human race itself,
Whose pathway, full of comfort she attends,—
Like man, only a little better, ever.
For he who knoweth woman, knoweth man,
He only who knows love, knows woman, too,
Time and the past, and spring and earth and heaven.

XIV.

Man in his complex Relations.

How various the relations of one man:
The king calls *him* his subject, whom again
The captain calls his corporal; and again
The clergyman calls his parishioner,
The alderman his fellow-citizen.
His parents call him "Son"; but then his children,
The boys and girls at home,—they say to him:
My father! And the mother* says: my man!
The oldest master of his handicraft
Calls him his fellow-master;—the physician
Calls him his patient; but the grave-digger

* That is the *German* "mother," the wife.

Calls him: our corpse; and mother earth, her dead;
And our Lord God calls him: my creature. Who
Can say, now, he is neither of all these?
And who can say that he is all of these?
Happy were he who could be all, at once,
And still, withal, remain a genuine man.

XV.

The Happiness of moderate Desires.

The poor man, like the sick man, must beware
Not to attempt what is beyond his power!
For then will he find out how weak he is.
His strength sufficed, so long as he lay still
On his sick-bed, to reach his hand and take
That which was nearest; for the first time, now,
He feels how much he wants, and heavily
And sadly sinks into his depth of woe.
Patiently in the circle, then, to abide,
Which God has marked out for us, gives us strength
Of strongest gladness, even of gladdest hearts!

XVI.

Yearnings for the Afterworld.

How many thousand human hearts once yearned,
In Egypt, in Eleusis, on the Indus, —
Yearned for the afterworld, — Elysium!
They longed one day only to see its sun,
To pluck one rose from that celestial spring, —
And then contentedly lie down and — die.
Deep in this longing lay the simple wish

For life eternal: — that Humanity,
That fair Humanity might live and love
Forevermore in an unfading spring.
In the bright realm of an unsetting sun!
Be it so! Ye mummies! be as men who died
With joy! be dead with joy! the earliest,
And latest generations by one heart
Are linked together! Therefore do I now,
Like to a herald of the ages, send
To your old world a loud and joyful cry: —
We are! Humanity has gained the shore
For which you once embarked! from holy heaven
Shines down on us even now the eternal Sun,
Blooms round the earth that everlasting spring.
Love lives! The living have their life in love,
And they that love live blest, — around us blooms
The golden grove of the Hesperides.
The Universe is ours! And ours is God!
The rose still lives upon its flaming bush!
The little violet hath not passed away!
The lark hath still the song and look of old,
Still the white snow-drop has the same green stripes!
And even the glow-worm's little lamp at night
That trails along the shadow of the grass
Is not yet quenched, — far less the stars on high! —
With joy we live, — be ye then dead with joy!
And as ye doubted of an afterworld, —
In which with full conviction we abide, —
Now then do we, too, of an afterworld
Not doubt! And as ye loved your passing world
So fervently and wept so for its loss,
And painted it for us so gloriously,
That world of yours we truly first possess!

And so two heavens at once encompass us!
And in the present, in these realms of space,
Lies a great deep, — immeasurably deep!
And in the immensity, within the heart,
Within the spirit lies our blessedness, —
In one man's life all ages lie contained!

XVII.

Reverence all Men!

With reverence greet thou every human head,
That comes to meet thee in the light of day,
Ay, every head, which, issuing from the world
Of cause mysterious, old as earth itself,
Young as the flowers, plays with them on the earth
So peacefully. For knowest thou who it is? —
It is a miracle, as is the flower, —
Only a greater and a lovelier.
And if thou wilt, go, also, greet the rose!
And if thou wilt, then kiss it: "In God's name!"
Not dull and cold pass by the stone itself,
For know, see, feel, and verily believe:
"They are!" Thy dream annuls no grain of sand;
It sleeps and shines before thee in the realm
Of sunlight. They and thou are in the same
Kingdom of heaven; companions of thy life
Are they, like thee in those firm magic halls,
Whence nothing bans them, naught exterminates,
Therein they still abide, howe'er they change.
Whatever is, is food for endless wonder.
And, if thou wilt, in silence bare thy head
Before the old man whom they bear softly by

In yonder coffin! Wilt thou drop a tear
For him, or for thyself, perchance for earth,—
Only forget thou not meanwhile, the bliss,
The miracle that forced it to thine eyes!

XVIII.

Practical Atheism out of Time and Place.

Man, nothing out of time! But out of time
The very days of this thy life may be,
If thou discern'st therein no spirit divine,
Who rules in every moment, and brings forth
Only with self-restrained omnipotence,
That which He will complete, and by this will
Must square His every act. Discern'st thou Him,
Then everywhere in Nature reckon thou
On Him, and count on Him in thine own breast!
And know for certain: He too counts on thee.
A milleped is not devoid of feet,
The spider's-web its myriad threads compose;
The giant fig-tree on the Indian plains
Supports its greatness round about with stems
Which it puts forth straight upward from its roots!

XIX.

Value of Old Age.

Say, when does life come to be something worth?—
When we know how to live and have lived through
Much in the wondrous mansion of the earth;
When we live thirty—forty—years each day,

And every thought comes laden with the sweets
Of earth, as heavy-laden as the bee
With honey gathered on the flowery mead,
Home to the brain; when every feeling stirs
A sea of feeling in us, made of all
That ever we enjoyed. For all that man
E'er thought, hoped, wished, wept over . . . . though in vain,
Stays by him faithfully forevermore!
When it comes back in thought, then is it true,
Fulfilled, and made a portion of his life;
Our fair, good things we do a thousand times!
Our very faults a thousand times amend!
Each is one day the man he willed to be,
And so becomes the angel, — that he is.
Spare, then, dear youth, thy life, till comes the time
When 't is no more a burden and a dream!
The time when even the beggar is a king
Of days, — (which now are days of blessedness), —
Of spirits, who now all minister to him,
Of his own life a master and a king!
The life of an old man is heaven itself!
'T is bliss itself! for in it dwells a God.

XX.

Godlike Contentment.

Godlike contentedness is his alone,
Who has a great and godlike consciousness,
That we are not that only which we seem,
Nor have no more than that which we possess.
The life of every man creates itself
Its opposite, and each in spirit lives

That which he lives not in reality.
Thus is the rich made poor, and must be so,
By poor who pass before him, — all his gold
Defends him not from this! The poor is made
Almost too rich by those ten thousand stores
Of wealth he misses! him his poverty
Harms not withal, — nay! through his tears the world
Shines glorified. The penitent beholds
For the first time the pure and holy God,
Because he is the sinner! So fair is life
Lived on this earth as counterpart of heaven,
Which as a picture floats before our eyes!
Covers us as a bell; and ev'n this fair
Picture, this counterpart, is part of man,
Linking his life to all existences,
And making him part of the mighty all.
Thus live we in the feeling of that whole,
To which the inner blessedness belongs,
And recognizing that, we are content.

XXI.

The Mystery of the Finite.

All is eternal, of itself. And hence,
The highest master-piece was: to create
The transitory, — that which should not seem
To have been before; should seem to have passed away,
Perhaps *have* passed away, when seen no more;
And, what is wonderful, should yet fill space,
And time, and undeniably exist.
The unfathomable lake of energies
The Master, therefore, once let overflow

In a broad, full, unceasing cataract
Down an immeasurable, steep abyss.
Silently plunges now the lake, and calm
The image formed by masses evermore
Speeding and gliding down the precipice;*
Bright in the sun it gleams; firm, motionless,
Above the eternal fall the rainbow stands,
And hides the horrors with its beauteous hues.
And we, — along the shoreless, unmapped lake
Sail on, inevitably onward still,
Still silently drawn nearer to its fall,
And as we go, sing songs, ay, farewell songs
To dear ones who sail after, far behind,
Who also, singing, soon shall reach the fall
And plunge, where we erst plunged and disappeared
In foam and thunder, — in the great world-stream.

Such is the immense prerogative of man:
Memory and Hope, and pain and woe, the death
Of all things beautiful and all he loves,
And his own death to feel as poignantly
As if he were himself the life that formed,
Ay, and the death too, that — destroys it all.
For, to be Nature's tried and proven spirit, —
And now with holy, awed, adoring joy,
Trembling to gaze on all the uncounted host
Of innocent beings who, without a word,
Come into life and pass away in death, —
This gives our human life its crowning charm.

* See Sterling's Hymn of a Hermit: —
"The stream of life from fountains flows," &c.

XXII.

Without Vision the People perish.

To have an object, clear and well-defined,
To long for that, to live for that alone,
Is the divinest power possessed by man,
Which only love and youth can exercise; —
The Spirit that not long since came down from heaven,
Of which, unconscious now, it still is full,
While yet it softly opens wide its eyes
On all earth holds of new and beautiful.
Has man attained the object of his heart, —
The heavenly stream still flows, e'en here on earth,
Wherein he has come down as if to bathe,
And soul and world are one, and death and life.
Has he not gained it, — then the soul wakes up
As in a living grave; the starry tent
Seems to him overhead a charnel-house,
And Spring's perfume a smell of mould; his death
Is but a flight, and without blessing it,
He leaves the world, wherein he blindly strayed.
What is the ideal then, whereof we speak?
And what do love and youth behold therein?
Love sees divinely the divine, for her
It wears no veil; in naked majesty
She sees with awe the work of God; she forms
Not the conception only but the man;
Whoso has loved, he only is informed,
And only he who is informed, has lived.
And though what dawned on him has disappeared,
That annuls not the world's divinity!
Man in his hoary age forgets it not;

He dies, — it goes down with him to the grave!
There where all things divine and beautiful
Abide, it meets him. He who never formed
A purpose, he has never loved nor lived;
In him, of him, is nothing to be formed, —
He cannot even die. For verily
Only the happy man can ever die,
In the sweet sense, the noble sense, God wills
The name of death shall bear to pious hearts.

XXIII.

Night the great Leveller.

Night doth discrown all kings; the Judge, the Priest,
Exist no more; philosophers and fools,
Doctors and churches, all have disappeared.
Ruins are now no more, Time's wounds are healed,
Nothing is any longer new or old,
No child is young, no old man full of days;
None is unhappy longer, no one begs.
The monarch's sceptre and the beggar's staff
Both sleep alike, forgotten for a night;
As in a grave, Humanity takes rest,
Eternal feelings sweetly lull its heart,
Eternal thoughts silently fill its brain. —
Could, then, Humanity, some morn, forget
What it had dreamed itself on former days, —
And could it still be what it was at night:
Harmonious and godlike, — ah, how well
Were it for man! then all were rich and free! —
But see, 't is so! time makes it so full fast!
Humanity already half forgets

That which it was in other times; all dreams
Of the old, heavy, superstitious days;
And what it once lived through in all the nights
Of its existence, in broad daylight now
Begins to dream! The feeling with which, oft,
Yea, many thousand times, on going to sleep,
—And what is dying but a going to sleep?—
It laid aside the soil and stain of earth,
And all the instruments of juggling sense,—
This evanescent and exalting mood
Makes fast its lodgement in men's waking thoughts,
And soon 't will not be Day that rules the world,
No, Night will hold the sceptre, great, free Night,
The equalizer, mother of all gods.
And whoso in the sun's bright light, e'en now,
Conceives great thought, with holy feeling thrills,
For him the sun and time have disappeared,
And like a God he stands in ancient night,
The magic glow of the great Spirit's all,
The warm, fresh, primal fountain, God himself.

XXIV.

Do the Duty which is the least Convenient.

Wilt thou, of two things, know which is the right?
It never is the more convenient one!
What gives thee the most trouble, *that* is it!
Or would become so, were it not! For so
Thou conquerest matter's ancient sluggishness,
Thou conquerest thine own heart. For, be it odd,
Or be it godlike, what is good for thee,
Is good for others; out in the great world,
There only canst thou thine own fortune earn.

XXV.

The Evening Star.

In Spring, there stood the morning star in Heaven,
Looked round on all the blooming earth and saw
Her children blessed with seeming endless joy,
Out of the halls unsearchable of Heaven
Enkindled on the earth. He saw and smiled,
And vanished in the young day's rosy light.—
In Autumn he came back as Evening Star,
And all the pomp of Spring had long been quenched.
Again he saw and smiled; but this time stayed
Till all earth's children softly sank to sleep.
As toward a lighthouse from the waste of waves
I looked across to him and said in thought:
Whatever comes to us beneath this heaven,
Whate'er such godlike creatures look upon
And smiling bless, that bless thou too, O Man!
Who does not, in his loved one's sight, with joy
The noblest, and with ease the highest things?
Who dies not gladly, when his King looks on?
Up yonder lives, thou knowest! another King!
There other loving eyes look down on thee!
And wert thou wholly and forever dead,—
When thou wert laid to rest, what were it more
Than when the child sinks in his mother's arms
To sleep, the father watching!—What a sight
For gods to see,—a childlike, pious man!
But lo, now! thou hast seen the Eternal Star
Which, each new Spring, returns so silently,
Sent by the Father as a monitor;
Who longs not for the eternal, loves it not,—

Can he remain immortal, if he is?
And he who in the Father's endless love
Lets his soul sink, who grasps eternity,
And loves the Eternal One,—*becomes* thereby
Eternal, *were* he not so! There is One
Eternal! Somewhere is an anchor fixed!
There is a hold to this world's fleeting show!
Thinking of this, clearly receiving it
Into thy soul, thou diest, thou canst die,
O loving, highly blessed and gifted *Man!*
Thoughts die not. If thou hast thyself become
Thought, love, benignity,—art thou not then,
Thyself the spirit that holds fast the world,
Humanity and—yonder Evening Star?

XXVI.

Value of the World.

"What may the world be worth,"—say'st thou, pure spirit.—
I know not; haply to the dead not much;
A little more than "not much" to the old,
Much more to youth, to curious interest more,
But everything to them that love it. Things
Are trivial, a small thing is life itself;
At last it is and was nothing at all
Except our dream of it, our longing for it,
The joy and pleasure that we found therein,
And our contentment with it. In our breast,
There lies the value of the world to us;
We journey onward through it, like the sun;
How bright we glistened and how warm we beamed,

How many flowers we called up from the earth, —
That tells how fair, how joyful was our day!
The moon will hardly speak well of our earth,
Because her cold face sees it but by night.

XXVII.

Spring Thoughts of Immortality.

At the approach of Spring I ask myself:
What is it fitting man should prize? — At most
It were the stars, if they but have the power
To bring forth anything immortal. Else
They sink in value, only to be prized
Because they are themselves long-lived, perhaps,
And then this earth too, were respectable, —
Like an old veteran of a thousand years.
But if the stars above us are no more
Than blooming islands in the ethereal sea,
Whereon in Spring-time flowers and summer birds
Alight and settle, and perchance fair men,
Then neither these nor they have any worth
Unless there is some home prepared for them!
Then naught is to be prized, but only man,
Who prizes naught else! only a pure soul
That builds up its own worth, — in lowliness,
And still, even as a tale, the world is fair!

XXVIII.

Nature's Method of curing Man's Errors.

To do the right in a wrong way, is wrong;
To take the right in a wrong way, is wrong;

'T is a sore wrong: harshly to hold the right!
Rudely to root out error, too, is error.
With gentle hands remove the noxious thing
From man, exchange it; first of all, with care,
Supplying in its place, the better thing.
Lo, each delusion, each mistake of man
Kindly and firmly Nature overcomes,
The illusion meanwhile humoring; as a mother
At evening clears away her darling's toys
Out of the chamber, gently extricating
From his wee hand, as in the cradle there
He sweetly slumbers, his hard horse of wood,
Sets it away and smiles on the dear child,
Who, in his empty little hand still dreams
To hold his treasures fast, — and fondly smiles,
For every, even the smallest, property
Is precious, rare, and irreplaceable,
And men themselves would weep unceasingly
Over their losses, like a little child,
When it has left its wreath among the flowers,
Did not wise Nature some new thing contrive,
Exalted Mother, who, with praise and stir, —
Like stormy Spring soothing the rifled year, —
Holds up to him a lovely spectacle
That charms and chains his vision, till at last
His little hand he reaches out for it,
In all the haste of long-denied desire, —
Thus forgets ever one thing in another,
And takes the tears of sorrow on his cheeks,
Shed for the old, the irrecoverable,
Into the brightness of the great, new joy,
And straight with new tears crowds them out again,
As on the tree young buds crowd out old leaves

In autumn. And with man 't is autumn ever
Round him! And in him an Eternal Spring!

XXIX.

Death of the Snow-drops.

"O vernal sun, and O thou vernal earth,
Let me too die! For what do I behold!
Scarcely the snow is melted, scarce the first
Dim canopy of cloud is drawn away,
Scarcely from heaven has a warm breath come down
To play and whisper in the old dry leaves
Of the late silenced autumn, scarcely has
The earth begun to put forth the young grass, —
When lo! I see your heads already pale;
Even now ye die, ye snow-drops! silently
And patiently ye droop them to the old earth;
Ye go! And not till now the violet comes,
The larks whirr upward and the almonds bloom!
How much you will not look upon, dear drops!
You will not see the apple-tree in bloom,
The rose, too, nor your neighbor strawberry,
Nor yet the cherry, — these are all to live,
To live a heavenly life above your grave,
When you are gone; and you, composed and calm,
You droop your heads upon the ancient earth!"
So spake I weeping! — But my Spirit said: —
You leave a world full of rich life, indeed,
And full no less of sad presentiments:
'T will not be yours to see the yellow leaves,
To hear the sigh of autumn's dying breath,
You will not, like the aster, live to see

The death of all things beautiful, you will not
Be the last flowers! O ye are fortunate,
Snow-drops! — and yet how much like you is Man!
Who, when he dies eighty years old, still breathes
His last in the first breath of endless springs,
Which all shall bloom when he is gone, — is gone: —
Freedom and Peace and tranquil Blessedness!
Snow-drops! Ah yes, ye are a type of man,
Called, in the dawn of a fair life, — to part!

THE LAYMAN'S BREVIARY.

MARCH.

MARCH.

MARCH.

I.

Maternal Spirit of Spring.

NOW, after long Spring warmth, a gentle rain
Distils by night upon the silent earth,
And all the myriad newly swollen buds,
And all young flowers, drink in so silently, —
As on the mother's breast the new-born child
Tastes the first drops, — so gratefully they drink
The pure, primeval, holy dew of Heaven,
Which, since the world began, has suckled all
The thousand generations, each in turn,
Their common mother's fresh nectarean milk;
And blessed now is Heaven and blest all they
That hang upon it with the lips of flowers,
While it bends o'er them to the very grass,
As if it wept a mother's tears of joy.
And such they surely are! But infinitely
More tender, beautiful, and fervent ones!
And so when thou, then, dear young human mother!
Look'st round thee in the spring, behold with bliss
Thy nature everywhere diffused abroad,
And see it sweetly centred in thyself,
And look down thoughtfully upon thy child!

II.

Be Temperate in all Things.

Be temperate in all things! — Let the stream
Of heavenly bliss flow smoothly through thy breast.
Condemn no feeling; let it have its course. —
Bind it with ice, — a freshet comes at last!
Be no oppressor! The oppressed will rise
With thousand energies unknown before,
And madly hurl their tyrant in the air;
No, thou wilt not! — Be ever mild and kind.
That love may not be partiality,
Unreasonable and unjust to others, who
Were once, or one day will be, dear to thee.
Hold on thy course unswerving, like the sun,
With equal light and warmth; and if the earth, —
If but a man, turn coldly for a time,
In his slant course, a false, wry face on thee, —
Still to thyself be true, and verily,
He 'll find himself again in thee at last.
Hope steadily; art thou too angry now,
Next time thou wilt too fondly, feebly love;
When thou hast sinned too much, then thou wilt pray
Too much. By overacting, in things good
As well as evil, an incontinent world
Betrays itself, whose noisy Sunday joy
Shows the still misery of its week-day life,
To which each day that comes gives ears to hear,
For which each day couches the cataract;
And which rejoices only in the old
Blindness and deafness, not in eye and ear!

III.

The Rose, an Emblem of Goodness.

Art thou not good enough to be a man,
Still be as good as the rose-bush's root:
Silently hidden in the earth, unseen
And unobserved, it gathers secret force;
Puts forth a stalk, then twigs, and on the twigs
Leaves, buds, and roses, even thorns; the roses
It nourishes, with fragrance filling them,
And if thou praisest, ay, or pluckest them,
It never stirs, — it feels, within, the power
To multiply itself a hundred-fold;
And even the thorns it beareth not in vain:
For when in spring the lamb tears off his wool,
It catches with the thorns each little flake
And holds it fast with patience till birds come
And peck and pilfer it to make their young
A soft, warm nest. And still it never stirs!
Be at least *as* good as the rose's root,
If thou wilt not be *so* good as a man.

IV.

Hope possesses the Future.

Whoever hopes and wishes, he already
Lives in the future, of the passing time
And things around him, scarcely taking note,
Using them only as they haply serve
For steps to lead him to his distant goal.
So sits the fisher in his boat and uses

The everlasting waters only as
The fulcrum of his oar-blade's pulse and play.
And lives with 's eye, already in the port
He only sees; e'en now with wife and child
Eats from the table by the glowing hearth
The fish that still flap round him in the boat.
Let each then hope for something, wish for something,
Years long he shall enjoy it in his heart,
And lightly sail the sea of heavy days.

V.

Be Patient, Content, and Calm.

Whoso could do without a wish, — a hope, —
That man were great! For nothing in his thoughts
Would hide from him that great world out of doors,
And he would take in its exhaustless good,
Its inexpressible beauty every day.
Hast thou yet rightly scanned no dead man's face?
What touches thee in him, is his *great* look:
He wishes, hopes no more! He will accept
With pure soul, unreservedly, again,
Whatever God assigns him, certainly,
As true as he is dead, and as God lives.
And wait thou too till then; for all will die, —
And dying is for each his greatest act.

VI.

Man's Pilgrimage grows Smoother.

Once, in the days of old, the traveller had
A weary time, climbing the rocky back

Of the old mountains; stumbled oftentimes
And froze in snow and storm, — and yearned for home!
Now, — pleasantly, at ease, he floats o'er all,
As o'er green cornfields floats the summer air! —
I sail above them! — and they rest below,
Like the sea's bottom, like the smiling coasts!
Sooner or later, good Humanity!
Nature sinks whatsoe'er once cumbered thee,
And thou, thou glidest peacefully o'er all,
As floats o'er grain-fields green the summer air!

VII.

God's Joy and Man's Yearning.

Supposing once a man were only God!
What lofty joy in that one thing were his!
Man takes delight as every artist does
When others copy him; to such we grant
Not only pardon, but ev'n love. And now,
If one should praise and honor so our works,
So prize and love them, that he would not be
Henceforward parted from them, evermore
Should fondly bear them in his mind and heart,
Ev'n as earth's children bear the works of God, —
O what a lofty joy would man possess,
If man were God! — But now see clearlier! —
Each man possesses truly as much joy,
And is as great, in apprehending God;
And God is, — what we cannot comprehend! —
Is his own wonder, — ay, our ignorance!
What lofty joy must God now take in us,
Who from the cradle even to the grave,

With childish, — childlike labor day and night
Busy ourselves, until we are worn out,
With all His things, and even rob ourselves
Of them, that they may exercise our souls!
Therefore He lets his works forever last,
And even those works, — which, of ourselves, we are!

VIII.

Live in the Present.

Spoil not thy present moment by the Past,
The Future, least of all by doing wrong!
If thou expectest better luck, — to-morrow, —
The brightest sun seems dim to thee to-day,
As if it would not be a sun to thee
Till after thou wast inwardly eclipsed!
Rise above every fortune, reckon none
The only or the highest one, that so
Thou still may'st keep eyes, heart, and senses free
To live in harmony with further days;
Cloud not the sight of thy past days with tears,
Nor yet block up against thyself the way
Of fond, familiar memory with remorse.
Thus with the spirit shalt thou always live
In the sweet, ever rich, eternal Now!
Not like the traveller, who enjoys no sense
Of blooming road, or greetings, as in gloom
He hastens to his mother's funeral!
But *thou* goest homeward to thy Father's heart.

IX.

Change and the Unchangeable.

On all things Nature lays her gentle hand,—
Gentle, but irresistible; she lays it
Upon the lovely shaping of a child
As on the rose-bud, and with restless toil
Fills out and ripens both, to man and rose,
So that thou knowest child and bud no more!
She lays it on the night and on the sun,
And plucks them like a pansy from the skies!
She lays it on the Autumn and the Spring,
On every year, on all that circled man
From earliest childhood, and grew up with him;
She lays it on the old man, his silver hair,
She lays it on the dead in earth's dark lap,
And turns their mouldering skeletons to dust,—
This is the most the worst can do to us!
But on one thing Nature lays not her hand,
She lays it not upon our heart's desires,
She lays it not upon our Spirit's wealth:
On freedom, love, and truth, and its fair things,
On these bold man alone, begrudging man,
Lays his hard hand to spoil for him the world.
And now if Nature but dissolves our bright
Into a brighter, if she takes our fair
And makes it into something still more fair,—
We still can keep our fond affection true
Ev'n for the doll that with great wondering eyes
Out of our childhood looks on us, as if
Astonished at our stature. How much more
Shall love abide with us! Ay, love for all

The freedom, beauty, truth, our souls have seen.—
More can we not desire from the best!
This the great lesson is, for man to learn.

X.

Be Thoughtful toward thy Kind.

Think often: "Who may be enjoying now
The good I did him once?" And though 't were only
The coat thou gav'st a beggar; the warm room
Where now in winter time poor children sit;
And if it glads thee,—then do good again!
Yet think too: "Who perhaps is suffering now
The ill I did him once?"—And though 't were only
The stone thou took'st not from the blind man's path,
The angry word a soft heart bore from thee!
And if that grieves thee,—then do good again!

XI.

Thoughts at Napoleon's Grave.

Friend Buxton, friend of mine from ancient Rome,
Who sailed'st to far St. Helena, there
To take the last cast of Napoleon's face,
Thou told'st me, when the pygmies now had dug
The deep, deep grave and lowered the giant down,
With a deep sigh the question rose from thee;
"What is the life of man,—the greatest man,
Since each one ends in dust and nothingness?"
O life is an immeasurable good,
While it endures; life is a deathless thing,

A holy, beautiful, abiding here
In a bright mansion of reality.
When at thy side I therefore asked thee rather:
Say, what is, after all, the death of man?
Or what is Nature's distant future, what
The future of each child of hers? That too
Is surely life, a glorious, widening life,
Hidden, it well may be, from human eyes,
Yet to the eyes of Nature bright and plain.
Because man's life is early closed with death,
Man's life is therefore not contemptible;
That only death could be; yet to say that
Becomes not men, — for that they do not know.

XII.

War, in God's Hands.

How many battles now are but a word!
Their very influences all extinct,
Abolished by the new and wider word.
What were they but a wish, even then while yet
They thundered loud, — two wishes, one of which
The Lord accomplished, only turning it
To higher issues! Then fight not so fiercely,
Ye heroes; for when scarce three days are past,
The fight ye won is lost again — to God!
And, as ye spared no man, none now spare you.

XIII.

The Exaltation needed for Humility.

The mount of sacrifice must always be
The mount of vision, — he who would renounce,

Must rise to the great realm of the pure Spirit,
The godlike, the immortal, and the good.
Who would not readily resign his will
To all things trivial and transitory,
What could be hard, henceforth, for him to bear,
Who — beareth naught! What enemy has he,
Whose spirit sees all things contained within
The deep eye-socket of a day that soon
Is quenched forever, shining on this earth,
Which he contains and owns, and not it him?
In the great Nature only dwells great strength.

XIV.

Moral of the Spring Flowers.

Innumerable flowers now start to life
That slept away the world a million years.
Lo, every violet is a new first one,
For the first time seen in the magic garden
Of the fair earth, and so it lives there new,
And for its sake all things are new and young:
The sun is only just hung up in heaven,
The earth is only just spread out for it;
And not a bud, nor an auricula,
Has heard a word of those old world-famed kings,
Of the long laid-by puppet-play, — of Xerxes
And Artaxerxes, Herod, and great Cæsar,
Who are not worth four daisies at this hour.
O the pure, beauteous life these flowers do lead!
The bees, too, ever humming round these flowers!
And then these larks, blissfully ignorant
Of all earth's idle gossip, old and new,

And yet to come, that sing and soar in bliss! —
Forgetting human discontent, we grow
As blest as are the violets, bees, and larks;
But keeping in our sight and in our breast
Humanity's fair nature and bright goal, —
That and that only makes man like to God.

XV.

God's Reflection in Man's Face.

How lovely seems the sun to us, — at night,
When his soft light dawns on us from the moon!
'T is the sun's light and not the moon's, although
She is so near, and he has dropped from sight.
Hast thou done some good deed, and therefore now
A human face smiles on thee through its tears, —
Then see there, too, the Godhead's mediate face
Soft-beaming as the *solar-lunar* light!

XVI.

Who has God has all Things.

Wilt thou possess on earth here something rare,
Divine, and wondrous, in the only way
Man ever can possess things, then conceive,
Nay, rather see, believe, and say aloud:
The Universe belongs to God; what I
Hold in my hands, directly from his hands
Have I received it all. Say to thy wife:
"The Lord hath shaped thee, consecrated thee
To me, thou dwell'st with me, thou lovest me,

And I love thee, while yet he keeps thee mine."
And to thy child say: "Dearest child of mine,
Thou art God's child, to whom the eternal heavens
Above there, and the earth below, belong;
His art thou, while with me; for I myself
Belong to Him, even as thou seest and lov'st
Me here; before I saw thee, I was with Him,
And with Him I shall be, when thou one day
Seest me no more!"—Thinking, believing thus,
Then honorest thou the wife within thy arms.
Then dost thou reverently kiss the child
There in his cradle, as a gift divine,
And of his Father's kingdom teachest him
Gladly as if he were an angel. But,
If death should snatch him from thee, calling thee
To lay him in the lap of holy earth,
Then hast thou faithfully restored a jewel
Committed to thy hands and kept by thee
To its true owner, who would owe thee thanks
Had he not made it a delight to thee
While it was thine. Then shall the heart-felt tears
Thy wife and children one day shed for thee
Be holy, tranquil tears; because in thee
They had a heavenly possession which
They shared with their true Father and with thine:
God only can forever be possessed,
A common property in every breast.

XVII.

Be content with the greatest Good.

Let him who has the choicest goods of life
Not yearn to add to them the lesser ones!

In large and in the whole God blesses him;
And if the sun makes light for him the day,
Why crave the light of every little torch?

XVIII.

Bribery the general Vice.

The all-prevailing vice is bribery,
Bribery of sense, opinion, and of will:
To be corrupted is the common lot.
Poor souls are daily bribed with gold, and gold
Is given by rich men spiritually poor;
Yet 't is not gifts alone that fetter man,
Gifts which the high, the covetous, and shrewd
Applies, to stamp his fellow-men as things,
As instruments and tools of his base ends;—
To let men do them favors, also gains
The scheming, the ambitious, and the low.
Woman is bribed by beauty oftentimes,
Still more by praise of her own beauty, yea,
By favors asked of her, and granted by her;
Which he who cares not for, is her worst foe.
The sage himself is dazzled oftentimes
By recognition, yea, unconsciously,
By honor done him, tempted to base ways,
Thinking he walks the true and proper path.
Good-nature leads the good man far astray,
And even friendship makes the friend a foe
To others. Ay, by noblest leading-strings
The sly, corrupt, rich sinner manages
Fools to befool, and laughs them then to scorn,
When with a ready will they zealously

Even against their will fulfil his ends.
From such disgraceful fraud no power can save
The lovely, wise, and good, but a true spirit,
Self-poised, clear-eyed, and steady in its aim:
Resolved to have no dark ways in thyself,
Nor yet to give consent, still less give cause,
That deeds of darkness shall be done by others; —
Serene composure; free from all false zeal,
Set resolutely against mere man's-work,
Based on a proper and profound alliance
With God, who gives thy heart and spirit light; —
The knowledge and conviction, deep and clear,
That all corruptors, be they great or small,
In large or little deal perniciously
And meanly. Be thy guard a steadfast mind
To do, in all things, no man's word or will,
Nor ever trust him whom thou hast not tried.*
He who has cheated others, certainly
Will cheat thee also, when it serves his turn.
— So shalt thou live to be what God commands.
O wretched creature, — a corrupted man!
Most miserable, — the corrupted world!

XIX.

Earth the old Toy-House.

How many tender things hast thou possessed
In childhood, which were dear to thee; in part,

* This will do as a prudential maxim: but Christian wisdom will say: —

"Better trust all, and be deceived,
And mourn that trust, and that deceiving,
Than doubt one heart, which, if believed,
Had blessed thy heart with true believing."

Thou hast preserved them, partly they are lost,—
Scattered, and gone to be laid up again
In the old treasure-house of human children,
The earth! Lo, many generations now
Have, each in turn, given back to earth again
Their goods and chattels all, both small and great,
And followed after them! Does then thy heart
Hold dear the little storehouse that contains
The remnants of the joys of happier days,—
So dear, I pray, and thousand times more dear
Be earth itself to thee! And look on it
As with a thousand kindred hearts and eyes!
Ah, then, how homelike will it be to thee!
Like to thy childhood's nursery,—to a palace
Transfigured,—yet filled only with thy toys!

XX.

The Claude Glass of the Spirit.

Thy spirit only makes life beautiful,
Thou must create it that which it can be.
In Rome thou seest the stiff tapestries
To Raphael's Cartoons; in Hampton Court
Thou seest the still more hard cartoons,—and neither,
As only what they are, are of much worth.
"And Raphael's pictures nowhere, then, exist?
Nowhere exists the beauty they might be?"
O yes, it does! but where? For see, now comes
A connoisseur, and in a . . . . looking-glass
Sees the cartoon clothed in such magical
And tender charm as picture never wore.—
Make thou that man thy master! Think, the world,—

The rough, the hard, the uncompleted world,—
That even the world is worth ten thousand times
More than an insignificant cartoon.
Well, give the day, the earth, thy life, thyself,
The worth it can have, in the landscape-glass
Of thine own spirit, which so warms and glows!
Therein the very storms, as pictures, pass!*

XXI.

No Impression is lost.

"We know so much as we are conscious of."
Yet whatsoe'er has ever touched our hearts
And charmed us, though it now seems sunk and lost,
All *that* shall memory one day give us back.
For not a deep, not an abyss alone,
Is this our soul! The sea, too, often bears
Its flower-gardens on its upper waves,
And its deep bottom thus is hid from sight
Even to a child, that then for the first time
Plays on the shore, much more then to a spirit
That trembling waits to see a miracle
Upon the strand of being's mighty sea!

XXII.

Diabolus the Doubter.

Diabolus, the Devil, is the doubter,
The caviller, the sceptic, who forever

* So Jean Paul's moral from the effect of an eruption of Vesuvius, as seen reflected in the Bay: "I said, lo, thus the muse bears in her eternal mirror the woes of humanity, and the unhappy look into it and smile at their griefs."—T.

Has doubts of being, love, and of the good
He ought to do; who in his dark distrust
Of all the truth that stirs within his heart,
Would fain exempt himself from virtue's law, —
From action! and at last ends in despair.
And would'st thou know who is the angel, now?
He who believes in all the good and fair
He finds in others, loves to find it there,
Finds love in God, and God's love everywhere,
Throughout the Universe, and gladliest
In his own bosom; who to satisfy
His honor, to be worthy of himself,
So lives, as if God always looked on him!
That man, and only he, who lives a life
Worthy of God, lives the true life of man.

XXIII.

Misery of the Miser.

The miser is an ingrate too; with him
It is hard giving, easy taking, — both
For the same reason; *he* must have, none else;
Receiving robs him both of speech and sense, —
That which another has, gives him no joy,
So long as that one has it; and when once
'T is his, — he finds no longer pleasure in it;
Why shall he then give thanks for agony!
Flee avarice, then! It is the uncreator,
The polecat of all good, it is the magpie
That grows, with lust of seeing, old and gray.
But learn thou to desire as ardently
As does the miser, only better things.

Be temperate, like him bend all thy strength
On one thing,—goodness; give as grudgingly
An evil word as he does money; learn
From him economy! Therein he 's rich!
Spendthrifts are seldom long-lived; habitude
Lets them spend days as lavishly as gold!

XXIV.

Blessing of Children.

Children are matchless! On the whole round earth
Naught can be distantly compared to them;
Without her children earth itself were naught,
And they in turn were nothing without theirs.
The virgin hardly dares to speak aloud
The sweet name "Child!" She blushes; ecstasy
Thrills, trickles ominously through her veins!
And calmly dies the old man, who lays his hands
On precious heads and says: "Children, farewell!"
The sweetheart ceases with the bridal night,
The woman ceases with the child, to whom
Her name is *Mother*, and to father too.
The labors all, and all the cares of life,
Point forward to a future race, the sons
Of fortune, liberty, and blessedness.
To fashion us was our forefathers' life;
And for our children to provide is now
Our life! In such mysterious bliss the sway
Of love holds on. That we are perishing,
That we are dwelling in a house of death,
This we forget, it half becomes a lie
Through children, who still live, when we are gone.

And so the pelican lays bare her breast
Suckling her children with her own heart's blood.
For even the roe, the nightingale, has children,
— The humming-bird has father and has mother, —
And even the lion loves his young like man.
What thousand-fold and noble life of love
Reigns evermore in Nature far and wide!
And in the overflow of gladness man
Gives children to his very God, though He
Lives without wife or mother, so he deems.
For none more blessed than a child! The world
To him is nothing else than Love: Love smiles
Upon him from maternal eyes; the Sun,
The Moon, spring 's coming, and the autumn's wane,
Does all that touch him? Scarce he sees it all;
The world all rapture is to him, — no word
Of magic, — everywhere so dear, so clear!
In father's and in mother's soft embrace,
His little hand in sister's curly hair,
All things are his, yea, all; and more than *all*
He never could attain, were he a god.
Could e'er a youth be foolish, or a maid
Light-minded, could a single soul be sad,
While yet in solitude he walked the earth,
If it were only given him to see
One of his future children! Could it come
Running to meet him, pluck his sleeve and say:
"I 'm here! Shall soon be thine!" O could he see
What bliss awaits him in life's distant paths
He would endure, and seek himself — the mother!
Could a man ever have hard thoughts, who thought
Softly of children? — And the childless man,
He the true poor man in a world so rich,

An outcast from the care of God, ... from life, . . .
And from the world, — dreams himself near the end,
Tormented and tormenting in return,
Back to his Father thus he takes his way,
A solitary child, — while others bring
With joy to Him a thousand grandchildren?

XXV.

Respect for Woman tests Man.

So much as one holds woman in esteem,
Purely or basely as he deals with love,
So much is his regard for honor, or
So little; such the honor he receives!
Who not *himself* respects, honors not woman;
Who does not honor woman, knows he love?
Who knows not love, can he know honor then?
Who knows not honor, what has he beside?

XXVI.

The Mystery of Evil.

Just as the blazing fire at last burns out,
Every misfortune helps consume itself;
As every little coal, that still might harm,
Betrays itself by its own glow, that men
May quench it, so the least distress cries out
Like the marsh-waking frog. And why ere now
Has not all trouble long been rooted out? —
Humanity is patient; once it deemed
Much the inevitable lot of earth,

Which was but bad men's burden. Now its eyes
Are purged, it sees distinctly, and has hoped
That from its guardians, help would come at last,
And still it waits, — restlessly, angrily,
And girds its own stout loins to help itself!
Only self-betterment, self-help alone,
Has worth, and God's own pledge of permanence.

XXVII.

The Heart a Diamond.

Like to a diamond is the heart of man,
It loves to fling out its divinity
Beyond itself, and hang it now on this
And now on that external object, pleased
To see its beams in outward hues alone,
And every charm the real world contains
It sees transfigured in the ideal light.
And thou, do thou no canvas give to man;
He 'll paint it full! and though the picture 's his
And his *own* picture, — still it is his dream!
Faith must not think to do what Love may do:
Transform itself and in its image live;
Confound not then together Faith and Love!
Self-consciousness alone is the true light.
Believe in God, in Him alone *as God*,
Believe in all beside Him as divine,
Man, in thyself believe too, and all men,
And in the light, — that in all diamonds dwells!

XXVIII.

The noble Dead still live.

The noble dead still live,—forever near!
The nearest neighbor, whom thou seest not, is
A ghost to thee, and only so can work.
When thou dost need good counsel, which just now
No friend can give thee, turn thyself to them,
The mighty dead, who still through all the world
A universal presence, live and move,
Who even within thee faithful wait thy word,—
And in lone quiet listening, ask aloud:
"What dost thou counsel me, Saint Paul?" or, "What
Dost thou advise, Saint John?" And thou wilt then
Hear voices speak in thee in ancient wise;
And Socrates shall join their council, too,
With Epictetus and Mark Antonine:
And in the sense in which they sometimes wrote,
And with the wisdom wherewith once they spake,
So shall they now still speak out of thy mouth
As from the dusky-glimmering evening hall
Of dream, or in the hushed and listening porch;
They even shall fall into a friendly strife,
For from the strife of wise men Truth comes forth;
Then shalt thou hear and know what thou hast sought!
Grateful shall press the hands of the world's friends,—
And truly, if thou dost what they advise,
That shall be well-advised, and prosperous which thou dost.*

* "Und wahrlich, wenn du thust was sie *gerathen*,
Wird glücklich dir *gerathen*, was du thust."

XXIX.

Man needs all Things.

Accept not fraud for truth, nor foolishness
For wisdom! Never be content, O man,
While and wherever thou yet lack'st one thing.
Step freely, boldly out and claim all good.
Thy life on earth, — that also is a Spring,
Which for its making needs its flowers, its warmth,
And all the new-born beauty of the earth;
What comes to thee of human good, alone
Makes thee a man; what thou attainest not,
Thou wantest; what thou losest robbeth thee
As man, and thou canst be a man but once,
And only here. Man must have many things
All his life long,* the sky, the sun, the moon,
The stars, the earth, humanity, the grace
Of changing seasons, a pure, open sense
For all of beautiful life has to give.
Much must have passed away from him, before
He starts at seeing the tracks of endless life;
The majesty of the once present spirit
That lived a thousand-fold, rich, heavenly life,
And left him but the golden nursery;
Father and mother, — only a short way
Must they attend him, teaching him to live.
Only old parents must he bury then;
The beauteous maiden must not till the close
Of his full dream of youth to meet him come
As woman, and then journey on with him

* "Man wants but little here below
Nor wants that little long."

Along the road of life to man's last goal.
His children, coming late, must after him
Live just so long as he himself had lived
Before they came (sweet guests) to glad his heart.
No parent ever should outlive his child;
That is the pure course of a rightful life.
And he must leave behind him everything,
To teach that naught was his, except his soul.
But if now the companion of his days
He has to follow to an early grave, —
If, some still morning, comes a man and bears
His child away, pale in the sunny gold,
Across the silent earth, to bury it, —
Ay, then is the poor man bereaved indeed
Forevermore; from him is snatched away
That which of human man, as human, craves;
And no eternal, no immortal life,
Will once, or can, make good to him what now,
As man, he on this earth has sadly lost
And sorely misses. Ah! Another wife,
Another child, cannot replace the dead,
No, never; they are new and strange! His heart
Essays in vain to take them for the old.
There is on earth misfortune, there is loss;
Through our own faults and our own ignorance
Through faults and ignorance of other men, —
Therefore so long, only so long, as man
Knows not, nor carefully obeys his law,
The universe's law, and no day more!
To teach the art of life is wisdom's work,
To exercise that art is learning's goal, —
Unhappiness is but a long "meanwhile."
Yet to hold fast lost treasures in the soul

Through love, through memory, (which not in vain
Nor yet in mockery by God was given,)
By strong affection to anticipate
The human good yet unattained, to make
The future present, to converse with it
As with a living thing, *this* man can do,
This man should do, who lives but once on earth.
Then be thou wise to win! strong to possess!
Brave to defend! and provident to keep!
Who lets bad pass for good, — he is a faint-heart;
Who lets wrong pass for right, — he is a blockhead;
Who lets that go which only seems to go,
Who draws not that which comes not, is a child,
Who flings his mother's pearls into the sea,
Whence they arose, but where they 're his no more.

XXX.

Thy Foes.

Hast thou arrived so far as to have foes?
I praise thee, then, for all are not yet good.
Though thou conceal it, yet be not ashamed
That thou hast foes, — for he who cannot bear
To have a foe, deserveth not a friend.
They must be foes to thee, who fear the truth;
They must be foes to thee, who twist the right;
They must be foes to thee, who swerve from honor;
They must be foes to thee, who have no friends
But only felons of their lawless lust;
They must be foes to thee, who have no foes,
Because, — to insure like pardon for itself,
The world too lightly pardons. They must be

Thy foes, whose friend thou art not. Strongly bear
The hatred of the bad! 'T is weak and vain.
And if thou standest like a pure, warm beam
Of heavenly fire, then shalt thou warm and cheer
The good, and they shall link themselves to thee.
Meanwhile be thou thy foeman's truest friend,
And cease not from him with the faithful word,
With looks, example, e'en with silence, long
Forbearance, though a sore reproach to thee!
He gains the highest praise of goodness, who
Knows how to win the fool to what is good.
And lo! the unhappy one has, pleading, for him,
His father and his mother, from the grave!
His loves all plead for him, — his children too, —
His own shy glances intercede for him, —
A God pleads with thee for him in thy breast:
"Desist not from thy brother, O my child!"

XXXI.

The Hall of Spring.

A mighty Hall of wonders opens now, —
The Hall of Spring! So great that sea and islands,
The magic lawns of Hindostan, the gardens
Of Alcinoüs, Circé's promontory,
The hills of Troja, and thy fatherland,
Like little children's gardens lie therein, —
So old that Abel well would know the sight;
So new that ev'n the silver-haired old man
Gazes upon it with astonishment,
Who eighty times has wandered through its pomp;
So warm that Bathsheba once more might long

To bathe herself amid its fragrances;
So rich that Solomon might long to see
The vine put on its buds,* the fig its leaves:
So light and clear the hall, that high o'erhead
The lark herself sees the gray lark below
Who broods far under her cloud-piercing song
In the green cornfields, on her silent nest;
So early closed, the very hyacinth
Hastens to bloom and then to fade away;
That every wave flows on unceasingly
As if it had no time for one small word!
So fair, that even Homer's old blind eyes
Might once more weep at it! — And ah! so sweet!
The dead old Priamus and Helena,
Carolus Magnus and Napoleon,
Would gladly in their narrow sepulchres
Have but one little window to look out
And take one rapturous glance at the blue heaven,
Or large enough to lay the ear to it,
And listen for a quarter of an hour
To all the hum of bees and song of birds,
To weep, and after a long sleep, refreshed,
Lay themselves down again to a long sleep,
The deep sleep of the dead! But thou, thou liv'st
The sweet life of the living on the earth,
In this workshop of delicate wonder-works,
In which no hammer ever rang,† no brush,

Or eyes. — SOLOMON'S SONG vii. 12.

† "No workman steel, — no ponderous axes rung,
Like some tall palm, the noiseless fabric sprung."
HEBER'S PALESTINE.

"There was neither hammer, nor axe, nor any tool of iron heard in the house while it was building." — 1 KINGS vi. 7.

No pot of colors, purple, green, and blue,
Was left behind, — no visible Master wrought, —
And yet all stands complete, — O wonderful!
Clouds fly away, that poured their water out!
Waters glide by, that made the meadows green!
And winds are lulled, when they have brought the clouds!
And smiling still, as if he had done naught
Stands the bright Sun in heaven, yet visible
To mortal men! But He who does it all,
The Master, never once is visible, —
He smiles not once Himself, — Spring is His smile!

THE LAYMAN'S BREVIARY.

APRIL.

APRIL.

APRIL.

I.

Spring: Birth, Death, Immortality.

OW Earth grows green again. What is to live
Comes on with still, resistless, ceaseless pace;
Crowds into being; flowers themselves spring up
Sooner than grass; the blossoms from the twigs
Burst forth into the light before the leaves,
Only a little earlier to exist:
And even the smallest spot is thick beset.
The dear deluded ones, they all are there!
And nothing now seems wanting that the earth
Ever possessed. It *seems* so, — but in truth
All that she e'er possessed is wanting. Naught
Of what has been comes back, or will come back
Though we should live forever. All is new,
That is, — all, all; even the very blade
Of grass, and every little breath of air
That sails down from new clouds to play with it.
The poorest of all mothers, is the Earth!
And if she had a heart, — 't were long since broke;
And had she many thousand eyes, — they all
Had long since been wept dry, ... but ah, her children
Have done her weeping for her faithfully!

We gaze admiring on all Earth's old days,
Full of unique and beauteous shapings, full
Of countless products of her workmanship,
Forms, to destroy a single one of which
In man were a scarce expiable crime.
And Nature, — takes them all and melts them over,
On earth she does it, and on every star.
Each human artist who, with painful care
Has wrought out works of beauty from his soul,
Preserves them, too, or if he lets them go
Into strange hands, men's reverence cares for them.
Nature retains alone the primal thoughts,
The die of man and animal and plant;
And every year, as with Mahomet's seal
Only enough to grace her hall that year
She prints, of all the lovely forms, in clay.
But we are Nature's thinking thought, and sigh,
"O were there but some mighty hall, wherein
Nature might keep, collected after years,
All things her cunning hand had e'er produced!"
But such a vast, immeasurable space
Seems wanting ev'n to her, — seems? nay, it is, —
And spirits to be there as lookers-on;
For the exacting present, crowded full,
Demands of her, as for a giant's fight,
All the old fires of kindled energies
And all the spirits, to stand by her now.
History alone still teaches withered names,
And artists shaped thereby their single works
In marble or in tints, and mournfully
Memory saluteth them as sunken gods.*

* Keats.

When once the world had reached that fair success,
Nothing remained but to destroy it now;
And holy sorrow is the highest life,
For it keeps bright all that was ever blest.

II.

The Mind is its own Place.

"In the green cornfield have I built my house,
And now I roam about, — how sweet it seems! —
From room to room, deep in high rustling crops,
And like the young of quails my children sleep
Curtained with crops!" The man before whose soul
Are hovering evil works which he hath wrought,
May walk in palaces, yet walks on thorns;
At noon he walks in midnight; and with dread
He goes to drive the — serpent from his child.

III.

One Generation cometh, and another goeth.

Thousands of peoples of the race of man,
Pass through the Earth's vast house, each by itself,
Like nations migrating from land to land.
Singly they come, and tarry all alone,
Unspeakably alone, here on the earth.
Only their fathers do they find here still
Of all their never-seen progenitors,
Only their children do they stay to see
Of all, all those that shall come after them;
And just as if Earth scarcely bore ev'n them,

So do they hover, and live hovering on,
Like white clouds, folded in the fields of heaven
By thousands, which, but just snatched forth from night,
Now find themselves at dawn together here,
And then blown off again by a light breath,
Like lambs without a shepherd, steal away
In silence! 'T is the old, great woe of man!
And the sore grief of burying in the ground
A child, a wife, would wear a milder look,
Did not the grave open to view that hole
Full of unknown, unknown yet precious dead,
As near akin to us, as eye to eye
. . . . Of one-eyed men. Meanwhile the earth beguiles
Our sorrow with her even pace; the sun
Charms it away with his still, even face;
And in the throng of fellow-solitaries,
This populous loneliness, none deems him lost;
The little legacy of old men dead,
Each takes, rejoicing in his share of life,
Reads the report they have drawn up for him;
And what of good he thinks, in turn, to leave
His grandsons, he writes down upon the wall,
Or lays it on the table, confident
That they will surely find it, when they come.
So light, yet sure, the bond that binds the world!

IV.

Hopes are Treasures.

Heart! learn to hope! The lesson easier grows.
What thou, as child, did'st hope fair years ago,
That know'st thou still; full well now see'st thou *this:*

By how thou livest, what thou hast become,
And what the world around thee, thou canst see
How much more wisely thou would'st hope all that,
With how much more, ay, even a seer's success!
What thou hast hoped within a year, a month,
As from the full and blossom-laden tree,
Likewise what fruits have ripened and what not,
That know'st thou now; — and what shall by and by
Ripen at last, that canst thou, by the signs
Of heaven and earth, thine own life and mankind's,
Almost foreknow. Auspicious for our works
Is it: to hope only what comes to pass.
Then, — is it small, 't is all was possible;
Or much, — still it can never be enough
For all thy wishes in all times and moods.
This one thing, then, I counsel thee hold fast:
Throw not away from thee the fallen buds,
As good for nothing more! How graced they once
That which is passed away! — Whoso can keep
All he e'er hoped, though it was ne'er fulfilled,
He only knows the worth of inward life;
The purest wealth of fantasy and heart
Is his unceasing income, — and he spends
No particle thereof on the worst fate.*

V.

Hope, Man's only fast Friend.

Hope's tender creatures are more true to thee
Than lovely maidens. Yea, they are thy daughters!

* "Bid him," is the language of Posa, in Schiller's Don Carlos, "when he is a man, reverence the dreams of his youth."

They weep with thee, they smile when thou dost smile,
They grow up with thee, they outstrip thy growth.
Only, when comes the day of serious choice,
Day of wife-hunting, time for wedding them
To life's rough forms, when the unlovely offspring
Of hard reality step in their place, —
Ah yes, they 'll fain supplant them in thine eyes, —
Before this poor fulfilment sought by thee
Their cheek grows pale; they vanish for a day;
Perhaps a night . . . . but then they come again, —
Like golden moonlight to thy silent room
And peer . . . . and blush with pleasure when they see
That Earth has not quite stolen thy heart from them;
That thou, possessing, art not wholly blest,
And lost to them forever. So they stand,
With wet eyelashes, drooping modestly;
But as thou stretchest out a hand to them,
Lo, joyfully they all spread wide their arms
To clasp thee, and they all lie down once more
In bliss upon the blest paternal heart;
And now thou 'lt no more cast thy daughters off,
Who, free, unwedded, never growing old,
Stay by thee till thy still old age creeps on,
Plant flowers e'en now in secret round thy grave,
And smiling, die with thee, when thou dost smile
The last faint smile, that sees the dawn of Heaven!

VI.

We are Members one of another.

Indifferent one, thou carest for nothing, save
Thy own affairs? Thy house and wife and child?

Scarcely has man a property whereon
Some strange hand has not an invisible lien.
Thou art thyself the world's; in thine own house
Thou dwellest, — in the land, on earth, at large;
Who has the land, he has thy children too,
And he who has mankind has also thee.
Then care thou for thy country and mankind.
Take part with voice and hand in what is near,
Take part, with heart and thought, in distant good,
What noble minds are doing, even for thee.
Let nothing die, — else thou diest with it too;
Let none be made a slave, else thou art one;
Let none be bad, else he corrupteth thee;
And if all think as thou, then can henceforth
The bad man trouble none, not even thee.
And when mankind can freely do the right,
Then every gift divine redounds to thee
And to thy children's children, for whate'er
Thy spirit gains is gained forevermore.

VII.

Losing all and finding all in Christ.

"What did I wish to find in yonder world?
Hardly myself; not for the *sake* of self, —
Who sleeps, sleeps off. All that I wished was Christ,
And next my mother and my father, ah,
And then my children, and my wife for them;
Then were I blest in having all I love,
That fondly love me, joined in endless peace.
That were my Heaven!" — This is what each one says;
Each wishes only, there as here, his own;

Of his grandchildren, of his father's father,
Of his whole race the wish of no one thinks.
But as each one does truly wish his own,
Each child to have his parents back again,
And as all parents wish their children back,
Man's wish runs up to the primeval world,
And snatches all the sleepers from their graves,
His wish runs downward to the afterworld,
Summoning all unborn dear ones to his heaven;
Love's yearning makes the whole wide world alive,
Ranging it round the Father in his Heaven.
And He alone, this most all-loving Father,
Shall thrust all back to the abyss again?
He who himself in all his children lives,
Shall curse Himself, ... the puppets . . . . and the shrine?
And grimly say to himself the horrid words:
"I let myself be slain upon the cross,
Exposed on the Eternal pillory,
And millions pass along and wag their heads
And curse me, saying: . . . . 'Thou . . . .! None of us all
Shall see one, *one* loved face again forever!
Nor Thou! Nor Thee! But we have power to die,—
Thou not! The holiest passion of the heart,
Love,—was our torment only, and our shame!
No devil can *of* a devil believe the like!'"
And yet, perhaps, 't is true! 'T is surely so,
If each, instead of the mere earthly form, ...
Instead of even Christ's mere earthly form,
Shall find the very Father, and in Him
Meet all his loved ones and himself again,
And God could not *of* God hold fairer faith.

VIII.

Honor all Men.

Before a Lily, that could talk to thee,
Profoundest reverence would fill thy breast.
A Beaver, that had built up all the works
That make man proud, would justly be to thee
Exceeding wonderful; an Elephant,
— The great, wise Mouse that through the palm-wood
creeps, —
Should he speak to thee as a friend, and show
Kindness to thee, and thoughtful, timely help,
And be thy servant, and support himself,
How would'st thou prize him! And a herd of such!
And yet before a man, good, glorious man,
His bosom full of all the gifts of Heaven,
Glowing with love for thee, — before his child
That plays alone, content in grass and flowers,
Could'st thou pass by indifferently, and not
Reach out a hand to him? Not cast on him
One friendly glance? Only contemplate men
As some rich-gifted, blooming growth of Earth,
And thou wilt feel thy breast at once enriched
With a great reverence, a still blessedness,
Till thou behold'st in man the heavenly one,
The Son of God, the godly one, and then
For the first time true love will fill thy soul.
I claim the inspiration and the love
Which has been offered to a Holy Child,
Loudly and boldly for *each child of man!*
When each is once revered as God's own child,
And loved with inspiration *livingly;*

When each thinks, feels, and lives, as God in him
With mighty agonizing yearns to live,
Then only shall begin at length on earth
The "Kingdom of the Father," then shall God
Live everywhere, distinctly, gloriously,
Then God comes down to dwell within your heart!
Yea, in your eyes! and in your very hands!
Just as you honor man, he *lives* to you:
— Look only at the King upon his throne, —
And God lives to you, as you honor Him.

IX.

Man's Criticism of God's World and Ways.

We human beings have a natural right
To pass a judgment upon all the world,
Death, Life, Joys, Sorrows, even man himself;
For we, we must be men and bear perforce
All that to be a man brings in its train.
A master builds a house, and when 't is done,
He goes his way! — But we abide therein!
A cook does naught but cook, — the guests must eat!
A lord sends out his servant through strange lands, —
Across the sea, — the servant learns the roads!
Whether the coffin was not somewhat close,
Haply the dead man best could answer that.
With all the unexhausted means at hand
Can the whole race of man insure itself,
Thousands and thousands of things truly good?
And when he has dealt honestly with all,
Himself and others, when by practice long
He learns to do this understandingly, —

To know the world, the house, wherein he dwells, —
Even as the butterfly shut up in some
Divine Rotunda, will no more go out, —
When he has searched and seen through frame and plan,
And master's mind, — *then* let him haste to judge!
But in the land you know full soon, ... the Master,
The way, ... the means, ... the very cook, ...
and coffin.

X.

Reverence the Child.

The child is of God's nature. Coming forth
From primal being, in his soul he brings
Knowledge and recognition of the things
Of God to earth with him. The highest things
And holiest he most readily conceives,
Finds time and opportunity on earth
To feel himself pent up and weak and small!
Honor him early! Treat him as an angel!
If he should trample one of his fair flowers,
Punish him (as one does a child) for murder;
If he has let a rose-bush die of thirst,
Poor mother of full many a poor child, —
Refuse to him the cup of clear, cold water;
Has he disturbed the nest of the young birds,
Let him sleep hungry on the hard, bare ground,
No mother, father, brother, sister, near.
And if thy child thus early has atoned,
With such divine severity, for slight
Yet dangerous missteps from right and truth,
Then shall he leave one day the grove of youth
With holy sense of this most beauteous world,

And dwell unfallen in a Paradise
Even here on earth; and all the heavy faults
By which men forfeit the true joy of man
Thou thus hast spared him, broken in the bud;
For he who spares the dew-drop on the grass
Will never wring out tears from human eyes;
Fancy keeps watch o'er purity of heart.
O count it not as play, this early, sure
Correction of the tender, trustful child!
To look upon the tender, lovely world
With love, to feel it tenderly, — is bliss, —
And bliss within the heart prevents all woe.

XI.

No Man liveth by, or for Himself.

Each one man's glory is humanity's,
If only that all comes to him from men
Of old times and his own, to win him to them.
Their very future gives him heart to work,
Not *his;* and all the human myriads are
The lesser mirrors, that make up for him
The one great mirror which exhibits him
Great as he is, and greater, great as all.
The living eats the fruit of ages dead.
And none can keep his doings to himself,
Nor would he, if he could. The best intends
His work for others; for a great mind feels
The world to be itself, itself the world.
The good man's evening-redness, — glory is;
Of great men 't is the ruddy light of dawn;
To the most great 't will be some time the day,

Yet not his own, but that of all beside,
To him remote, unheard-of. So can pure
Love for humanity yield only deeds
Long resonant, which all men love to tell:
"How great is man, — how beautiful is earth!"
Achilles chose fame for divinity,
And even he gained not the fame he gave:
For we now have it, we enjoy it, ours
Achilles is, and ours too his renown;
Under his name the flower blooms (that is all)
Homer once deeply planted in his heart.
Who honoreth is enriched by him he honors,
The lover is made rich by the beloved;
Every fair thing enriches its admirer,
And man himself lives for the God on Earth.

XII.

Worth of great Souls to Humanity.

There are, at all times, but a few great hearts
Who clearly understand the world, and clearly
Distinguishing the true and good therein,
Clearly reject and hate the bad and false.
Esteeming beauty as a holy thing,
They lift it up before the people's eyes, —
(As Moses did his magic serpent, which,
Mortal itself, yea, dying, healed all those
Who looked on it, by their own power of faith), —
To make them well thereby; their love becomes
The love of many; what they hate inflames
The people's hate; forever reprobate
Is that which the great heart has reprobated.
The sun shines up in heaven, that flowers may bloom!

Geniuses only war with geniuses,
Crossing their weapons o'er far centuries;
And earliest-comers slay the latest ones!
And oft the first fall only by the last!
And to *their* graves they drag whole myriads down.
The flowers will bloom, while shines the sun in heaven.

XIII.

Expectation is Possession.

Expecting is itself substantial joy.
In expectation lies the entire form
Of that which thou expectest, hundred-fold:
What it shall be; what it will really be,
And all it may be for the world and thee.
The thing itself, then, comes as a detached
Phenomenon, — a shell without its sea!
A drop, from out the golden evening clouds!
The fairest, richest *present* needs to be
Artistically congregated in the breast;
The *future* lies, one whole, within the mind.
What thou expectest, that thou hast, and longer
And better, than when once 't is in thy grasp.
This, only, makes the present bearable;
T is this makes youth so lovely and so rich!
To look at things over the shoulder is
The poorest way to see them, — age's way,
Which by experience grows wise — and dies!

XIV.

Spirits and Bodies.

There are innumerable grave-diggers,
Vampyres without number: — evil men!
They *are* such, for they would be, — feel themselves
To be such, — and the mind* is the true man;
How much of horrible, flesh hides! The world
Is but the place, where mind transforms itself
To whatsoe'er it will, materials
And means thereto being at hand for all.
Man is and makes himself whate'er he will;
Only a ghostly being here and now,
But in a new existence, haply he
Shall be rewarded with a body, too, —
And in the resurrection I rejoice!
Not for that there I may behold revealed
The hideous monsters bad men truly are;
No, but that I may see the heavenly shapes,
The lofty, godlike forms of shining ones,
Who, here humiliated, crushed, and poor,
Feeling this life their burden, dumb with woe,
Have risen from boors to citizens of heaven,
By their own will uplifted. In the realm
Of the free will is man omnipotent,
Yet often is content to be a *king*.†

* *Mind* is here used in the Scriptural sense. — Tr.
† The first half of this piece reminds one of Lowell's "Ghost-Seer." — Tr.

XV.

How to know Nature.

The wisest way of learning Nature is
For man to live his round of human life;
He knows that circle, that he can fill out,
When the absorbing WHOLE would cripple him.
Now what each creature is to learn and prove,
For that Nature herself has fitted it.
What 't is to be a lily, or a bee,
That man can never know nor comprehend;
But the bee knows it and the lily too.
Time is immeasurable: Nature's world
Can wholly be learned out; thousands of ways
There are to prove all her felicities,
Masks, dresses, small and great, innumerable,
And light in each department, every nook,
That one may clearly see, and even be, all.

XVI.

All Creatures dear to God.

What may be, is; what may spring forth, springs forth.
Thus there *may* be one mind, and therefore is,
That in itself contemplates and enjoys
Through an invisible, pervading chain
All that the scarcely separated beings
Of all the worlds enjoy, see, think, and are,
That is at once, what they are, each and all,
And, at the same time, infinitely more.
So a good mother in the summer time

Hands round to all her children strawberries;
But one she tastes beforehand with her lips
And gives it to the infant in her lap,
Which they forgot, — because it lay so still!
And yet she truly tastes upon her tongue
How to her every child, and even the least,
The sweet strawberry tastes upon the tongue:
And as they smile, she smiles, with joy, for oft
Her childhood knew the flavor of the fruit:
And, if thou wilt, note kindly this one thing:
The image of "the Mother of us all"
At Ephesus, the fair, majestic shape,
Was but an earlier statue, piously
Hewn out by men in marble, of "*Our Father!*"

XVII.

Why does the new Bride weep?

Why weeps the lovely bride, who knowingly,
Willingly drawn by a resistless charm,
Has given herself, a pure, chaste virgin now,
Forever to her youth, her dear one? Ah,
She flieth, sobbing, to her mother's arms
And weeps out like a child upon the heart
Which lovingly has watched her destinies
Up to this very day. — Why *does* she weep?
These are not tears of sorrow and of pain, —
She is too glad to comprehend her bliss;
Nor yet for her dear mother does she weep,
Nor for the home, the garden, and the trees,
Which, to a ripe young womanhood grown up,
She now must leave, and with another walk.

Nor weeps she yet for joy, — for ah, her mother
Weeps with her too, and for her daughter weeps,
Whom she, — sole thanks for all her pains! — must lose!
Must yield her up into another's arms,
Forced from the old, familiar track of life!
Nor does she weep with trembling, as for fear;
For there is naught to fill her heart with dread,
Not for a noble spouse, a rich estate;
And children, in presentiment beheld,
Would surely only make her blush and smile!
— "Why weep'st thou then?" — a faithful sister asks,
And takes her hand, imploring. — "Ah, I weep," . . . .
She says, ... "I stand on one of those bold heights
Of life! By imperceptible degrees
Have I, with infant's, child's, and maiden's step,
Climbed hither, — and amazed I now look down
On the long tract — thousands of years — which I
Have left behind me, — and before me lie
Thousands of years of untried coming life, —
And in the midst, here in this hour, I stand
Leaning upon a mother's heart! My hand
Clasped in a brother's! as if heavenly spirits
Attended me! — and must this beauteous hour
Pass by? This too be naught? Nay, it shall be
The highest, loveliest, most blissful one
Of my existence. Yea, in this poor life
The holiest to my heart. O mother, mother,
And brother, ah, there is a life eternal,
Whereof our fairest hours are only tones,
Echoes, — that wake a shudder in the breast!
But the whole soul is not yet quite awake,
And so, before the bliss which weighs me down,
Like a poor flower beneath the drenching rains

From full spring-tempests, do I bow and sink!
The inexpressible, ... I feel it now,
I have it! You I have! And you have me, —
And have so little, ah, in my poor self!
And why I weep, — if truly I divine:
I weep from deepest human modesty."
— And so the holy hour had likewise passed;
And now had we, as from a mountain-top
Of outlook wide, descended to the vale,
And went to sit around the nuptial board,
And there serenely the old moon looked in.

XVIII.

The Virgin coming from the Churchyard.

The fairest maid that from the churchyard comes,
Has lost all charm henceforth for the day's eye:
Now as a mortal she appears, a shadow
From yonder deep, dark ground of azure blue,
Which men call heaven and eternity,
Veiled with the glory, from that world, she sheds.
All meek and lowly walks she at thy side, —
All melancholy walk'st thou at her side, —
Who would make her his wife? For he to-day
Desires no mortal wife! To him life seems
Not worth even just beginning, — and lo, there
He just now saw it ended, thousand-fold.
She softly prints a "good night" on his hand;
"To-morrow I will come again," says he.
"To-morrow!" she replies; and none can say
Thou bring'st not, gracious Sun, new days to men,
Making all life immortal in thy beams.

XIX.

The Child in his Paradise.

He has been playing all day long; has sate
With flowers, and given them food and drink, as if
They were his little children, and has closed
The very eve with pleasures; and so now
Sweet sleep comes over him so speedily, —
The little soul seems as if breathed away!
And yet to-morrow he 'll forget it all,
And live again, filled with a new-born day;
Full to child's ecstasy of endless life.
For when his mother shall become one day, ...
One day, as small again, as he himself, ...
Then will he bear her on his arms, and all
She 's done for him, he vows his little hand
Shall do for her, and seals it with a kiss!
And even now he weeps for joy, poor thing!
Not knowing, *whom*, one day, — in mother's stead, —
God in his arms shall lay, ... Himself, as child.
Thus is there still a Paradise on earth,
Still in the midst of us and at our side,
At hand! within us! For we feel it nigh!
We, — we can weep, too, even in Paradise,
And suffer, like the child, — (for children suffer
Much greater, sorer inexpressibly,
And bitterer woe than we), — we can behold
Even Nature's frailty, — see her fade, and die;
Yes, see her die, and yet remain in heaven,
Just as the child in his sweet heaven abides.
That makes the power of love! The power to see
That, like the heart, all nature is divine;

That time exists not, — naught but blissful work;
Nor space, but only one wide heavenly life!
Buoyant as childhood must the pure soul be,
Busy as childhood, without care or fear,
Nursing not distant thoughts, but near and deep,
Filled wholly with a present majesty;
Then, then, shall we too, not unconsciously
But unconcernedly, without a hope
Of better things, or yet a fear of worse,
Or looking for an end, — enjoy ourselves.
The clear enjoyment of the free, whole soul
That is complete enjoyment; consciousness
Comes after bliss, — Living, alone, is life!
Not re-collecting, ... stringing empty shells! *

XX.

Honor the homeliest Callings.

Why wilt thou mock at poor humanity,
That this one is, forsooth, a tooth-puller,
That other one a Doctor; that the joiner
Will, for whoever shall bespeak the same,
Prepare a coffin in the sweat of 's brow,
And beg his future custom heartily;
That the grave-digger lives by burying,
And often murmurs too at the hard times;
That yonder man upon the powder-house
At risk of life sets up a lightning-rod;
While here the constables come bringing in

* It is just to add the original: —

"Erinnerung nicht, . . . Zusammenreihen! . . . Sammeln."

The robber with the block upon his foot.—
Behold! all do an indispensable work:
To-day 's required task, with tranquil mind,
A calmer mood than thousands can command,
Who deem themselves too good for such low work!
The little men do the great things for life,
By the enormous power of their chain,
And lead it onward to its shining goal.
Do thou not think for others! Feel thou not
For all men! Do thy work as quietly,
O heart! Then shalt thou feel like joy in thine!
Be thou content to *know* what others *do*,
Who hardly know it,—and admire them!
Self-mastery makes the master,—and the man!

XXI.

[Matthew xxi.]

Humanity made God in Christ.

Much had He thought and suffered, in whose road
Ye strew, as for a king, a wall of palms,
Your sorrows he had conquered, and his own.
He saw what 't was you did, that full of joy,
Ye consecrated him to be a king.
Such is he still! Of all the tribes of earth,
Ev'n of all kings, who bow the knee to him,—
Or sink before him, ... if they *scorn* his word,—
For *every* good man's word demands obedience.
Thus has the carpenter Joseph's foster-son
Lifted himself from out his lowly hut,
By seeming to desire so near to naught:
Not land, nor people, house,—not even a stone

To yield his head a pillow, for the night, —
For *that* he left next morning in the field.
And yet he did desire all things, of all;
Only he could not own all that at once, —
And so possesses all things by degrees.
He was too great to sit upon a throne;
A king of men, who 'd reign in palaces,
Must wear the chains of 's time, he must be small,
And seem still smaller, limiting himself,
Holding himself a prisoner by his care
And thought for bread, for neighbors, land, and life.
This he gave up! No people did he find
Made for him, — he created for himself
A people, and creates it evermore: —
Humanity! And *it* must be a man
Like him. As he. The Son of God. Even God.
Who gives a glass of water to the faint,
Gives it to God. Whoso denies it him
Leaves God to thirst, who thirsts for love, whose thirst
Love and a lovely soul alone can slake.
Then gladly lose thy personality, —
Which thou, as Thou, hast not, but may'st become, —
In the most high and holy person, — God!
To no one be thou subject, but thy God,
For God is thine, more than thy heart and arm:
Nor be ashamed of this: to disappear
As in the sea the drop, — nor yet be proud,
For to partake of God is but our nature,
As every flower enjoys the heavenly dew, —
And every flower sends up its prayer: "Our Father."
It does far more than praying it aloud, —
It shows it forth, by tender, heavenly grace,
It *is* the prayer, — it is the child of God.

—Now go and walk a little in the garden
Of Spring and hear the chime of Easter bells!

XXII.

Stealing.

Last night, by dark, the poor old woman came,
And from thy pantry stole a fragrant loaf.
Well! and shall I be angry, then, that she
Was hungry? Shall I laugh, that she, thus driven,
Took what *I* had not given her, unconcerned
For the poor people and their poverty!
No! let me rather pity her whose soul,
By my hard-heartedness and other men's,
Was forced to such a pitiable act!
Let me take pity on myself, who, having,
Cared not and thought not who around me starved!
And,—that we may not twice commit a fault,—
Go, give her double, in advance, and further,
Bid the poor woman come again to me.
The rich, hard-hearted man who gives not, steals.
The poor man only does it in his place.
The strong, the blind, and the unmerciful
Bear the world's guilt and all its misery.
To meet the one just as we do the other,—
Laying on all alike an equal load,
Of hardness, chastisement, yea, even revenge,—
Would hardly pass for justice down in hell.
He is the just man who gives each his due.
Thou, therefore, then, and only then, art just,
When thou, as man, giv'st thy whole self to each,
A perfect goodness and a perfect love:
For that is his in thee, and thine in him.

XXIII.

The Greatness of Man.

Who tells, how great is man! For earth supplies
No standard. By proportion we may guess.
Of monstrous creatures the most monstrous, — such
That Nature makes us look on her with dread
And horror, — the most fell of hideous shapes,
More frightful far than the gigantic snakes,
More loathsome than the crocodile, more still
And stealthy than the foul hyena, gnashing
Their teeth of mastodons, more strange and grim,
With their mask-heads and scaly coats of mail,
Than Ahriman could e'er invent in dream, —
Thousands and thousands of such creatures, seas
Swarming with such, — man daily eats and drinks.
He sees them not. Yet had he a god's eyes,
How great would they appear to him, — how great
Would man appear to man! The human face
The magic disk of a gigantic moon!
A wood of hollow snake-trees covers it.
Like far snow-mountains shining in the sun
His forehead gleams, a heaven of ivory,
A sacred arch covers the laboratory
Of soul and brain, as in warm March white snow
Covers the teeming bosom of the earth.
The mouth a grotto with stalactites white
Of teeth appears, — and in it dwells Chimera,
The tongue, free-moving, fettered in the abyss.
Thence, as of old from Delphi's sacred cave,
From the dark spirit-castle of the world
Oracular words sound up, and voices of the gods!
Two precious stones, blue spheres, unscalable,*

* Unübersehbar, — not to be looked over.

Repose, ... nay live! . . . . themselves inspiring life,
Each under cover of its shady grove,
Sparkling like lakes, Diana's looking-glasses,
Bright, fathomless! and out from them gleams forth
The power of the glance, the soul of love,
As the sea gleams by night with inner fire;
And great drops of clear liquid, — such 't is said,
The chaste wife of the Brahmin yonder drew,
Gather themselves and globe themselves, — to tears.
Man, like the world, admits no measurement.
Hence, to the fine-souled Greeks, the face serene
Of man, in all his glory and his strength,
Appeared and was their highest God: their Zeus.
Not greater than majestic, strength-crowned man,
The Indian figures to himself his God,
Reigning omnipotent through purest love.
How great now should man's body be esteemed,
Who stands upon creation's farthest verge,
. . . . A hermit on the spirit-ocean's brink, ...
Thousands below him; and above him none! —
Wrapped in the human race are thousand kinds
Of higher beings, heavenly natures all, —
For where 's the line shall sound the deeps of mind?
And were it possible to find bottom there, —
What measure e'er can reach to Virtue's height!
Of Love who measures the pure blessedness!

XXIV.

Rest.

"*One* rest alone is possible," yet not
The rest of indolent slumber in the grave!
True rest is the calm energy of Mind,

Which, in the world, yet high above all worlds,
Hovering serene, all evil holds in chains,
So full of good that it knows not the bad,
And yields to love pure sway. To it belongs
The liveliest life! unmarred tranquillity,
Conflict with all the world: the deepest peace!
. . . . The all-pervading Power that ceaselessly
Its boundless work continues in profound
Primeval stillness, — wilt thou to *that* power
Deny repose, tranquillity, and bliss?
To God? — And God's rest is not in the grave!
I must go through the grave to come to Him,
And hope, in love and labor, to find — peace!
God is no better thing than thou — canst be.

XXV.

Man the Child of his Time.

Each is a child and creature of his time.
What grows around him, he drinks in, and grows.
What in a later age unfolds itself,
That sweeps, like wind and rain, with godlike might,
But fruitless, o'er the head of the ripe crop.
Youth only is the fructifying time,
As is the spring to budding trees; what *then*
Bloomed not as man, was not impregnated
By floating pollen, *that* he ne'er puts forth,
To that he never ripens, for himself
Or others, that expect thou not of him.
The works of man, when he grows up, become
Only what he in youth, yea, childhood, was; *

* See a beautiful passage in "My Early Days," beginning, "The clew of our destiny, wander where we will, lies at the cradle's foot."

For what he thinks and feels and loves and lives,
And all his further doing, but unfolds,
Elaborates, and completes the child — no more!
And when man dies, his works are buried with him,
And their first influence. O then call not Death
"Nothing at all!" 'T is something verily
To leave one's work unfinished in the midst.
The world 's full, roaring stream rolls on its wealth,
Crowning therewith the newly broken shores,
Meanwhile the old shores stand there petrified,
And full of petrified forms that once were men,
Holding aloft their works upon their hands,
Which, like the hand, are also turned to stone!*
And only spirit with its wakening power
Opens again the book, full of the breath
Of withered roses, fresh no more; for it
The divine Spirit's human Avatar,
Its transit across time, is here arrested,
Full of a truth and beauty of its own,
Yet not the highest, not the Eternal one;
Sacred to men as the time-hardened rut
In which their ancestors, when living, went;
And blooming flowers breathe fragrance in the track
As in sarcophagi of risen men!
Who cannot rouse, remains himself entombed,
To him the old world lives, but not the new;
For life itself waits to be animated!
But he who rises from the graves awakes
Thousands of dead. The life-giver is gloriously
Enriched with that to which he giveth life,
And all its worth he, too, himself is worth.

* An apparent allusion to the Memnon statues by the Nile.

XXVI.

The Mother at her Child's Burial.

Lo, where a solemn man, and silent, ... clad
In a black mantle, ... in the golden morn,
Forth to the green and grassy place of graves
Walks, carrying a little coffined child:
And though half hidden, still the morning sun
Espies the little coffin, and from heaven
Graciously gilds it for the few short steps!
How e'en the old man is touched by children's death!
And yet none follows this one with wet eyes!
Only, be certain, — the poor mother there,
Standing before her house, weeps bitterly,
Strains her sad gaze and seems to beg the man
To let her darling down right tenderly!
And veils herself for grief. — At length she sees
For the first time, scarcely distinguishable, . . .
The little grave far off, clad in fresh green, —
She weeps aloud and flies. For she, she knew
The child, — yea, knew it as she knew herself!
. . . . And seest thou, seest thou, heart, who 't is that
love?
They love, who know! Who know well, truly love!
Acquaint thyself with men, and with the world;
With strangers even, and the foreign world,
And thou wilt love them as the mother loves
Her child. For to its very mother once
The little child was strange, — was new! and yet
As near akin as she is to her child —
So near art thou to God and to the world;
So deeply bound to be acquainted with them!

— Go now, pluck flowers! and twine a little wreath
And thankful lay it on the little grave.

XXVII.

Honor thy Father.

Thou honorest not thy Father, proudly saying:
"All being from itself derives its worth,
Each one creates his life's worth and his own!
The boy soon learns to find it beautiful
For pleasure's sake; the father holds it dear
Because of his dear children; and the mother, —
To her 't is priceless for his sake and theirs;
Each day its worth enhances; coarsest men
By custom come to be in love with it,
Till it grows wellnigh indispensable!
— He thought but of himself; how then of me!" —
Experience exempts from special thought.
Just as the human dwells in God, the old
Head of the family to us and all, —
The impulse to become and be a man, —
So in the mind and in the sense of man
— Of human kind, — male woman, — female man, —
Already dwell, mysteriously inborn,
The dear and cherished forms of spouse and child;
For else the woman would not seek the man
Nor man seek woman, and, by woman, children;
As on the rose-bush he, in lovely May,
By right already hopes, expects the rose.
So has the father long fore-dreamed his child
The while it lived in him, as the fruit's bud
Secretly lives within the parent-tree;

Thus has he known thee, loved thee, ere thy birth!
And when thou camest, fondly gazed on thee,
And said to thee exulting: "Art thou here?"
But he who bare existence gave to thee,
Gave thee therewith all that which afterward
Made of existence beauteous life for thee.
He who a naked rose-twig sendeth thee,
Has given thee, surely, all its roses too, —
'T was just the roses he presented thee!
Not the bare rose-twig, plainly; for he knew
That in the twig a thousand roses slept,
Which thou should'st one day gather and enjoy.
But He who gave thee being 's fruitful twig,
Gives thee, beside it, earth, sun, warmth, and rain,
And a whole heaven of bliss and loveliness.
Thou art to be a man! That thou would'st be
He knew and well commended it to thee!
And art thou thankful for the gift, — why then,
Thy common bread becomes a precious joy.
The ungrateful makes life ashes! Gratitude
Could of itself create its God, and Father!

XXVIII.

Happiness that survives Youth.

If 't were to be that none should longer live
Who love no longer in the worldly sense,
Who nothing crave, but objects of pure choice;
If none were longer happy, all henceforth
Unblest, whom beauty could no more befool
As once, when, for the first time, the young soul
Looked upon beauty with astonishment, —

Then must the mighty multitude of men,
Soon as the uncertain days of youth are gone,
Be carried to the grave! Then none should live
To know the blessings of the further life
Which youth was but the entrance to, the time
Of preparation, and apprenticeship;
All man had earned were smoke and vanity;
The large, the tranquil look out into life,
The sympathy with richly-dowered humanity,
The knowledge how to dwell in the Gods' house,
At once an inmate both of earth and heaven.
—But no, 't is only the unloved thou seest,
Only the inwardly uncultivated,
Drag o'er their youthful passions into days
Which bring to others new and radiant joy;
And now, unsated and insatiable,
Cold to the heart, corrupting and corrupt,
Only not utterly despair, because
Used to their load. But the great people of men,
Following in life's procession, ev'n the poor, ...
Yea, poorest, (they who do not glut themselves
With feelings they are ever warming over,
And painfully imposing on the world,)
Them thou behold'st like fruit-trees, fair and prosperous,
Bearing what their bloom promised; letting fall
What they have borne,—full of new buds again!
The young man's rosy cheeks, the father's boys
Now wear, as if their kisses from his cheeks
Had stole the rosy hue! The young bride's laugh
Is laughed now by her girls! Meanwhile the mother
Smiles only! Mildness is her greatest joy.
Her deepest sadness is sobriety;
Yet is her mildness blest; her soberness

Is holy! For 't is pictured on the face
Which God in the beginning stamped on man,
And said to him: "So shalt thou then be glad,
When making others glad thy gladness is,
And drying others' tears makes thy tears flow!"
Then let delusive show delude not thee,
For there 's a natural sweet in vice itself,
What scarcely lengthens out the base man's life, —
It is not that which gives the good man pain,
Sore sense of loss. And feel'st thou discontent
At times, think it not strange that thou should'st feel,
As his new life the unsheathed butterfly,
The daily transformation of the man
Within thee, and of men and earth around,
And the infinitude of life itself!
The genuine man is happy all the time, —
Yet happiness has its own sadness too!

XXIX.

What produces its like is Mortal.

That which brings forth its equal, new and young,
Whether it be plant, bird, or fish, or man,
Is mortal: for to lengthen out its life,
Perhaps forever, — it renews its youth.
And therefore are all tulips called — the tulip!
And therefore are all swallows called — the swallow,
As if they were but one, and are but one,
The same that comes with the eternal Spring!
They that produce what 's earthly, pass away
Like summer-plants, and do not winter here,
Require continually new shoots, new springs,

In order not to perish with the year.
But,—that which dies not brings not forth its like;
For having life within itself it stands
In thousand children's stead, like sun and moon
And stars. Wilt thou, now, be immortal, man—
Then bring forth naught but that which is divine
In beauty, truth, morality! naught else
Than what thou art thyself and of thyself
Mayest become:—this is art's noble work;
This the true word,—the good deed; many a one!
This shall abide like thee,—its dwelling-place
The Kingdom of the Sun;—it shall abide
Forevermore in that mysterious realm!
It propagates itself, with heavenly increase,
Yet lasts, itself,—like sun and moon and stars.

XXX.

The Auricula's Children and ours.

Thus early from the Auricula, still in bloom,
Loosening themselves again, behold, ... her children, ...
Future auriculas! And now when they
Strike root in turn, then will they need no more
The mother-stalk; and yet without a pang
The flower-mother sees this and lets it pass!
But yonder,—see! that very little girl
Makes her a doll! so soon! and with alarm
I look upon it! For the doll, *that* means
To her already her own future daughter;
And as she plays,—that is, in earnest lives,—
She thinks no longer of her mother, save
In play! .... And with a smile the mother sees it all.

— So good are parents, so disinterested!
So void of truth is man from childhood up!
So artful is he, and withal appears
So innocent, ... and the soul feels so too;
For every being is ordained to this:
That it exists. And this to help it do,
Is of its parents the — unconscious — task.
Lo, where a bride goes yonder to the Church,
And from the Church home to her husband's house,
And not till now the mother — father — weep!
Although long since in secret was that heart
Loosed from them, that best heart, — so full of love!
Yet will they smile, out of a great, deep swell
Of natural feeling, when, one of these days,
The daughter's little daughter comes to them
And in her lap — makes the new doll again!

THE LAYMAN'S BREVIARY.

MAY.

MAY.

MAY.

I.

Time divides, — Thought unites.

THAT Time is all *one* time, that years are naught, —
O say not so! Thou bitterly shalt feel
There was a world before thee; centuries,
Years, were, that now with adamantine walls,
Though not unkindly, yet inexorably
Part thee from men, — who would have been thy friends,
Yet who, beside thy brown hairs, even now,
Gray-haired and blind, go tottering on the staff, —
From trees, — that having closed their life, e'en now
Decay in thy green prime. But not the less
From children, beauteous children, who in sweet
Confusion look on thee with their black eyes,
And smile, not guessing what thy sadness means,
Smile and yet sigh. For darkly they divine
That solar ban, which shuts each mortal up
In the fixed bound of his appointed days:
Majestic man and the sweet race of flowers,
The blooming bush, the lambs upon the mead,
The silent cloud that sails along o'erhead,
The very blade of grass, and all that lives,
That has lived and that shall hereafter live.
— One comfort only know I in this grief,
Which is no grief, but folly, to light minds:

That we, with vigorous senses, placed between
That which has just gone by, and that which comes,
Behold the fading and the budding one,
And reach a hand at once to each of them!
And, — that what dawned, and has kept pace with us,
Mirrors the foreworld and the afterworld,
In form and essence answering perfectly,
Full of peculiar charms enough to wake
Both joy and woe, when found, — when sadly lost!

II.

Lowest and Loftiest need each other.

Set man as high as e'er thou wilt, but leave him
Still on the earth! Mated with ox and ass,
Man, as in Bethlehem once, must still be born.
Not without cow, not without salt indeed,
Comes any one to Heaven, for so none comes
And stays upon the earth. Were there no sponge
There were no cordial, without wood no cross.
Thus even history grows, — out of the woods.
And stones must be, to make morality true;
Wherewith, then, would they, before Christ, have stoned
The woman taken in adultery!
All that exists, fits, and belongs together,
E'en man and cloud, no less than child and nurse.

III.

Love kept alive by Imagination.

Sure, self-based and our own, is happiness,
And all things purely felt remain in us.

How indispensable to our love we deem
The loved one! and lo! soon the fatal years
Divide us from her, and no more her form
Lives round about us, — and yet first love's rapture
Abides within us still, just as the light
Of day continues, when the sun is hid
Behind the clouds. And so we reach old age,
With riches won from youth, from our whole life!
For all our feelings were but golden keys
Unlocking for us earth's wide store-house, full
Of beauty's treasures: not for things we cared,
But for the inner growth and coming forth
In heart and mind. And wilt thou follow me,
Then kindle oft within thee feeling's flame!
Her office even conception shall refuse,
Unless thou often wak'st her images;
Yea, thine own mother's face shalt thou forget,
Dost thou not often call it up to thee.
"Thou carest nothing for it," Nature thinks.
But whatsoe'er is holy to thy heart,
To her is also holy for thy sake.

IV.

Nothing dies to the Soul.

Why must life's lovely visions, like yourselves,
Phantoms as well, be gradually lost?
Heart-truth, true love, is not the only truth,
There is a truth of spirit in loving, living,
To every blossom and to every rose
That beckoned to us travellers, passing by,
And said, "Remember me! — Think of thyself! —

For even this bright to-day, the day, is thou!
And lo, just now, for one short instant, I
Was thou! — Remember me! — Think of thyself!"
And how they love to appear in us, — the forms
That linger in the soul and slumber there!
How they, with cheeks all rosy-red from sleep,
Awaking light and gay, as children do,
Open their great eyes full upon their friend,
Who let them sleep, like children, all the time
While he himself journeyed, and loved and lived.
And yet you see no tear-drop in their eyes;
The little sister reaches out for thee!
Thy little child, whose little beaming face
Is quenched to thee, begs to be taken up!
Another smiles on thee, as if not she,
No, thou, ... a little child, — were just awaked;
She longs to press thee to her bosom, — thou
Canst never press her to thy bosom more, —
And to stir still more deeply thy sweet sorrow,
To quicken with diviner life thy love,
They vanish from thee down the vast, dark deep
Of thy soul's realm! But thou, as Moses once
Beheld the burning bush, in heavenly fire,
Hast seen once more thy being all aglow.

V.

All live for each.

To make a single nail requires a forge,
A fire, an anvil, bellows, and a master;
A drop of rain requires a cloudy heaven,
A single rose requires the whole wide earth,

The sun, the powers of Nature all combined,
Though but a moment, and as in mere play.
To make a man takes the whole spirit-realm,
To make one child, takes the whole human race
Up to the first creation-day of time,
When that primeval power, that old Master,
Sat there aglow, and coined the creatures fair
In heavenly fire, in the magic workshop.
This is no dream, no fable, but cool truth.
Then freely breathe, heart, wellnigh stifled now
In yearning pains at sight of all that flood
And pomp of beauty! Thou, too, art, — art one
Of the divine creations, bearing still
A holy kindred to those wonders all.
For thee, too, is the universe, and shines
As truly, steadfastly, and gloriously
As the blue heaven, for each, yet all for thee!
So wholly thine, as if 't were thine alone!
The little green-finch in his slender nest,
Claims a whole wood for his; the little smerlin
Has a whole lake for his; the little rose,
The loveliness of suns, and the whole sun
With all his power. — And thou, and thou, dear man,
Thou by thy thought and feeling hast them all,
The entire spirit-realm. — Behold, amazed,
The power that, magic-like, bequeathed its house
To a thousand children, ... and the whole to each!

VI.

What we do to Others, we do to Ourselves.

Whate'er thou doest to thy fellow-man,
That very thing thou doest to thyself.

For he is — thou! One spirit are we all,
As light is everywhere one light. One flesh,
As bread all kneaded of a common dough.
The good thou doest is for thy good, the bad
Is bad for thee. Therefore thou bid'st the beggar
Come back again! and fosterest the sick lamb.
And every heart that wounds another heart
Feels the blood steal away from its own breast!
And so the murderer cries, while the dead man
Is silent as with heavenly shame. — And so,
A child is silent with astonishment
When for the first time from his mother, — her, —
God's image, — he receives an angry blow!
And paleness overspreads him, as one dead.

VII.

The Measure of Life.

By what shall life be reckoned? What event
Of time, or what experience of the soul?
The whole of life itself has no result
That can be seen; no child, or youth, or man,
Or old man, anywhere attains a goal,
Finds other human end, — than human life.
None of them leave behind them anywhere
A mask; slough off a skin, as does the snake.
Only, at last, the dying leaves — the dead!
Lightly they glide through metamorphoses,
Continually, yet imperceptibly
Even to themselves, changed to new beings, yet
Under the same, old, ever youthful sun.
By charming visions, wild, enchanting nights,

Nay, by good deeds, no noble spirit counts;
'T is little that the best can bring to pass.
Whereby then shall we measure life? By years?
By rapturousness of joy? Can images
Of fairest hours hide haply the bare walls
Of age? Can that which scarcely is remembrance,
Bare satisfaction, can it, self-sufficing,
Like gold, be dragged through sorrow to the grave?
— Dream not of reckoning, O vain man, with God!
Yet wherewith, then, shall life so fill itself,
That at each hour it shall be rich and whole?
Man's bliss comes never to him from without;
The rich man buys his pleasures all for naught;
The loftiest oft stands hollow as the poor, —
Love fills the soul, and keeps it full, of help
For others, sweet refreshment to itself;
The good man has life's fountain in himself;
Wherewith he gladdens all within his reach
From early dawn till night, and even in dream
He still holds out the cup! He sees; he hears;
He stays; he journeys; he is young; grows old;
Is old; is poor, — rich ever in the same
Good-will, the same *inspired, divine delight*
In the fair creatures of the first-fair, God,
For whom, as a true lover, he is still
Ready to die, and ready, too, to live!
Life has no goods, it has no goal for him;
Such living is itself a holy good,
Is God, as every sunbeam witnesses.
Knowledge of Nature, — I have called its name;
For love grows out of it, as fruit from bud.

VIII.

Love of Nature makes us one with her.

Study of holy Nature re-creates
In loving reverence the great Master's work,
And from the full love-bathed, love-dripping work,
Love breathes, it trickles down into the soul,
Whose yearning gaze would fain survey it all!
The gardener bears the scent of the spring flowers;
The dyer has, himself, as heaven-blue hands
As his dye-kettle's contents are heaven-blue;
The young physician gradually learns
To love his first sick maiden, and himself
Grows sick with love; yet with what heightened charms
He sees her as the well, the grateful woman!
The friend of flowers, who sought the flowers alone,
Is fast chained even by the loveliness
Of the sweet science. Whoso understands
And penetrates a matter to the bottom,
Is to the bottom of his heart, life-long
Drawn to it, loves to teach and practise it.
From the best master only must one learn.
Thou learnest from his work the master's art.
A work thou understandest not becomes
Mysteriously dear to thee, when once
Thou knowest, 't is from thy Master! 't is his best!
Boldly think thus of Nature! And create
With tender reverence, after her,—herself,
A lovely image in thy soul's pure glass,
And thou wilt love her with a human love.
For what thou comprehendest, that thou too
Wouldest have done, and ah, thy spirit whispers:

Thou art thyself His work, the lofty power,
All that thou art; and ah, thy spirit whispers:
Thou too had'st once a hand in this great work,
As sure as thou art spirit, old, primeval,
Eternal; else how could'st thou grasp a law
Of such a work, just as if thou thyself
Had'st written down the paths the stars should take?
And now love's longing rises to the heart!
Yet rapture rises higher, rises highest!
For lo! the beautiful and loving one
Who wore thy mother's mask and lineaments,
Who was it then, — when the grave snatched her from
thee, —
But she! She, — Nature's self, most intimate self!
And then the man, who took so faithfully
The semblance of thy father, who so oft
Kissed thee so fondly with his human mask,
And looked out on thee with such loving pride
From those great eyes of his, — he, too, was she,
He, too, was Nature's self, a living work
Proceeding from the full, the magic whole;
And ah! who then may all the others be?
Those sweet, familiar forms, men, flowers, moon, stars?
Who may'st thou be thyself? If thou dar'st guess!
Who may the workman be and who the work?
If thou for holy dread canst guess the truth!
So, then, from love of nature streameth love.
But what may love itself be, holy Love?
The master's life and being, and thine too.
— If now thou wilt, canst love, or if thou must,
I will not say the word half way: "Have love,"
Nay! rather feel that you yourselves are love.

IX.

Each for all and all for each.

The greatest vantage for humanity
Is this: that each does everything for all,
And each in turn receives from all the same.
How little one contributes to the whole,
How much, however, one receives from all!
How true a guard humanity to each,
How little more is needed after all
For concord, bliss, and peace, and the unmarred
Freedom of all men, than the will of all:
To seek with life itself the good of each!
'T is with the slightest means God will effect
The greatest purposes, — but through the greatest
Of sentiments, through the divinest: Love.

X.

The Star in the East.

There stands the Star of the Three Holy Kings,
Who long ago rode home and turned to dust, —
The star in sacred beauty still shines on.
Yet they too, sacred in our hearts, shine on
Who sometime sought the child, the child alone!
For by the elements and spirits richly
Endowed as by the highest godfathers,
By all the wondrous gifts wellnigh opprest,
There in his cradle lies the new-born babe,
The human child that can do naught but weep.
And yet it is a spirit; 't is love itself!

And in its heart brings with it silently,
As a sealed book, heaven's treasures, nature's law,
Knowledge and understanding of all worlds
And every mystery. And he by and by
Unfolds the book and reads from it aloud,
Reads out aloud to earth and to the sun.
On earth his word is heard, is treasured up,
On earth no work is seen, no temple reared,
No statue, city, tower, or masted ship,
No, not a ring hangs in a maiden's ear,
But all of it at last comes from a child.
For even the others, too, who haply helped
Unroll to him the writing of the stars,
The script of flowers and the papyrus roll
Of holy Nature, helped prepare the works
And represent them, — each was once a child!
Thus all at last comes only from a child:
The inexhaustible fountain's golden mouth, —
And the child seems almost adorable.
Therefore the poorest father is made glad,
When in his hut a child is born to him,
Like to that richest father, Him in Heaven;
And rapturously the poorest mother takes it
Upon her breast and feeds it with her life;
And if so poor as not to own a shred,
With her own body then she covers it,
And thou, who seest this, art left in doubt
Which is more touching, beautiful, and glad:
The child now! or such homage paid to him!

XI.

The human Face divine.

Were there no sun in Heaven, what void were there!
And yet would I live on, if one could live;
But take away the human face, and earth
Were lone and dark as death. O human face
Divine! fair lotus blooming on the deep
Of heaven's great sea besides this earthly shore!
World-mirror, spirit-mask, God's counterfeit!
Thou, thou, enlightenest sky and firmament,
Else dark! Beholding thee, man is no more,
E'en in the wilderness, alone, — all heaven
Has now become as near and beautiful
To every child, as is the world to man.
God stands before us and looks out on us
From the sweet countenance of every child.
The soul were naught, — e'en love itself were naught,
And naught were word or wisdom without thee,
Key of the world, ... though from the hair-crowned head
Of man the very tones of angels rang.
O beauty, thine, thine is the highest prize,
And every face that bears beneath itself
A pious heart of childlike purity, —
As the clear water holds the imaged sun, —
Is beautiful. The human countenance
First made disclosure of the hidden bliss
That in the heart of Nature stirs and throbs, —
And overflows, — in smiles! Upon the face
First shows itself the deep and mighty woe
That thrills through nature in her Holiest;

And when a child is born, when once it lives, ...
When, with its myriad flowers, encircling spring
Is now made new and young, ah, child and spring
First live divinely in the human face,
Live there as nowhere else. The face of man
Like a sun-dial of life shows but bright shadows;
It shows us youth, — which blooms not on the stars,
Nor in the rose so full of trustful charm;
It shows old age, — of which no mouldering tree,
Nor faded leaf such touching truth proclaims,
As the pale countenance, — the silver hair, —
The weary eye of man; and even Death,
The holy, serious, solemn death itself,
Appears in all its wondrous majesty
Only upon man's face. And one thing more:
Thou seest, as through a lightly woven veil,
Through his transparent face the blessedness
Even of the dead, of them that have gone hence
To where the still source of all being is.
— Then let each human face be holy to thee,
Thou never wilt repent revering it,
Be thou field-marshal, surgeon, even king.

XII.

Man's Greatness.

A lamb feeds softly round me on the grass,
A so-called *innocent* creature, — yet is he
A horrid monster to the flowers he crushes,
Mangles, devours, almost more ruthlessly,
Than even the very tiger throttles lambs.
How great is, to these flowers, the very lamb!

What awe inspires the lamb before the dog,
And to the dog how like a God is man,*
Who visibly walks round him, as almighty,
Visibly feeds him, guards him, is his friend!
But thou, O man, standest so bare of God,
So shieldless, over thee the empty blue,
And all that lives, all lies beneath thy feet!
Alas! if only the great child of earth
Had also such a demigod, — such father,
As his own little children have in him?
How great, archangel-like, arrayed in might,
How wondrous, fair, majestical, long-lived,
How blessed would he be! How full of blessing!
And lo! This miracle, — this giant is!
He lives! Yea, a whole race of giants dwells
With men, visibly walking on the earth.
Man has his gods beside him on the earth
Which in his company they daily tread,
And to the same pure sunlight lift their eyes!
And that we may believe them, — they grow up
Amidst the race and in the form of men!
As from the lizard-tribe the alligator,
As from the race of trees the giant-palm,
As platina-grains appear in gold! They are
Guard, guide, stay, solace, to the sons of men,
Round whom the boys so cluster, and on whom
The men look gladly, listening for their word.
Who are these giants of the race of men?
— As not all lumps of gold ore are pure gold,
As love is God's eminent godliness, —
So are the loving, wise, and good of earth

* See the remark of Burns, heard by Scott, about the fidelity of the dog to his god, man.

The truly godlike, demigods, and gods;
And so in olden Scriptures are they named.

XIII.

Atheism of Sorrow rebuked.

"O impudence unrivalled, — in yon heaven, —
Thou shameless, pallid face, thou sun's-eye, — no!
No eye, but only white, unfeeling star
That turns down on the earth a deathly stare
On the great swarm of ghost-like living men,
On graves as grains of sand innumerable!
I have not seen a single happy man,
Nor heard of one, — no, not a single one!
In such a world as this, there can be none,
Each has already suffered, but is yet
To suffer, as if 't were for the first time,
The very child upon his mother's breast;
Not one has gone down to the silent grave,
But some one tore his hair with grief for him,
None, but that wept, himself, when he went down,
Such tears as no one sheds for joy! O world,
So is thy beauty, then, love, riches, joy,
And peace, ay, even the grave, all emptiness!
And yet is that blue vault up yonder, still
Called heaven! — The old, unhappy, ill-starred stars
Are still pronounced: the old, the eternal pomp!
I grudge you not your everlasting bliss.
Come down for me and fill the grave, O Sun,
With thy great lustrous head, — not I for thee
Climb to thy throne!"

And speak'st thou thus, poor man,

Who has just buried his twelfth and only child!
Thou art not wrong, yet neither thus art right!
One word! — The fulness of Eternal life,
What brings it forth? Its last consummate fruit —
Is Death! — What does the richest heart, like thine,
On earth here in the midst of Heaven feel? — Grief!
The most unutterable, the highest woe, —
Longing! — Which has already in itself
All that it yearns for; nay, would fully have it
Then only, when in the most utter want.
Blest sorrow is the pith of the world; its life
Is bitter earnest, — yet mere show! mere dream!
Such a deep dream 't was no light thing to ordain;
For on the columns of the world the stars
All hang, like lamps on the fair temple-walls
Of dream, — the dream from which none ever wakes:
Only we dream, that we *do* dream, — and smile.

XIV.

Moderate Expectations blest.

The heart of man moves always heavily.
Here on the earth the spirit feels itself
Caught like a bird beneath a crystal bell
Wide as the heavens: his wishes, his desires
Not years can satisfy, nor yet the grave,
From the far distance glimmering faintly green.
Thus, whoso now is young and rich and fair,
And seems, for all in all, a happy man,
Has growing care for trifles in his heart.
And he who has to care for daily bread,
For wood to warm his children, even for

A sickly child, that will not let him sleep
Nor even weep, he is the happiest
Of our unsatisfied, insatiate race;
And above all huge fears and huge desires,
Above his dim, low days, the good man's heart
With mild beguiling lifts him far away.
So does the excessive fervor of the Sun
With all the over-rich juices of the earth
In spring bring forth but flowers: it lines the brooks
With a green fringe of grass; o'erspreads the trees
With blossom-snow, — and, doing so, does enough;
For moderation always hits the mark.

XV.

The Value of the Days.

Hold not, I pray, thy days on earth so cheap,
Because so simply and so silently,
So all unknown they glide. Dost thou thyself
Know them? O learn to know them, and thy heart
And mind shall feel, — their glowing life within.
Thou dwellest on the ground of the old world,
By the old loom thou sittest even now,
And holdest the full shuttle in thy hand;
The distant mountains send thee down the rills,
The river, that makes green thy meadow-land:
The unseen oceans welter to and fro
And send thee up the clouds, that visibly
Feed now thy little pears upon the trees,
The very colewort in thy garden-ground;
The winds from their far birthplace sweep along
Across a hundred vales and lift and bow

Thy billowy harvest! Suns, moons, come to thee
From far, far deeps full of primeval bliss,
So near to thee, even through thy window-panes,
And darkly shadow out upon the floor
And wall thyself, thy children's little heads,
The heads of flowers, in lovely images;
Thou livest alive with live ones, who are thine,
Here in this seemingly forgotten vale,—
And far back in the depths of space meanwhile,—
Stars are extinguished, arches crumble in,
And through new seas, new constellations, full
Of joyous life, glide by as tranquilly
As fishes in old meadows swim the ponds!
My heart, *so* small and insignificant
Thy days are, that thou should'st with solemn joy
Give thanks for each of them on bended knees.
Yet, teachest thou meanwhile thy little ones,
Providest for thy house, thinkest pure thoughts
And lovest strangers, giving this one drink
And guiding that one who has lost his way.—
Then have thy days been even divinely spent.

XVI.

Life a Picture.

How magical the ground of human life!
Far more ethereal than the canvass, yea,
The bright enamel for a Raphael's
Transfiguration.
Not more enduring is the spider's net
Than the bright-gleaming web of this our day,
Spun for the creatures by the motherly Sun,

Lightly suspended, lightly shifting, lightly
Drawn, like a veil, aside! Behold how Spring
Spreads its green flower-embroidered carpet out
Before the children's eyes! How winter spreads
The snow-white mat beneath their sportive feet!
And in the magic element, the while,
In such magician's cave of the bright day,
We sit as spellbound, in a fairy tale,
And how and whence we came here, none can tell
A thousand summers since, we were not here!
A thousand autumns hence will find us gone,
And now, to-day, so undeniably
We do exist, so undeniably
Imaginary beings: and our children
Imaginary children; and our homes,
The kingly palaces and holy temples,
Imaginary, legendary, all.
Yea, fairy trees, — no more, — are our fresh trees
That loudly rustle in the wind, whose fruit
Rolls loud as footsteps down to me e'en now;
And the lark's songs are legendary songs,
A fabulous song the herdsman's harvest-lay.
Yon sinking sun itself, — is but a tale!
The wonderful jars not upon our life,
It takes no hold, — I am a wonder, too;
It makes each man a solemn apparition,
The little children in the cradle heavenly,
The days all brightly marked, the nights all blest.
The lovely maid is truly lovely now!
Her eye enchantment, and her love a blessing!
And even the bad, the odious man, himself,
The stone, the grave, and misery, and pain,
Are lovely to the tranquil, pious soul,

Which wafted up as on a golden flood,
Stands as a moon of God in God's great heaven.

XVII.

Enjoy thy Life, not thy Mode of Life.

Now, in full blossom stands the apple-tree,
All white and red, as if its blossoms were
The leaves that lay asleep in buds of green:
And lo, the starling in the blossom-house
Has built himself a nest and hatched his young;
And now surprised that from the little eggs
Such yellow bills peep forth, and with loud cries
Of pressing want so plainly call him "father!"
He flies with joy to find his children bread.
Was ever Emperor nested with such pomp
As is this starling in his apple-tree,
Which, like a flower itself, with taller stalk,
Stands as Earth's fairest flower in tender green!
And here, too, on this green and lofty tower
With its white bell, — here in the lily-cup
A golden chafer dwells so rapturously
As never proudest human creature dwelt.
And what exalts the chafer above men, —
The starling with his wife and darling brood, —
Is, — that they worship not their dwelling-place!
For joy, for love, for busy earnestness
In the still, holy labors of their lot,
They never think how heavenly is their palace,
And that, because they dwell there, they are blest.
O world, O beauteous, beauteous world of spring,
That glitterest like a tree with golden stars,

And bloom'st eternal, so should man forget
Thee, too, and only just be conscious of thee,
For reverence of his human work; then first
Man lives as man, — e'en as the starling lives
In his blooming tree, as the gold chafer lives
Beneath his lily-tower's white cupola.
Then hail to him, him who can thus forget
Spring-time, and earth and sun and night and heaven!
For what divinest treasures that man knows,
And only he, who can so clean forget
Such gladness of the eyes, such stir of beauty,
As if naught else were living or would live
In all the far or near immensity
Than he alone, he with his heart, his love!

XVIII.

Vanity and Vexation of Spirit.

A private word, which each one bears with him,
Sets a whole host astir through countries! war!
A few old phrases in the soul suffice
To kindle all humanity to war,
Waging the unbespoken fight of life, —
A little piety, a little wisdom,
It takes at morning for the coming day,
As food and guide, and very seldom that,
And so begins anew such wild turmoil!
How many thousands would not live at all,
Nay, there lives not a man, could bring himself
To set his foot, to move an eye or hand,
If thought and judgment had to do the work:
Not one would have a hair grow on his head,

Not one would have a heart beat in his breast,
If he himself had to arrange all that
Which bare existence needs, to set in motion,
Say, his own soul's and body's organism;
If God and Nature had not worked for him,
Had not hung up the silver lamp on high,
And the green battle-field adorned below;
Did not a rich humanity live for him,
Had it not lived, and made his path and day.
The baggage-train is ever merriest!
And all humanity 's a baggage-train!

XIX.

Sympathy for every Form of Human Life.

I 've seen in hundred places, women, children,
Farms, gardens, houses, horses, cows, and dogs
To me repulsive, and right odious all,
And have thanked God they belonged not to me!
Yet in their places did I see them all
Prized highly, even loved, and sorely missed!
Only because I, too, held dear and loved
That which was mine, did I forbear to count
Such love in others foolish! Look around
And see how dear, uniquely prized o'er all
The wealth of realms,—things all unknown to thee,
Scarce noticed, even the tree before his house,
Will be to every man, there where he dwells,
And lives and loves and knows and recognizes!
Yet let not that depreciate thine own things,
Nor blind thou thine own self to them, nay, rather
And better: with the worth of all thou hast

Enhance the worth of that which others have!
And if thou canst do that, make all the worth
Of all the treasures of the loving ones
Around thee richly swell the worth of thine!
Then shalt thou haply recognize and feel
Some part of what each human lot is worth
To God, and what it should be worth to man.
Yet modestly be silent thereupon.
For to the modest good is magnified,
And beauty glorified a thousand-fold,
And when thou, by thy modesty, hast thus
Exalted it, then, if thou canst, at length
Hold it as trivial, — human. — God is great!

XX.

It takes all Men to make a Man.

A man is not the thousandth part of man.
It takes the human race to make the man.
In him resides all love, in him all art,
All knowledge. Every one bequeathes to him
His private store, then dies and leaves it. Each
Takes all from him, all his humanity,
And every single man is wondrously
Like to the whole in light and bliss and truth.
So lives he a completed man; thus all
Live, through all, as a human family!
And each one when he dies takes a whole earth
Away with him, — as in a symphony,
Which all the hearers played, the players all
Heard, in their turn, in silent rapture drank,
Till every voice, as each plays out its part,
Puts out its light and silently goes home.

XXI.

Blessed are they that Mourn.

Would'st thou see weeping, — see the poor man weep,
Who verily in feeling sees himself
Stand weeping in the sight of God, — and smiles!
And so his tear to heavenly incense turns,
And his loud voice grows low and faint and choked,
Thought fails him now, and for a moment he
Transforms himself into another soul,
And whoso sees him dry his tears, to him
Ah, holy is their flow, with God so near!
How rich the poor man is! How rich can he
Make others! How much has he still to give!
— If *he* is not to give, who has not much,
He who is poor, right poor, — who then shall give?
Who *does* give truly, then? if giving means: —
That which thou really needest, — not to need,
When, blessing others, it makes thee more glad.
Expect not then such comfort from the rich,
No, not from them, the comfort of the poor, —
They know not poverty, nor giving's worth;
How he who would receive, how he can give!
So gives the poor man only, and is blest,
How poor and miserable soe'er he seem.
The many thousand poor alone sustain
The many thousand poor, ay, even the rich
By their still services and poverty.
So is it, and in this way life is rich!
And hearts are rich. And gladly as I look
Upon thy tears, I bid thee, soul, weep not!
They whom thou pitiest are more blest than thou.

And so be not astonished! wonder not
At the long-suffering, inexpressible
Patience of the unnumbered tribes of poor,
Who with the giant-strength of thousand arms,
With all that light and easy play of power,
Snatch not earth's treasures from the groaning boards,
Grudge not the few rich men, but gladly grant
Life's golden table gorgeously bedight;
No "blood-soiled flesh," no "oxen of the Sun,"
Do they desire, "that low upon the spit,"—
From the mere wont of being poor and strong.
For a chaste purity, a holy feeling
Of heavenly descent, a sense of God
Dwells in the bosom of poor human kind.
Then let them weep, and weep not thou, O soul:
In silence, softly, scattered far and wide,
Let them give life its beauty and its grace
In the most pure of ways, as man beseems.
The individual only may repent,
The human race remorse beseemeth not,
But greatness, beauty, worthiness, alone;
And of its day assured, in modest pride,
In a pure path it seeks earth's purest joy.

XXII.

War endangers the Soul.

When thou dost strive about a thing, so strive
As not to harm the thing for which ye strive;
Yet what is worth so much as that one thing
Which always *is* harmed in men's strife,—thy soul!

XXIII.

Recipe for Contentment.

"Say, by what art shall I secure content?"
As day is but a consequence of the Sun,
So must contentment be the effluence,
The clear effulgence of a sunny soul.
The bride must first be wooed and won, ere thou
Possessing her, wife, mother, children hast.
I am content, it seems to me, if I
Am in the same mood one day as the next.
And as no day is like the last, as each
Loves to bring something new, of joy or woe,
—And brings it up, too, out of our own breast,—
I must feel tranquil, and for that secure;
Must stand serene in all the ceaseless change,
Must therefore bear within me something higher
Than aught the hour can bring or take away;
I must possess the soul's supremest bliss,
A spotless heart and love for all that lives.
With this one feeling evermore the same,
With these unchangeably beholding eyes,
I can accept,—I can reject the world,
Endure it, set my heart on it,—against it;
What happens round about me,—*in* myself,—
Can guide to good, can mildly conquer, bless.
I must press onward to a great, glad mark,
Which time's events give me dim glimpses of,
Scarce show, but daily urge me to pursue!
The conflict, too, is half the victory,
And where the deed falls short, the will makes good.

Once hear and do with all thy heart the word:
I am a man, — and thou wilt be content.

XXIV.

Man writes his Life for Eternity.

Had it been given me to write down my life
Or only its beginning, but two lines,
Upon a solid tablet of pure gold,
How had I paused! how pondered o'er the task!
But even now, as children on their slates
Write what is easily effaced, each man
Writes with light hand but ineffaceably
His life upon the heavy mass of days
That towers behind us, dark, immovable,
An up-piled cloudy wall — of adamant,
Infrangible, more solid than mere gold;
He writes it, as a fate, on human hearts,
He writes it on his own with iron pen!
Then, writer! think, create, engrave with care!
The lullaby we sing the cradled child
Preludes a picture of his coming days!

XXV.

Fight against the Wrong thou doest, not receivest.

What sorrow smites thee at Fate's hand, endure!
What wrong befalls thee at men's hands, forgive,
However heavy it may be, forgive,
As a sure help, and noble. For to fight
Against it, though 't were noble, were as vain

And as impossible, as to fight against
The arrow shot off yesterday, and makes
Wretched indeed, sufferer and doer both.
Only against the wrong which he himself
Has done, — would do, — let man life-long contend.

XXVI.

Contemplation of the Dead.

The bell's sad stroke that tolls the funeral hour
Is, among all this feverish world's alarms,
The last that ever can disturb the dead.
Henceforth he lies unmoved, forever still,
Amidst this loud, tumultuous roar of life,
As the pale sleeper on the field of fight.
He is far hence, yet seems still near, like moonlight.
His soul is near, yet seems remote, like stars.
Thus is man buried, — as a drop in the sea,
As the faint streak of dawn in sunrise-glow,
Even as a sand-grain in the mighty waste.
O soul! thou poor, poor child, how lonesomely
Thou far'st, a pilgrim, through the mighty realm
Of life! So solitary art thou born
Here on the earth; so all forlorn thou tread'st
Thy solitary, dark, and dismal path,
As the dark moon moves onward to new light,
Where it will burst upon thine eyes; when thou
Like a slave-child shalt be once more brought home
Into a hut! nathless thou faintest not,
Art here and there with beings, who, like thee,
All lonely, yearn to thee and thou to them,
By naught attracted and by naught consoled,

And blest by naught, — except by love alone!
Then whoso hates, he is alone! for he
Shuts himself out from this great realm of life;
That man must have more than the power of God
To draw henceforth another breath of joy,
Whereas love's fount has power with one sole draught
To make the poorest life and longest rich
And fill its parting dreams with endless bliss.

XXVII.

Sorrow a Treasure-pointer.

There, where a sorrow comes upon thee, where
Thy tears are made to flow, there certainly
A treasure lies awaiting thee, which shall
Richly repay thy sorrow and thy tears;
Some true thing hast thou there to find, some thing
Of beauty there to see, some good to do,
Some wrong to right; or at the very least
Thou hast the fairest recompense of all:
To learn what life is and to try thy heart,
And freshly, freely, to look out on heaven!
Thy very tears shall open wide thine eyes,
Thy very sorrows shall wake up thy heart;
Then mark the heavenly signals, — and be glad!
And where thou sufferest, feel a joy to come!
In woe be glad, glad of the very woe,
That thou canst prove by it thy happiness,
Strength, wisdom, love, tranquillity, and toil!
Then, and not till then, art thou truly man:
Then is thy happiness a steadfast thing.
So shall thy spirit lightly bear the pain

That Nature gave thee for its health. How blest
Is he who only wills that which is good!

XXVIII.

Day is a Part of the great Night.

The blaze of day is also but a night,
The one great holy night that reigns through space;
The very Sun in heaven is but the lamp
That proves it, with those thousand lamps hung up
From the necessity of driving back
Darkness, and yet the Sun fears not the night,
Which seems to come each morn so near to him.
He will be surely there! Will be himself!
And thou, O man, thou wearest on thy breast,
Just as the miner in the mine-shaft's night
Wears his bright safety-lamp, a still more bright,
An inextinguishable lamp with thee;
And dost thou shudder at the gloom that lies
Upon thy way out in the distance there,
Which thou alone must pierce? — Be of good cheer!
And though it were the gloom of death itself,
Yet step by step and even in the light,
As here, so wilt thou reach that stage at last,
And each will be made bright to thee, e'en death,
The grave, and where, beyond, thy road may lead.
Thou wilt be surely there! wilt be thyself!
And how much more at every stage of life,
E'en in dark hours of pain and melancholy,
All way of refuge seemingly cut off,
Wilt thou be present with thy soul, thy light,
And clearly see, by the strength given to thee!
Then courage! Come what will, — Thou comest too!

XXIX.

Lesson of the young Apple-tree.

Scarce had I planted me an apple-tree,
Scarce had the stones grown quiet at its foot,
Scarce had the tender fibres of the root
Been covered now with earth, and the young stem
With willow-twigs bound to the firm-set stake,
Scarce had the tree stood up, as born full-grown,
As brought by magic 'mong its sister-trees,
Filling a small space only with its crown, —
When lo! a finch came gliding down along
Its budding boughs as one familiar there,
And trilled his old song on the youngest twig!
At morn a spider had already hung
Thereon her net, so fine and delicate!
And had the spinner been a god, he could not
Have woven more finely, more artistically!
And if the spark of dew had been the god,
He could not on the twig have gleamed more bright!
And had the apple-tree itself been God,
Not finer purple snow could he have bloomed!
But the finch came and trilled, as yesterday
He trilled! and will for ay! His little tree
Already was an aged thing to him!
— Then said I to my spirit, deeply shamed:
What would'st thou be, how sweetly innocent
And happy, wiser than the greatest men,
If thou could'st only do as this bird does!
Were the clear sun so wholly thine of old,
Were the old earth to thee so ever young,
So lightly trod, enjoyed so on the wing,

The human race and all its life, so full,
Complete, abundant, and soul-satisfying;
Its fresh existence ever in the bloom
Of pristine beauty and eternal youth,
Its knowledge, intuition, feeling, art, —
And did'st thou, like the bird, sing primitive songs,
And like the spider spin a master's works,
And like the young tree from thy earliest bud
Put forth, with godlike ease and gracefulness,
The fair and fragrant bloom of purple snow!
— And my blest spirit whispered low to me,
How far, indeed, lives man from the divine!
For, did he feel God near him! livingly!
Like God would he create, — as dew from water!
Like God would shape things, — as the blooming tree!

XXX.

Study God's Poem.

O then that one might shape a living poem
As God does in his work, this beauteous world!
That one might so project all into life,
An actual, a life-generating life,
That one might so spread out his thought-filled soul,
More living than a robe from Persia's looms,
Whereon each rose nectarean fragrance breathes,
Each nightingale throbs out enchanting trills,
The blushing mountains purple clusters crown,
The vine-dressers sing gayly as they pass,
And glowing with a little new-made wine
The rosy child sleeps sweetly in the shade!
O that one had such colors and such stuffs!

Such lofty art! and such a soul withal
As the old pious master's childlike soul!

Ah, vain and idle wish! ask but for eyes!
Thou need'st but eyes rightly to see his work,
A soul, a soul to understand it all,
A heart to feel it simply as it is, —
How will the loving soul thrill through thee then
Which he has breathed into the eternal work,
Into the beauteous face of man and flower!
How wilt thou feel the high morality
The patience and the truth, that lives in all,
That even the cloud and rain-drop exercise,
The brook-side flower and every blade of grass.
Truth is the very basis of his world,
And all things show just what they are; the lark
Sings honestly just what is in her heart,
The violet exhales, the lily breathes,
From its pure cup as God has bidden it,
And not a leaflet's tell-tale tongue tells lies!
Not one of all the fairest of the works
With vain complacency exalts itself,
But each the master only glorifies,
Although the peacock shows his gorgeous wheel,
And sets yon sun in like magnificence,
And in the rosy wheel stars show themselves, —
They come forth with soft step, and patiently
Let the first night cloud sweep them from the sight!
And over-night a thousand blooming flowers
Fade gracefully without the slightest sound,
And, even when faded, clothed in touching charms,
Bow their meek heads contentedly to earth.
But it beseemeth man to understand

What God doth speak out loudly through his works.
And when thou comprehendest it, dear soul,
Then go, and do thou too compose a work, —
If thou hast courage for it, pious soul.
But suffer me a little longer yet,
To gaze, in holy contemplation blest,
Till holy sleep sinks down upon my eyes,
Till my cold hand in wonder folded close
Not my best friend shall longer loose, nor shall,
Absorbed in blissful wonder at me dead,
And awe of God, wish any more to loose!

XXXI.

Self-possession.

Precisely as man never saw himself,
Never possessed and understood himself,
As an arrested, fixed, imprisoned fact,
So Nature has him! So Humanity!
As man complete, and even as man scarce-born:
As child, as man, old man, and dead man, too;
And not his trees, his children, and his house
Alone does he possess, — just as one may
The shells of the pearl mussel and great roof
Of the sea-tortoise, — or what he has wrought,
Just as one may the silk-worm's web entire,
No! Genii-like she has his very self,
Just as the earth possesses still the Sun's
Image and power and life, when he has set.
And out of the unnumbered genii
Of the departed ones a realm is formed,
A bright, fair kingdom of the dead on earth,

In daylight, visible to the soul's-eye
Of all; accessible to every one
Of earth's new-comers, — like a heaven below,
A hall of gods and an assembly-house
In the light-realm of Suns, as formerly
The genii, all, sat in the realm of spirits.
And therefore, as there are more days than suns,
So live there far more genii of the dead
Than the one multitude of living men,
And whoso treads humanity's hall of gods,
Of heavenly spirits, as a living man,
Enters their heavenly society;
On him they pour out all their stores of wealth,
He is made king o'er all the genii,
He lives among them in the realm of light,
A spirit and a ruler over spirits,
He is a judge as of the under world,
A servant, too, as of the highest world;
And whate'er names of whate'er Genii
Thou ever nam'st of highest, fairest, richest,
Still is the very beggar king of them,
And every king is but their minister, —
And evermore on earth this mystery holds
A patent, undeniable, visible sway.
And so wilt thou, then, godlike, pure, immortal,
And mighty, join thee to the Genii.
And every man is one day taken up
Into their silent realm, to live as they.
Yet hear thou also now the solemn word:
As thou hast never once possest thyself,
So dost thou still possess in this thy life,
Nature and life, God and humanity,
As Nature, life, God and humanity

Have never seen, will never know themselves!
Thus hast thou even here with such divine,
Such singular power girded thee, O man,
To live a singularly beauteous life
In thine own spirit, in thy human form,
As never yet the universe possessed,
As ne'er has seen or felt the universe,
So long as heaven existed, while heaven stands.
To be one's own, and be unique forever,
As every man and every violet is,
That is the eternal triumph of the all!
And the denial of its strength and love
Is its most glorious Epiphany!

THE LAYMAN'S BREVIARY.

JUNE.

JUNE.

JUNE.

I.

Rejoice in Tribulation.

HE life of mortals seems so hard, so bitter,
So full of toil; and so indeed it is;
And yet in seeming only! not in truth.
That man beside the anvil, forges long
With heavy hammers and with heavy blows,—
The sweat still trickling from his brow, he goes,
The iron in the tongs,—and shoes a horse
For the gay rider there, who sings his song,
And merrily mounts to bid the wedding guests!
The weaver works till far into the night
And weaves with painful toil—fair table-spreads
For many a joyous feast! The song that oft,
The while he wrought, against his will, has made
His heart to swell,—it was life's joyous spirit,
That visited, looked on him smilingly,
And through him sang! He by the furnace there,
Hot with the glow,—blows many a glass for wine!
This other, stooping oft, digs out the earth,
And sets the cherry-tree for happy children,
Who standing round, look on and beg him plant
One more, only one more: "Dear Father, do!
And apples, too, for the long winter-time!"
And is the man now tired?—See, he digs
Still more! and in his pains feels pleasure still.

So lovely is the sense of life! None toils
So mere a drudge that from his labor joy
And welfare do not spring for *one*, for one!
So to her cells laboriously the bee
The virgin honey bears. Yet she herself
In the sweet spring-time sipped it! From the flowers!
She bore it a sweet morsel in her mouth!
Man 's not an axe! a hammer! or a spade!
He is a heart, that feels for what he toils
The livelong day, and through this holy life!
And e'en the ox that for the farmer ploughs
The furrow, understands the holy power.
His holy voice has in its cry, who is
The sire of many children: and behold,
Though weary, willing, ploughs his acre through.
And whoso tires himself, has done it, sure,
For one he loves, who makes the busy work
An aspiration, not a stint, a goal!
And every golden evening brings to each
The twilight-holiday! the lovely hour
When he has done enough for to-day, and now
Can come back to his dear ones, — to himself, —
And rest and live; and feel the hours thrice sweet
After such toil. So sweet, how sweet the kernel
Of the world is! So loving is a God!
That to man's joy he adds the pleasant dream
That he is, nay, creates somewhat himself
When he is but a child, who, by free grace,
Receives from Heaven that thing which he creates.
And each may quickly prove his life hereby:
Who finds not pleasure in his work, has none,
Not one, he loves! And no one who loves him;
Else would he certainly love others too!

His aim is evil! For he seeks his own,
His private pleasure and his private gain,
His pleasure heaps up for him woe on woe.
And would'st thou work with gladness, thou must love
Some one somewhere, — and happy wilt thou be,
Even in the troubles life brings, — only then
Completely blest, without them only half!

II.

Joy in Sorrow.

Heart, trust thyself, and this one thing believe:
That joy is hid in sorrow, life in death,
In suffering, love, riches in poverty, —
Know this, and happier shall it be with thee!
Yonder they bear a little playmate home,
Who has been sorely wounded in the head,
While playing ball. Forth his pale mother runs
Shrieking. He bleeds. Her kisses also stain
Her lips with blood. She sets him on his feet,
The little boy stands staggering. Now he knows
His mother. See, he smiles. And she with joy
Clasps him, and taking comfort bears him home.
And yet I know that this poor mother has not
A loaf at home; that the poor little one
Owns not his ball, but only borrowed it!
But she cares now for nothing save the fate
Of that one child; and more than rich in him,
Has put all other treasures far from thought!
And at this moment only feels for pain,
With love; yea, love alone is all she feels.
Riches are naught and poverty is naught,

Naught is but love, — that feels with glad and grieved,
All else is darkness, all else misery.

III.

The Strength of Tenderness.

My child! Thou hast a dread of being good
In such a world, in such a swarm of men;
When a good work is to be done, each counts
Without a question, in advance, on thee!
Thou seemest to thyself to be a reed,
A green twig by the way, each child may pluck;
A sheep, a good dog, teased by boys, and driven,
Whither they will; drowned in the pond, perchance!
Whoso plays with the cat, with him the cat
Plays too, the dog, the man, the demigod;
Thou followest only one, in following all;
Thou mindest one, when thou art minding all,
Thou dost but one thing, though thou doest much.
And is thy work, because so still, no work?
Is not the pyramid's base invisible?
It seems not there, an idle, useless thing, —
And it alone bears dumbly the whole load
Up to the topmost stone, with restless force,
With busy, restless, tense, defiant force.
So thy still spirit bears the whole world's weight.
Sleep looses from thy neck the yoke of toil,
The softly gliding, tender web of sleep!
And need I tell thee of the might that dwells
In tenderness? 'T is Nature's chiefest strength;
Only the tenderest is not to be torn!
Thy spirit is more delicate than the ether, —

And lo! the air evades the nimblest blow;
The thunder hurls his bolts at it in vain!
Like to a goddess it defies all wounds,
Still stands before him, and its laugh rings out
Over *his* death through all the vales and glens!
And who can overtake thy soul? Lay hands
Upon it? Who can crush it, shatter it?
The infant in his cradle cannot speak,
And yet his very look, one little glance
That scarcely dares flit o'er his little face,
Shall move the mother, stir up all the house!
Two friends stand, sundered by the roaring sea,
Each on his lonely shore; yet naught on earth
Can rend the bond that binds the twain in one,
The tender look, that, shot from eye to eye,
Saw joyfully the man in each; the low,
The tender word: "I love thee evermore!"
And thou, my child, thou stand'st here on the shore
Of earth, and over yonder there stands God,
Thy friend, the other side the broad blue sea;
Thy call can scarcely reach him; thou must die,
And so pass over to him, — and yet who
Could e'er blot out his look in thee, thy low,
Thy tender word: "I love thee evermore!"
My child, the silent power is terrible:
More than the threatening thunder-cloud in Heaven,
And never let the bad man tempt it forth!
For as the good man loves, so hates he too,
Hates crime, hates all things evil terribly,
Invincibly, invulnerably, despite
All weapons and all poisons earth can yield!
My child, so fear not therefore to be good,
To be a sheep, a good dog, whom boys tease!

IV.

Greatness of Little Things.

The smallest thing thou canst accomplish well,
The smallest, ill. 'T is only little things
Make up the present day, make up all days,
Make up thy life. Do thou not therefore wait,
Keeping thy wisdom and thy honesty,
Till great things come with trumpet-heraldings!
To each direct thy undivided nature,
Thy whole heart, mind, and soul, all love and truth.
The stamp which thou hast set on each, thou seest,
It shall one day come back to thee again,
As old coins come, each from its several age,
Bearing thy image, and make glad thy heart!
So does the Sun on every smallest flower
Bend his whole energy, — a little while;
Earth lends it all her force, for a brief space,
And each rewards her care with beauteous bloom!
And so she conquers, day by day, the year.
He who has only gained the day, has gained
The battle! Do thou gain the moments, man!
For when thou hast subdued unto thyself
Each moment, thou hast won the whole of life!
Hast made the whole of life a beauteous thing!
Made time's enormous burden light to thee!
So chip by chip, the child bears off a tree!
Life is not heavy to the ever-good!
To him alone who is but seldom good,
Or only often good, is all a snarl,
As to the weaver who has dropped asleep!
Life is so light when man is always good!

V.

The Sceptic's Laugh rebuked.

"Earth is not worthy of one serious thought!"
Thou say'st without the sense and glow of life;
And yet there 's Beauty here! — *That* thou must needs
With deep and solemn earnestness revere.
He who can laugh in mockery at a flower,
Can laugh to scorn a loved one's beauteous face,
Is blind, is heartless, or completely crazed!
And yet the Good is here! — That canst thou never
Make light of, to neglect at any time,
That summons in good earnest all thy strength,
Be thou unhappy, happy, young, or old,
Or on thy death-bed, — 't is an idle word:
"Earth is unworthy of all serious thought!"
For where mind is, be beauty, love its thought!
And yet the Truth is here! — Thou wilt not laugh,
When once it seizes on thee, wretched fool.
To hold the great in small account, is small;
To feel the little to be great, is great.
In sooth, the spirit that fills the ethereal round,
That breathes and lives and loves and feels, as here,
In the least creature on the furthest star,
Cannot be small. I never heard from Heaven
Loud laughter shake the stillness of the night!
Never from out earth's caverns have I heard
Mysterious voices laughing at our earth!
And wilt thou dare up at that Heaven to laugh
And at that earnest, calm, and silent Spirit?
Lo! every little flower God magnifies
With solemn stillness, holy earnestness,

He shapes each blossom, every blade of grass,
And seems as if he stood before the pink,
Not yet content till he had faithfully
Traced on it every stripe and every point.
Where do we see thee show such diligence
And such devoutness in thy works, thou man!
And wilt thou laugh at God as at a child
That busily paints flowers for his mother,
And weeps when thou hast spoiled a leaf? For him
The work of childhood is made great by love;
So God doth magnify child and everything,
And every day and moment, each to Him
Is blissful, weighty, precious, and unique.
Because He is so great, He feels all great,
And looks upon the glint of dust as suns.
And thou wilt look on suns as glittering dust,
And on this earth as on a children's ball!
I therefore, could I ever scorn, would say:
Thou earth-worm, miserably hollow dream,
Ungodly is the beggar who derides
The staff that props his steps, derides the child,
That gives him with his hand the crust of bread.
Ungodly is the king who ridicules
The sceptre in his hand; who will not make
The people prosperous and blest so far
As love and human understanding can,
And yearns to have them; as the human race
— The flock of God, — is worthy to be made;
Ungodly he who staring up into
Heaven's vault, will wait in idle wretchedness, —
Wait till this earth has vanished silently,
Like to a drop of water, like a mote
That plays in sunlight, — and will then begin

To wish and hope, create and execute
Good for himself and for the human race,
There where it is no more, and he no more
As man! — A holy awe comes over me;
Here, here is God! Here is the earth! And here
Is man! Here build, O man, the Kingdom
Of God. For this He made Himself a man,
For this alone He daily comes on earth,
For this alone He gives thee now His eyes,
His thoughts, His spirit, power, and nature gives, —
Nay, see, He is the All itself in you.
And now, then, rest thee not, till everything
Perfected is, and stands upon the earth,
Born visibly of the spirit, as a child
Out of its mother's womb, — held in her lap!
And never more in laughter say the word:
"Earth is unworthy of all serious thought!
Thy native land and every native land,
Thy house and yard, thy field and meadow-ground,
And every stalk thereon and every tree
Within thy garden, every child therein,
Thy wife and thou thyself, thy life, thy soul!"

VI.

Man's Helplessness.

Among all creatures the most helpless one
Appears to thee, no doubt, the new-born child,
More than the little daughter of the lamb,
Just standing in the grass and nibbling flowers!
More helpless than the little darling bee
Whom buzzing brothers and sisters sweetly feed

With golden blood of flowers and violets' hearts!
Yet who is richer than the human child
Through mother's love, and the fair human bond?
The little bed and dress lay ready for him,
Long, long ere yet the little guest appeared.
And would'st thou call man heir of misery,
Because so many hardships fence him round?
Because he haunts the earth, a looker-on?
Because he feels the pangs of death and parting;
Which pass, unfelt, in silence o'er the flowers?
The flowers, — that know not tears, but only dew!
Yea, thou hast said: he is a looker-on!
There lives in him the wise eye of the world,
In him the sense and joy and peace of God,
For him too, as a guest, is all prepared
In life, and none e'er failed to find his grave;
And trulier than a mother once at night
Watched with low lullaby her darling's sleep,
Up yonder the good Spirit watches him.

VII.

The Greatness of Manhood.

Intelligence is worth the pains it costs;
A heart informed, a spirit full of light,
Shall make the world and all its treasures thine!
Clear understanding is abiding gain
And makes the longest life serene and fair;
The sun that has arisen within the mind
Descends not till a late and still old age;
What thou hast learned goes with thee all life long,
Whither thou goest, as a cultured friend,

And gives thee new perceptions for the world,
Acquaints thee with it, even as with thy wife.
A heart in life's fresh morning early decked,
A mind, in youthful days made sweetly wise,
Is like the fruit-tree. Planted once for all,
Spring after spring it puts new blossoms forth,
And autumn after autumn bears new fruit.
Be wise betimes! that thou may'st be a man
The sooner, surer, in the good old way.
Upon life's threshold, in the days of youth,
Man's errors are the greatest, longest, worst!
The older any one, the less his fault;
Not till the eightieth year to break one's limb
Is scarcely a mishap, makes lame not long!
To lose one's little finger, as a child,
Is a misfortune that lasts eighty years!
Stupidity and badness bring no worse
Danger nor punishment than just themselves,
In time's vast range, no penalty of death,
Endless damnation, — no! A worse: the life-
Penalty, just to live a bad, dull life,
To lose one's life, to die unripe, on earth
To have lived a man, and yet not *as* a man,
Not to have been, nay, worse: to have been wretched!
The mole has then been more and better: — He!
The stone more blest! as neither dolt nor knave!
Thou 'rt bound to be a man, wise, pure, and good,
Thyself a man before all other things!
It helps thee not, that other men are men,
And good and wise ones, that the round earth blooms,
That the whole human race is prospering
In joy and righteousness, that goodly works
Of painters, sculptors, poets, fill the land

With grace and glory, riches and renown;
Not all earth's beauty and the love of men
Can help thee, all the world's perfection still
Leaves thee imperfect, foolish, base, and blind!
Then boldly, full of courage, strength, and faith,
Set thyself forth as end of the great whole!
Fulfil its will within thee faithfully
By thine! Lay deep thy base! Build thyself up!
Thou 'rt useless to the world, if to thyself!
Thou 'rt useless to thyself, if to the world!
Wilt thou then prosper in the outer world,
And be right happy in and through thyself,
Then bend thou all thy powers upon thyself,
Thyself alone, as if there were naught else
In all the world but thou. Then wilt thou find
The world at every hour all ready, ready
Even as the mill-wheel, when the stream roars down;
Nature meanwhile will take a mother's care
Of thee, will be beside thee every day,
Upon her path, which thou hast made *thy* path,
Will lead thee, ripen thee while journeying; not
Misguide thee to a desert where no dates,
No waters spring; and say with scornful laugh:
"Here die now, thou that hast relied on me,
And on thyself! I care for all; not each!
Yea, him I cast off who will be a man."—
Thy iron word be always: Take no step
Away, aside from thy humanity!
Draw not a single breath, raise not thy hand
Except to be, and to abide, a man.
Thou art God's earthly image, let not aught
Have power to tear thee from thy pedestal,
Let not the treasures of the whole wide world,

Not all the honors or rewards of men,
Tempt thee to swerve from thy supreme reward,
Thy highest honor: that of being a man!

VIII.

Why are Partings hard?

What need on earth of saying farewell! All
Goes, after all, to a good place. Behold,
Where the young finch flies lightly from his nest
And comes not home again; as there it hangs,
In the dry leaves of autumn, a dry thing,
He scarce can see it without bodeful thoughts;
Flies the gold-chafer from the chafer's feast
On quick, light wing, glad as a youthful god!
The winged maple-seed, and thistle-beard,
Float on the breeze light-hearted, caring not
For so much earth as might a rain-drop drown,
To serve them for a cradle, for a grave!
The dying flowers part calmly from the flowers,
The blossoms snow down calmly on the earth,
The leaves drop calmly from the leaves, no sigh
Breathed upward to the tree where once they played!
The birds quit calmly autumn's leafless realm,
Nor look back to the wood that harbored them!
Man only follows restlessly his fate,
And sorely parts, because he has not faith,
And has not, as a pure child, tasted bliss.

IX.

Not to be unhappy is Happiness.

Mere freedom from misfortune is good fortune!
Is man's great wish! No sorrow then bows down
His head to earth; no tear bedims his eye
And veils the fair world from his sight; no fear
O'ercasts the radiance of the sunny days;
Nor yet does ev'n a hope contract his breast,
And fix his spirit's eye on earthly things.
Free from misfortune, man can live in bliss,
With gladness can enjoy what makes this life
A thing divine to man: for as the rose
Is laden with sweet perfume, so the world
Is laden with beauty and felicity.
And even a god cannot impart to man
A higher joy than God has given to him
Who lives in purity an unvexed life!

X.

Honor Beauty and Goodness everywhere.

The good in others, O conceal thou not,
The good, both what they do and what they are,
The beauty they themselves are, and create.
What? by concealment thankest thou the God
Who gave the feeling for the fair and good?
Thankest thou thus the man, who offers it
With soul inspired by native modesty?
For such a soul is his, who bears so much
Of what is good and fair, that like the fruit-tree

He must bow down to reach it out to thee.
Acknowledgment of God exalts thyself,
It makes thee good; and beauty makes thy soul
Beauteous like his by whom 't is brought and worn,
Where much is to be praised, there thou may'st blame,
But to be silent, — 't would disgrace the frog,
Who speaks the praise of Spring, as best he can.
— Far otherwise the morning star in Heaven!
He has sailed through the tepid summer night,
Has looked upon its splendor near at hand, ...
The highest spirit in highest silence throned, ...
The sweeping constellations, and the ether
Like a deep well-spring full of gentle life, —
And yet is silent! — They too who have seen
Him yonder, they in silence muse alone.
His sparkling eye, his glance that shoots afar
Clear as pure gold along the heavenly space,
That is his call! He is himself his hymn!

XI.

Oil on the Waves.

The seaman pours upon the storm-tossed waves
His cask of oil, and they compose themselves
All round his ship. And now he smoothly glides
O'er a still plain, round which the tempest roars
And rolls high waves that come not near to him.
With surer, softer influence works on men
The spiritual might of gentleness.
Then pour it out, like gentle moonlight, man,
Upon thy path, and tranquil will it be
And lovely; as the moon adorns her path
With the same light that guides and gladdens men.

XII.

Everything beautiful in its Place.

Seen in its place, is nothing so august
Nor vile as far off and alone it seems;
Perchance the Sun itself is not so hot.
Thou journeyest to see the giant palms,—
And Nature leads thee gently up to them
Through lines of cedars and of cypresses.
Thou seek'st the jungle of the elephants,—
And lions, tigers there she lets thee meet.
The tiger's spots suit him as naturally,
As do the delicate pink its tender streaks.
The setting only makes the object clear
And needful, as the tree's bark to its pith,—
So from the hoary, holy days of old
Comes down a people! and its smallest custom
Is, as the oak-leaf by the parent stem,
Borne fresh and living in the age's sky.—
'T is a sweet solace to the friend of man,
That all which anywhere has lasted long,
—And though 't were death,—being so familiarized
To human feeling, and grown mild by use,
Its harshness long worn off, means less and less,
Nay, often wears a fair and human look,
Made beauteous by those bliss-laden flowers
Strewed by a faithful God through all our days!

XIII.

That which is unseen is eternal.

The breath that from the tepid heaven, unseen,
Falls on the blossoms here, so that they thrill,
And softly dies away, — does it decay?
Is it of flesh? or is its influence wood,
That it must moulder, undergo a change,
As flower-seeds do even in the best of earth!
The word, — the deed of man are not of earth,
Not earthy. Were he so, even then he were
Indissoluble, incorruptible,
As element! But what subdues and sways
The very elements, — creates on earth!
Creates ev'n in the silent spirit-realm,
It even shapes itself and roots itself.
A look into a human eye dies not!
A word once spoken to a good soul lives:
For incorruptible, indestructible is
The element divine in which it fell.
Then always think thou this: There may be One,
Who writes down everything thou say'st and doest!
And canst thou trust thyself, there really is
One who engraves thy every word and deed,
Ay, every thought! That Some One is — the Spirit!
Think always, then, the good, the true, the right.
O live in the most loving sentiment,
And shape unresting beauty in thy heart!
'T will crystallize, 't will grow a precious stone,
Fairer and costlier than the diamond,
'T will grow a sun, the sun that spirits see.

XIV.

The Expressiveness of Silence.

What touches the most deeply a man's heart,
Ay, and a lover's? — 'T is the silent proofs, —
Not the loud-spoken words, — that testify
A true heart's beautiful and faithful love;
The dead, — their lips are silent, — yet they speak
With a loud voice! their eyes are shut and sealed,
And yet behold us! mildly smiles their face, —
And we, we weep to look upon that smile,
Which a dead loved one leaves us as a proof
How gladly she would still have lived for us! —
And yet how gladly she had died, that so
She thus might say: "I loved thee unto death!"
Then reverence the holy, eloquent
Silence of sun and earth and every heart!
For everything most noble and most fair
Is still, and chiefly when unuttered, works
With heavenly might unutterable things!

XV.

The Euthanasy of a Day.

See where the day burns out! Its ruddy blaze
Strikes to the clouds, and now they glow with fire.
In ashes sinks the day, 't is dark all round,
The holy palace fades away forever,
And see, the clouds of sunset weep great drops
Dyed with a purple glow, as red as blood.
O soul, is it a folly, is 't a crime

To ask?—O ask, then, only once ask thou:
The past, say whither, whither has it fled?
Where is it, where? What has become of all
The treasures, wonders, all the stately forms, ...
The beauteous, piled-up structures of the air,
Creative Nature's lavish hand dispersed?
And does she only scatter? Ne'er restore?
For verily they were! Yea, bodily!
Thou hast, hast with these very eyes of thine
Beheld them, with these very hands of thine
Hast touched, hast handled many a blooming twig;
The summer flowers and the fair maiden's curls,
These hast thou touched,—and scarce believed it when
The thought came: they are all a dream,—are naught,—
Soon they will pass away, will all be gone
Into the gulf of Being,—of Have Been.
And lo! already they are gone! all gone!
Yonder the Spring burns out! its blaze of hues
Expires in clouds, and thou, too, weep'st like them.
And every beauteous face, each little face
Of childhood, is a new, original work,
Else has no painter painted, sculptor shaped,
Nor heart e'er loved, nor stands there anywhere
A human treasure-house full of man's works.
And every bud was an original thing,
Though the tree's child, and though the tree itself
Was the earth's child, and earth again in turn
A child of heaven. I pray thee tell me, where
Shall holy Nature's treasure-house be found?
And had she many thousand times too many
Treasures? Her starry spaces, were even they
A mere child's table, all too small and narrow
To spread out wide her riches on, or even

To heap them up on, as a golden mountain?
And does she now, having just shown her things,
From all the enormous spaces sweep them off,
And is then every star made, every day,
A wholly new, clean table for her plays,
Whereon she spreads them out successively
To please her children? and the play is up,
So soon as she has kissed and sent them off
To bed? how silently the flowers do sleep!
I miss the store-house, my heart misses it,
I miss the show-hall, my mind misses it,
Where Nature treasures up the host of works,
Which she with never-tiring industry,
With highest art, with touchingly-still love,
Creates to-day, created yesterday,
And has created from eternity.
And if *she* wants such, — then she wants and wants
Forevermore her fairest Sanctuary. —
Methinks, thou now art ready, sacredly
To pay the reverence due to all that lives!

XVI.

Learn Wisdom from the World.

My Son, be wise and make the world thy school.
For knowledge of all kinds 't is over-rich;
As thou considerest it, it teaches thee
Each thing in turn and so thou learnest it.
Wilt thou now learn compassion, for the present
Avoid the beggars, and the poor and sick,
Farewell to hovels where the afflicted weep,
Stay not to list the wailings of the oppressed,

Constrain thyself, see not unrighteousness
Do her misdeeds, be silent 'mong the sad;
Think now: thou livest in a perfect world!
The human form is finished, like the earth!
Upon the fairest faces feast thine eyes,
Linger in golden chambers, look thy fill
At the gay pomp of great ones, eat and drink
To fulness of their viands and their wines,—
Then, go learn Freedom! both in act and thought,
Live, where one honors all alike as men;
Visit fair countries, cities richly built,
And if thou wilt, look upon ruins, too,
And on old graves, till it comes home to thee:
How soon the fairest human life is gone!
Hail the bright Sun; and think of Him who said:
That *as the heavenly kingdom was in Heaven,*
So should it be on earth,—and brought it down!
With such an eye, with such a heart behold
Humanity, its ignominious flight,—
And if thou hast not for a heart—a stone,
Then hast thou pity, know'st what pity means!

XVII.

Man never knows himself till the End.

Thy frame, O man, as child, as youth, as man,
As old man, is a vessel, ever-new,
Which with continually changing thoughts,
Emotions, wishes, purposes, desires,
With changing moods for all the changing days,
With changing soul for all the changing hours,
Draws from the well of life for thee on earth.—

Thou errest, then, in thinking thou art right,
Only when thou dost hope one thing, or all;
That thou art right only when thou enjoy'st
One thing with zest; or only then art right,
When thou rememberest it; or only when
Thou hatest, lov'st, despisest, prizest it!
Think always, man, that thou art many men,
A thousand-fold man by unfolding ever.
A whole man art thou not; *that* nothing short
Of a whole life can make thee. Know thou then:
Man is invisible; his total being
Never appears. Child, youth, man, old man, never
Unite in one. Man never sees himself.
And none sees him. The swimmer in the sea
Shows now a shoulder only, now an arm,
A foot, a hand,—until he climbs the bank
And stands majestic there, a man complete!
Then never, in whatever mood, supinely
Give thyself up,—be sure it will not last;
Nor in the height of fortune be at ease
And vain,—it cannot last. But thou shalt last,
To men and to thyself invisible.
Only thy soul shalt thou behold entire
In the great hour of death, and not before.—
And if a man can, like the glowing grape,
In one short summer fill himself so full
With precious richness,—then how precious rich,
How passing rich the universe must be,
That sweeps along before the human race,
With myriads of suns, with such a sea
Of energies, that unveiled laboratory
Full of the naked, manifest art and toil
Of Him, the veiled, yet plainly busy Master,

To whom the human race sustains as near
Relation, as the eyes do to the light,
As intimate as thought does to the mind,
As head and members do, as sea and shell,
As shell and pearl, nay, more, as intimate,
As that which makes the vine and cluster one,
Co-working for the full, the clear ripe glow.
Let man be never discontented then
In evil fortune, — nor in good content.

XVIII.

Wherein shall Man live?

Wherein shall a man live? — Nōt possibly
Here in the body. For thy very eye
Bears thee o'er garden, valley, mountains, far
Away; out of thyself. With eye, ear, sense,
Thou dost already, like a demigod,
In the great house of Nature, greatly live,
Up on yon clouds; out in the starry night.
For how could man e'er live a mortal life?
Thou livest even here as an immortal,
Beholdest all change come and pass away,
And in the body still remainest thou.
Thou would'st live better then out of the body.
Thou livest in the spirit the true life.
Light is invisible. So mind and sun.
Their very image, like a fire, illumines
And colors; therefore do the world and life
Illuminate thy spirit. Hence thou livest
Out of thy spirit, a warm, bright, cheering life,
High and harmonious. Yet the spirit's fire

And force is love. In love thou livest now
A rich, fair life, — yet out of love thou livest
Divineliest, for thou livest out of God.

XIX.

Add to Goodness Beauty and Joy.

The child would give his pretty pigeon food;
The mother strews its food, — but in the shade!
And but one pigeon pecks the golden grains,
No play of light enwreathes his mottled neck,
No shadow of the pigeon paints itself,
No lovely, living image. But the child, —
He strews his golden kernels in the sun, —
And lo! two little pigeons peck the food!
And sunny-bright his darling shines for joy.
Now that was just the dearest little folly;
Yet would that thou wert like the child in heart,
To take one short step more than thousands do,
A hard step, oft-forgotten in the hurry
Of life: from vanity, or spurious pride!
The good thou doest, make pleasing, beautiful!
For naught is good, that sheds, not joy, but gloom.
Thou hast in this a genuine test of good,
What thou receivest and doest, and of thy goods,
The goods of life, — yea, life itself and death.

XX.

The three Sacred Rights of Man.

Three things belong to every man, which none
Has any right to wrest from him or harm:

God's gift of being and of happiness, —
The help of them who share this life with him, —
But the third only makes him fully man!
The right to reverence God and love His children
In trouble and in death. For without love
This great house of the world must needs collapse,
And every human house and human heart.
Sooner than lose this right, then, lose thy life,
To exercise it, welcome death itself!

XXI.

The Creature's Gifts often his Ruin.

It is the costly tooth, — the ivory, —
For which men hunt and kill the elephant;
The mussel that men open, till it dies, —
Must thank its pearl for that! The beauteous bird,
The Tsu, is caught, — for having handsome wings;
The art of talking lays the fetter on
The parrot's foot and binds him to the cage;
They seek the tortoise to secure his house;
The musk-ox might have grazed in quietness
Had not his musk alone made man his foe;
Even with the works of art, it oft holds good
That what gives worth to them destroys them too;
Thus does the sound wear out the bell, the torch
Consumes itself ev'n by the light it gives,
And ah! how often does the selfsame thing
Happen to man! Let him then who is wise
Think upon this at all times and take heed:
That his endowments hasten not his fall! *

* Originally from the Chinese.

[Of course every one is reminded of Italy's *fatal gift of beauty.* — Tr.]

XXII.

Divine Consolation for the Erring.

Even Error's devious ways make error plain,
But opposite to Error, evermore
Stands Truth, majestic as the rainbow stands
Fronting the Sun. 'T is born of sun and rain. —
There is a joy in woe; it springs from it,
As darts the lightning-gleam from heavy clouds, —
Nor is it always day upon the earth.
And still we call our earthly dwelling light.
We know, even in the night-time, where we dwell,
For none forgets, who e'er has seen, the sun,
Then, only *to have been* made happy once,
Only to know that some one loves us, one
Who, if he lived, would love us alway, — that
Is comforting and cheering at all times,
And One in all times lives and loves us, — God!
And every one *was* blest, — he *was* a child!
The star of youth is the great Evening Sun.

XXIII.

The Aged Sceptic at the Grave.

"You talk to me so much about the seed,
How it must moulder, e'er a germ of life
Can spring from it anew; and so man's frame.
But from this body no new body grows
The first spring, and still less will grow the last.
The seed-corn lies there dead, till it is sown;
Livingly works the body, till dissolved,

— (The soul, as being, can only disappear) —
And, while it lasts and lives, still bears its fruit —
The soul, — which veiled by it so quietly,
So gracefully, has worn it for a dress,
Has shaped it to itself, then thrown it by,
A cast-off garment. If, then, in the time
Of the soul's bodily life naught has transpired
Deep in the soul itself and from the soul,
The case is bad enough; for from the grave
Naught can arise, not what you laid therein,
Still less what you have never laid therein!
The soul! which I possess, remain, and am."
— So spake an old man lightly on the graves,
And sought himself a place among his kin,
Leading along two grandsons, fair as day,
And fresh as life. But their eyes turned aside;
For on the gravestone, lo! the worm began
Her chrysalis, and rocking with her head,
She spun the threads to form her silken couch;
The sun went down; her lovely day was up, —
Still, dead-alive, she hung there by a thread,
And grew a Psyche in the golden body,
Newly enkindled at the ancient spark.
From the well's bottom through the liquid clearness
The little gnat came up from his red cell;
His feet he planted broadly under him,
And like a new-born kid he stood erect
A moment on the surface in the sun
And prinked his untried plumes for the first flight!
And scarcely guessing yet that he had wings,
Flew lightly out into the evening-glow,
While the clouds softly thundered overhead,
In token that up there, too, there was life!

And awe and reverence filled my soul, that I,
I too claimed kindred with such miracles
That in primeval, hoary time had reigned
As if but yesterday, and will, as if
But for to-morrow, reign unceasingly.
And from my eyes the burning tear-drops fell,
They were the tears of Nature for herself,
The thunder's voice, the old man and the child.

XXIV.

The Lost Child on the Alps.

A stranger child has lost his way and now
The highest glacier's silver castle climbs,
That with its tower stands high above the clouds.
Hope fires him; for up there he will behold
His home, his father! He will climb to Heaven,
Will enter it from there and tread its walks.
For there is where the Sun doth daily rise,
The stars, too, over yonder, every night
Rest like a flock, there gleams the purple gate,
Through which the shepherd, evenings, drives them out,
Through which the shepherd scares them in at morn.
So climbs the child, — climbs wrong, and baffled sits
High up alone, alone there in the storm,
That blows the *gray* hair wildly round his face, —
For suddenly he has grown old with fright.
Cut off from help he sits there on the peak;
He can no more go down into the fields
And flowery lawns he played in, cannot even
Distinctly see them, for his eye is dim,
The green earth down below there lies so far,

No human sound can longer reach his ear,
Not even the voice of the good foster-parents,
Who followed him a furlong with fond care,
Then cast one tearful look and suddenly
Sank down beneath their load and turned to dust.
This to the child a quiet Spirit tells,
That lingers with him. Now the night draws near,
Now heavy storm-clouds tower up black in heaven,
And now his frighted glance no refuge sees
In, out, or down, but in the grim abyss, —
When suddenly grow on him golden wings,
And as he walked before, — so now he soars
And flies to his father. —
Man, that child art thou.

XXV.

The Temple of Dream.

The ancients, dimly conscious yet of self,
And hovering with vague thought through Nature's realm,
Built special temples for themselves, wherein
To dream of Man, Futurity, and Truth.
In such a temple man himself is born,
Walks, talks, and dreams therein with open eyes,
He comes a wonder, and a wonder goes!
And only not the dream-house seems a dream,
Because new dreamers ever dream therein,
And its roof arches over all who sleep.
And so the dreamers and the dreams therein
Seem then more weighty and more wonderful,
Yea, truer, than the hollow house of dream!

XXVI.

The Divinity of Man.

Man is divine, in him dwells manifestly
A God, the beauteous soul of God himself!
And even man's frame is visibly endowed
By Nature's fair and holy elements,
In sooth they constitute it, — it is they.
But ah, the God on earth, — is very man,
And weeps already as a new-born child
Upon a mother's breast, — that goddess's,
Who, but a few days earlier, also came
On earth, to be to him a human mother,
Softly to cradle him with anxious heart,
To love him and to be by him beloved.
And lo, as if departed out of Heaven,
Nay, as if banished, so is man on earth
An incomparable original,
A strange, mysterious, awe-invested thing:
Even like the diamond hidden in the flint!
Like to the bee within its amber-prison;
Like the twin-image in an Iceland spar,
Like to the double berry in the cluster,
Each with its special juice, its special stone.
Man, — human kind, — *as such*, is but a show,
A fleeting light, a phantom of the hour,
A ghost, the shadow of a Spirit, God;
And yet the shadow only says the truth,
Saying of itself between its tears and smiles:
"Man is divine! In him dwells manifestly
A God, the beauteous soul of God himself." *

* This reminds one of a thought of Pascal's. — Tr.

XXVII.

The Rich Man and Sleep.

"A rich man bade his servant wake him up
At every hour of night, that he might feel
Full often and right vividly the sweetness
Of sleep, of going to sleep, of half-awaking.
This man had many children, and he wished,
Large as their number was, so large a joy
To feel in often and in half-awaking,
And to impart the same to every child;
And to this end with careful hand he drew
A magic chain round all his children's beds,
— Who at his pleasure fell asleep and woke. —
But the chain's lock he laid beneath his head.
And so, a mute enchanter, he enjoyed
The pith of pleasure, sleep; the dream of death.
And lo, the golden chain led silently
Dreams also to the brain of every child. —
Come, name me now the children! and the man —
The mute one! Name me the mute servant too!"
A conjurer in Egypt said to me.
And I replied: The rich man, — he is God.
The silent servant, Death. The children, — well,
They are we two! and all men, all that dwell
On all the stars that round about us shine.

XXVIII.

God All in All.

To say that all know all things, recognize,
Experience, yea, live through, themselves, each state,

Each fate, the entire round of woe and joy,
And think, themselves, each thought of every one,—
That every feeling thrills through, constitutes,
So many beings as there are on earth:
The earth itself, the waters and the winds,
The rocks, the grass, the blossoms and the fruits,
The fishes in the sea, the beasts in woods,
The flowers and trees and all the birds and men,
The very Proteus in the earth's dark caves,
The flowers in the deep garden of the sea, ...
And that for ages they have been all this,
And quietly will be for ages yet;
And that the unnumbered stars through endless space,
With all the wondrous creatures thereupon,
And with their thousand wondrous powers of sense,
Have known, lived, been, and thought whatever is,
And know, live, and experience it to-day,
And in themselves will live it through all time,
And that in this way all best know themselves:
Call'st thou all-knowingness, all-consciousness?
That all know all, call'st thou omniscience?—
That were to crush the diamond into dust!
To dissipate into sun-dust the great Sun!
To change the great heart into drops of blood!
To make the universal eye a fly's-eye!
The spirit of all can of himself be all,
And He himself is all, as true as He is,
And He?—Shall He alone then not exist?*
O shame! Nay! He himself is also God!
Nay, He is all! not *beside* each is He,
He is entire in every single one,
Alike in them and in himself entire,

* "He that formed the eye, shall He not see?"—PSALM xciv. 9.

He knows us all, even as we all know him,
And therefore He is, just as we—*is* We!
And we are, just as He too is, not He!
Nay, we consist of Him, and He of us,
The life of all that is, makes out His life.

Now dost thou know, methinks, the blessedness,
The silent, inward, present blessedness
In all things, that to-day is and forever,
Proceeding ever from the holy life
That billows round about us like a sea!
For all this magic loveliness and grace
Of the unnumbered creatures, as of flowers
And men, and of the male and female sex,
In every kind of creature that hath life, ...
The joy that day awakens, every day,
The bliss that night awakens, in all nights, ...
The gladness of all creatures in themselves,
Their gladness in their hearts, and doings all,
And in all others round them everywhere,
Even in the stars and in the starry night,
The immeasurable joy of all the young
In every kind of creature that hath life,
The finding, laying hold upon, possessing,
Contemplating, exploring, recognizing, ...
The love that fills and overflows each breast,
The love of brides, the love that mothers feel
Towards their children, and the children's love,
The love of each one for the universe,
Hope, memory, and the very sorrow felt,
The very tears shed over what is lost
And now lives only as behind a veil,
The exalted sympathy of dying men,

The smile that welcomes the new-born to life,
The smile that hails and crowns a worthy deed,
The smile that greets the coming of a spring,
On one face only! — And all this through worlds
Repeated without number, without measure!
And without change repeated through all change, —
O were not that felicity enough
To fill *one* man? What say I? Is not this
The rapture of the One great heart that feels
All beings, as thou hardly feel'st thyself! . . . .
It *is* felicity! Felicity
Is ready for thee too, so sure as thou
Shalt lose and shalt forget thyself: the man,
When God is no more man, no, Thou in God,
God is no more Thou-He, henceforth He-Thou.
That life may be, — is blessedness ordained,
That blessedness may be, — for this is life!
Once more then in the highest sense I say:
He only who hears out the entire voice
Of Nature finds her to be — blessedness!
And, man, for God's sake live a godly life!
For such a life is all else through and through.

XXIX.

God's Use of Man's Faults.

This seems to me the most divine in God:
The turn He gives even to unrighteousness;
The picture which He paints even for the blind,
And sets before him till he opens his eyes!
Thus man is even by his faults made blest,
Thus only, with life's fairest, truest bliss,

Blest as and whence he never hoped to be,
Nor yet deserved; not through his failing, not
Through that which was a veritable fault
In *his* thought, — but in Nature's thought and sense
The right, the true! And such man owns it then,
And reverently accepts it as his life,
As he accepts long-slighted, grown-up children,
That were not owned as his, and yet were his,
And now stand round him, images of God.
So, too, a God rewards the dream of wrong
In which *one* child of His endured and wept!

XXX.

The Aims of Man.

Our aims are many. Many a one succeeds,
And many a one seems baffled; yet the world
Softly and surely all our working guides.
What we had thought of least, one day receives
Our name, though that which seemed the best, perhaps,
Was labor lost. We live as if we were
Others, we think we are; we even seem
To be such, — and Time makes us other men.

THE LAYMAN'S BREVIARY.

JULY.

JULY.

JULY.

I.

Sincerity.

PROOF of heart-ripeness, clear and heavenly
ring
Of the pure breast, — Sincerity, thou com'st,
Of all the virtues, never till the last, —
(As the rose comes the last of all the flowers), —
To him who walked not in a steadfast course
Of childlike innocence! And, thou dear Soul
Of Truth, how good and pious thou must be,
Childlike and good to childlike openness!
With what sweet grace and truth the child himself
Carries his erring thoughts, his little faults,
And even his hurtful wishes, to his mother!
But thou, O man, how sorely, with what long
And bitter pains, thou winn'st back honesty,
Now that thou seest thy faults, confessest them,
First to thyself, with shame, and slough'st them off
Painfully, as the snake his spotted skin,
And lurest the long frighted genii
Back to the good ones that still stayed with thee,
Till, like a bell, thou hast attuned thy breast
In unison with the holy chime of Heaven,
And made thy tongue the tongue of the just balance
That weighs the true, the genuine, and the right.
Even earth herself opens not her pure bosom

Till with the little crocus's golden head,
With hyacinthine bells that shake abroad
The true spring fragrance, — with the countenance
And eye of pure and radiant flowers, she comes
Forth to the pure and holy light of day!
Full of chaste shame before even human eyes!
The founder cannot, surely, show the bell
That in the mould still boils and smokes and glares;
Who would lay open the pomegranate's apple,
While yet, instead of ripe and purple grains,
It teems with naught but green and bitter milk?
Who lets thee see his eye yet red with tears,
Till first, in secret, he has cleansed it dry?
And who, in fine, can let thee see his heart,
Till, as a silver chalice, it is pure?
O heavy load of silence and reserve!
O heavy pain of false and idle speech!
— Through a pure will alone comes childhood back.
Happy, who can at length rise in the morn
As if no padlock on his lips were laid
By evil spirits from the ancient night!
Into whose eyes the sun's glad radiance shines
As through the poppy's light, new-opened house,
Where lies no captured bee that died o'er night
In agony, no speck of dust! His heart,
And only his, has like the rose's, power
And right to bare itself to men and gods.
Thy worth, sincere one! is immeasurable
To thee and men. Thou hast a light, secure
Conscience within. Who always speaks and lives
As inwardly he thinks, chimes with himself,
With God, and with the Universe around,
With good men gladly, even with bad men well.

Frank-hearted one! Thy look is free! Thy hand
Cheers with its grasp! To him who looks on thee,
A genuine man, God's image, hath appeared,
He is no more alone! To thee all hearts
Unfold in beauty and in joy. Thy word
Unlocks the richest treasures of men's souls.
Thou canst confide! so blest art thou alone!
Thou never art alone! for in thee dwell
All the good genii; Truth and Faith and Love
And Joy and Hope, dwell in thee without fear!

II.

Night.

Heavenly is night, a miracle divine!
But loveliest is the part man sleeps away.

. . . . .

So almost meanly Nature doth esteem
Her very greatest things, and holiest,
That she herself gently shuts-to man's eyes
From the brave sight, that so she may call forth
His sweetest life, his bliss, his dream alone,
And by and by she softly closes them
For the last time upon her majesty,
Making her highest sacrifice, — and gives
A sweeter sleep, the beauteous sleep of death.

. . . . .

Heavenly is night, a miracle of God!
But loveliest is the night man sleeps away.

III.

"*He calleth them all by Name.*"

At dead of night, when, in the magic dusk,
The old star-grotto overhead once more
Wide open stands, illimitably wide,
And yet with its far-twinkling little lamps
Sheds but a feeble, sparse, and niggard light,
As if some poor man might have lighted it,
So dim, as if a child at twilight-hour
Had lighted up his little tapers there,—
Or on the red-hot shovel sprinkled round
Fine brimstone dust, which sparkles up and glows
With inexpressible beauty in the dark,—
And when a silence deep as death, and holy
As death itself, through all the grotto reigns,
Then, after long and dumb astonishment,
My blissful spirit whispers in my ear:—
How many thousand names *one* star may have
On all the many thousand stars around,
How some one on the star *Zubenhakrabi*
May name the star in the Bear, *Kalbeleked*,—
And how *Kalbeleked*, in *Benetnasch*
In *Rukkabah*, in *Ras-Althagne*, sounds,
And what in *Kochab's* speech is *Markab's* name,
How many thousand names and thousand tongues
On all the stars through the vast grotto's round
At once the star *Capella* designate,—
(The elephant of stars, among the lambs,
Monster,* 'mong all the starry pasture feeds),—

* The star Capella is 600,000,000 leagues in circumference, and our whole solar system, with the intervals and orbits of its stars, would find room and to spare within its girth.

This knowledge brings no fruit to thee and men;
To know even how an angel names the rose
With such a name, as, drawn from Nature's depth,
Reveals at once its very essence, too,
Were beautiful, yet leaves the soul untouched.
But ah, to know how God, how God names man,
That were momentous! Such a name should thrill
Through the whole soul, that loves to feel itself
Free, great, enduring as the Universe,
In primal beauty clothed, and purity;
And full of restless yearning stirs itself,
As does the child within the mother's womb,
Or in the tub the wine, when the vine blooms.
One word would grandly for all earthly time
Decide the fate of earth: Does God call man
Son? Child? Or does He to a dead man speak,
Or *of* a dead man, or of death, to men,
When once again a man comes home to heaven,—
Does He still call him Thou, or says He "I" . . .
I *was on earth!*—And Hope shall die for joy,
Shall fall down dead before this oracle:
"God was on earth!" that is the name of man.

IV.

Children gathering Strawberries.

Now come the children with their little hands
Full of the red and fragrant strawberry,
To them more precious far than mines of gold!
Their little clothes and fingers are perfumed
With stains of rosy blood from the ripe fruit,
Whereto heaven's juices have been so transformed,—

It seems as it had crept from out the earth!
The children's mouths breathe perfume as they praise
The mother who has brought them from the wood:
O look not on this joy so slightingly,
Nay, but with heightened, with divine delight!
The walk this mother took has cost the earth
A journey round the Sun, ... hast cost the Sun
So many thousand beams! . . . . these thousand beams
How much blue oil, from yon blue ether drawn!
And when thou once canst measure and hast weighed,
In thought, a single summer's godlike work
And godlike bliss,—and earth's outlay and heaven's,
Then hear, astonished, this my whispered word:
The strawberry costs what a summer costs,
And what a summer costs this Universe,—
It is a joyous work of that sore toil!
The children are a hard work of the mother,
The mother is a hard work of the earth,
The earth is a hard work of the great Master,—
Now then rejoice once more! With heavenly joy!

V.

The Creation of Woman.

When woman came from God's creating hand,
When he had finished now her graceful shape,
Endowed her with a soul, the effluence
Of his own pure and chaste and holy soul,
And, pausing, looked aside with smiling face,
Awaiting what would next transpire in her,
Then, as a rose bursts open from the bud,—
A sudden glow suffused her cheeks; she wept,
She wept, self-conscious, at the first fresh glance

Of her enchanting form, — that magic work
For magic workings; and it seemed to her
She were but such a work, with show of life,
With flowing hair, with eyes of brilliant light
Endowed, endowed to wander, — to and fro, —
To fold with gentle pressure in her arms
A clearly-presaged something to her breast,
To be whatever might be made of her,
To be whatever might become of her, —
Then she herself became sweet modesty,
The veil of her own person, shrinking shame,
Which like the invisible garment of a God,
And making her invisible, divinely,
Divinely grew to be her beauteous self!
And now she dreamed that she herself no more
Existed, yet her heart beat wildly still!
And as she thus before Him naked stood,
The Lord said, as if He, too, saw her not:
"Where art thou, woman?" — Sinking at his feet,
She whispered: "Here I am, Lord!" — and He said,
"So be thou! Soul self-perfected, as I
Trusted it should be when I gave it her.
Be for my works, the greatest wonder-work;
Be for the vision, loveliness; for love,
Be love itself; — yet (and He shook his head)
Thou still to me and to thyself art naught,
Art naught to him who sees and thinks as I.
I call thee, virgin modesty! sweet shame!
That shall henceforth be woman's name in Heaven;
And never in the world forget thy name:
Not for the world! . . . . Else thy old sire shall weep!"

. . . . .

Whoever now assails or impiously

Mocks, scorns, and curses the divinity
Of woman, — Virgin modesty, sweet shame,
And like a faun, — a satyr, — thinks to catch
Fair woman, when he scares that guard away,
That bold blasphemer has torn woman's name,
And over him the old sire in silence weeps.

VI.

God's Memory.

'T would be denying memory to God
To say, God did not know, — that man once was;
Or would not know one day, that thou wast once
A man, that He had once been thou on earth,
That thou still art. Can God forget what is?
To be, is to have been, be going to be:
God, — He is life! Is everything that lives!
And whatsoe'er is dead, all *that* He is;
How could God e'er forget, then, that He is!
And see that thou forget it not, dear soul!

VII.

Compassion.

Soft-souled compassion! Best, most heavenly
Of all the heavenly ones, — with thy good heart
What could'st thou be in yonder perfect Heaven?
Where thou, feeling with all, with none could'st suffer,
Could'st dry no tear of sorrow for the dead,
Could'st mitigate no grief o'er treasures lost,
Nor soothe the lost, forsaken, and forlorn,

Nor comfort nor advise a downcast soul,
Nor carry help in need to one poor man!
Nothing art thou to blessed ones in Heaven,
On earth alone art goddess, there complete!
Love art thou, too, that pure original love:
In sorrow's whelming flood the happy one
Who makest happy each thou smilest on,
For when thou comest, he sees heaven open,
Sees in thy person all the gods draw near,
He sees them weep over a mortal man.
And all is well now, — some one pities him!
Thou art from Heaven, — and yet thou dwellest here!
Here, thou art blest, and blest is man through thee!
— And should one day unalterable health
Part thee from man, now grown so dear to thee,
Part men from thee, now grown so dear to them,
Then scarce could Heaven with all its treasures give
One to make good thy place, their truest friend,
The fond and fair companion of their woe;
And but one longing would remain, — for thee!
Thou givest me thy hand? — dost weep e'en now?
Dost look upon me with thy beauteous eyes,
Sweet sadness hovering about thy lips,
And hid'st thy trembling head upon my breast?
Courage! — We shall not part! not yet! not we!

VIII.

Optimism.

Thou human soul, thou art the heavenly one!
And helping, soothing, is a rare delight!
Man is made richer than the gods themselves

By pain and agony, by tears, by death,—
In and beside long, full felicity.
The earth is made a perfect thing by love,
By love is man himself made perfect, too.
Life will be always what it is to-day,
Else were 't not so! Else God had wrought in vain!

IX.

The universal Will.

Whatever thou beholdest, and wherever,
In the wide circle of humanity,
Is only Will; yet not a stony will,
But one that enters into life and earth,
One that comes forth with man's and Nature's force,
That woven and working deep, with mystic strength
Now deals a visible blow, amazing thee:
Yet no less valid out in Nature and
As Nature, still is ever only: Will!
See now the huts of men in yonder field!
Behold the city's walls and battlements!
See yonder the old towers and temples, there
Mark the gray arches of the aqueduct,
See up on yonder hill the windmill's wings
That rise so softly in the evening-red,—
They all are just the same old human will.
I see, too, brides walk by,—young women, too,
Now pale ones, moving slow, with heavy gait,—
And mothers now,—with children by the hand,
Who carry to some neighbor wreaths of flowers;
In them, too, simply has a will been done!
And now, methinks, if with the self-same eyes

Thou would'st one little moment look aside,—
And through the space between those human towers,—
Would'st in those mountains, still as pictures now,
There also recognize no less a will!
One Being's Will! and if in yonder cloud
Which a light breath sweeps by in heaven so fast,—
As if it had, so late, still far to go,—
Thou also would'st observe the self-same will,
Observe it in the stream, and in the sun,
And in the flowers all round about thy feet,
And when thou hast descried a will in all
That is in heaven as well as on the earth,
Haply, ay, certainly,—and with what joy!—
Then shall the veil fall softly from thy eyes,
And in the will of all and each of these
Thou shalt discern the will of One alone,
Who, dwelling in the whole, as gently wills,
As surely, as thou willest in thy brain!
Who bears along as lightly earth and heaven
As the soft breeze bears yonder the light cloud!

X.

Sundown.

The Sun is down!—And yet with magic power
Still holds aloft the rainbow in the air,
Which *without* columns stands as on a thousand,
And lends a grace to heaven and joy to man.
—How shines on us the power of olden days!
Arches across the heaven! and sways the earth!
The lingering glow of long, long sunken suns
Gleams o'er us yet; an influence touches us

Of spirits long since vanished from the earth;
And we too, when we long have passed away,
Shall touch the generations yet to come
With spirit-power and be what once was "we!"
Become, what has, as power, gone forth from us!
The good man has a long and mighty arm,
Far longer than the outstretched "hand of kings";
For good men's kingdom is the Universe!

XI.

Causes.

Of many things and incidents we seem
To see a clear beginning, — only *seem*,
We see it not! Beyond us evermore
It lies far off, deep in the abyss of time.
Of all that makes the Universe of things
Each to each other ever lives, and near.
Still floats with mighty echo every word,
Still points with mighty meaning from the grave
Each dead man's hand into the present day,
To-morrow, and the last of earthly days.
The lightest cloud, the briefest breath that curls
And vanishes, — the lightest blade of grass,
Have seed and growth, direction and effect
In the long-buried, silent, holy grave
Of the elements, the power-crammed Universe,
For which in turn the little grass-blade lives,
The cloudlet sails, the light air stirs and dies!
Just as, in years long since gone by, the storms
Bowed down the branches, so they stand to-day,
As if struck stiff by sense of holy power,

Before the Lord's behest, and so they bloom!
The course of things seems free, too, flexible,
Controllable, — yet sternly sweeps us on!
As others thought before us, as they did,
And were disposed, so are we wrought upon
By them to-day, and so we carry on
Their work, and blend our influence with theirs.
There is a web, invisible, but firm,
That, woven round us by a spirit's hand,
Entwines inextricably every head;
Man, too, is but a product of the time,
A fruit of the great life-tree full of fruits,
And none escapes the spirit of the world, —
Full of mild power is the mild Universe,
And one thing only is our own, — our heart!

XII.

Fate and Freedom.

Believe not in necessity and fate,
But in constraint at most, if thou art weak
Dost ill and wrong, nor honorest social force.
Fate is the spider in the web which all
Free wills and individual powers have spun:
She has not made the web, the web makes her.
Yet 't is all one; although no spider 's there,
We fall into the net and perish still, ...
And still live on, ... in misery, — or in bliss.
Caught in this web, each flutters round and round,
Buzzes and struggles, and whoso has much
Pure will and vital force lives longer there,
And even the good man bears the bad man's will

In token that Humanity is man!
By liberty is man alone oppressed!
And yet to feel oppressed by liberty,
Art thou ashamed, for reverence of thy lot,
Till all men's freedom is the good of all.

XIII.

Divine Metamorphosis.

Whether the gold ring is destructible,
If wise, thou provest simply by the gold.
How can a ring grow ever into gold!
Inquire then: Can the gold become a ring?
And then, if man was not made out of air,
Inquire: Can God take flesh and be a man?
The immortal one appear in mortal shape?
And He appears, — Thou art! God *is* made man.
And *how* the gold can run into a ring
That the old art of the old Master knows,
Skilled to transform himself, make himself small,
Shiver himself to splinters, diamond-like,
And then to a great diamond grow again, —
Seem mortal, being immortal all the while.
— And knows He not that art, — what does He know,
What can He do, — He who is all in all!

XIV.

Earth the Home of Man.

Earth is the home of man, there still he finds
His homestead; even though on other stars

Were living other beings like himself.
The soul is not the man, the body is not
The man; to make him soul and body join;
For soul is equally all else that lives;
Soul in a human body is the man.
Thus is the earth his fair and goodly home,
His workshop for his individual life.
The heavenly spirit lives on earth, and man,
Inhabitant of earth, yet lives in heaven.
That which is one, is always like itself,
And what is like itself is one and whole.
The water-drop cleaves to the water-drop
With ease and joy, as brother does to brother;
The river seeks the ocean, as a child
Runs to its mother; up to heaven's blue sea
The dew ascends, as to its ancient sire;
The iron to the magnet flies and clings
As to its Saviour, and the swallow hies
Into strange countries, as if hastening home.
Ay! Look abroad! with what a rapturous,
Heart-thrilling bliss, all feels itself at home!
The fragrant lindens, in their rustling green,
They are at home! . . . . these blushing rose-bushes,
They are at home! . . . . these lambkins on the mead,
They are at home! And nowhere, nowhere else
Are they at home. As little children run
Into their father's garden; with soft voice
He calls them, and they hasten like the clouds!
— And yonder cloud is only here at home, —
'T is everywhere the self-same Father's-call;
The same obedience of the loving child!
And everywhere the one great common home,
The Father's home and all the children's, all!

And in the great home each one has his own
Peculiar and familiar little home:
The nest, the house, the grove, the brook, the sea!
The head, the body, the blue sky, the stars!
The mussel has the handsome golden shells!
The nut's sweet kernel has the rich brown shells!
The jet-black apple-seed within its core,
Its apple: white world of white apple-flesh, ...
The purple heaven with its lustrous stripes:
The spicy rind redolent of dewy eves,
And with its brothers in the nursery dwells
Confidingly as man abides in his, —
The body, which in stuff is like the all;
And all, throughout the Universe, inhabits
Its nursery: the spirit, which is like
In essence to the universal spirit,
And to each ray the spirit-sun darts forth,
And God is God in heaven and on earth.

XV.

A Lesson from the Sun.

Behold the Sun at morning and at eve!
The sun knows naught of thee, he sees thee not,
And yet he does thee and will do thee good.
He signals with vast might out through the blue;
Spends he his good on the blue void alone?
He hits his mark! He grows in man and flower
And blossom, to the ocean's deepest bed,
Nor is one ray in all its journeyings lost!
And *thou* must know to whom thou doest good?
To distant strangers wilt refuse thy love?

To men and flowers that come long after thee?
And dost thou truly know the very man
Who stands before thee? Were he in himself
No mystery, he would still be such to thee.
For when thy being is completely filled
With goodness and with love to him, believe me,
Thou seest him not, as the sun sees thee not,
For glow of heavenly warmth and perfect light:
Thou need'st but this to glad thee! that he is!
The rose is gloriously rewarded for
Her fragrance by exhaling; and the Sun
For his effulgence, by the light! And man
For all his loving finds a rich reward
In love itself; man is repaid for life
Amply by living. Learn thou this of Heaven!
And learn it too on earth, from all thou dost!
Distinguish no one, then, of all that live!
Not him who names himself thy foe, or friend;
Distinguish naught that lives: let fruit and tree
Be one to thee, the shepherd and his flock,
The lambkin and the grass, the grass and dew,
The dew and its refulgence. In the midst
Of the vast universe of love, unmoved,
Keep thou thy place! and only live and love!
Behold the Sun at morning and at eve!

XVI.

Be worthy of thy Place.

Whate'er deserves not that the sun should shine,
That God should have invented light, and framed
The eye so magically; whatsoe'er

Deserves not that the earth should roll through heaven,
That God should have created sound, contrived
So curiously the labyrinth of the ear,
Deserves not that the little hammer's blow
With spirit's tongues should tell it to the soul;
Whate'er deserves not that thy heart should beat,—
That thou should'st be a man, that through the world
A moral sense should thrill; whate'er deserves not
That God should be, or that the hand should be,
—The Master's masterpiece,—*all that*, dear man!
Do thou not see nor hear, nor do nor think!
Far better were it that the soul's pure bell
Should swing in peace and silence, than announce
E'en that which is unworthy earth, instead
Of gladdening Heaven, to the immortal ears.
Whate'er is worthy of thy being man,—
Of God's being God,—that see, do, hear, and think!
And if thou canst not close thy eyes nor ears
Then look upon it with the eyes of God!
So looks the sun pure and serene on all:
For 't is an easy thing to hear and see
What is *divine;* the very child, the beast,
The villain can and does and must do that;
But to behold, to hear *divinely*, that
Is hard for mortal man! who thinks, forsooth,
To die,—thinks, without God, to be a man!
Yet easy is it, like all hard things, to him
Who recognizes *Him* as his true *Self*,
Who is the man within him, and so now
Has come to know himself and be himself.

XVII.

The least is great.

What, now, is worthy aught should be? and all?
That all the stars should wheel in heaven above,
That thou should'st have come forth here on the earth
From deep, unutterable wonders, full,
Thyself, of wonders, as a man? What is it?
This, unmistakably: That thou art man,
And that thou dost the smallest human thing!
That thou instructest, warnest, clothest children;
That to the well thou takest daily steps
For water; that thou eatest, sleepest, toilest,
Art glad and grieved, even as men are glad
And grieved. The very word within thy mouth
Whereby thou comfortest to life again
A sad one, — yea, the rod within thy hand,
Wherewith thou chastenest thy little ones,
Is worthy that a holy law should be,
(It is itself the law incarnated,)
Is worthy, day and earth and heaven should be
(It is the world made into life, the right
The genuine world), — is worthy that in Heaven
There should be joy, — yea, worthy God should be:
For he is Lord and Master of all good,
Father of life is He, and Life itself.

XVIII.

Theology of the Hand.

Look on thy hand, and tell me now, I pray:
Whence comes thy power to raise a finger there?

Now get thee to the desert, pray and fast,
Search, speculate, guess, prove, and make research.
Investigate all powers, explore all wonders,
The mystery of will, thy will, a will.
Yet wilt thou never know the holy power,
The Omnipotence of metamorphoses,
The duplicating power, the one in two,
The one in thousands and *as* thousands, nor
The thousands joined as one, until thou say'st:
"'T is I *myself* that make my finger move."
"Myself am I." The Word createth man,
Creates the world. Thou art; there is a God.
The Word destroys too the created world,
And speaks of Being, its Nature, of existence
As Nature, and of Nature as existence,
As Being, and of Self, as I and Thou.
Now raise thy finger and point up and say:
"He there on high has *formed* me here below."
Then fold thy hands and pray and utter thanks!
He who cannot give thanks, feels not himself, —
Gratitude is the highest joy, — existence.
The beggar thanks thee, — now he lives, — and thou!
And some One else who takes a silent joy,
In secret, and who, as a tear of joy,
Flows softly from the eyes of both of you;
Nothing but Love itself believes in Love,
And love is only clear self-consciousness;
Yet if a man might venture to name God,
Ah, then would I name Him with lowliness:
Primeval source of maiden modesty!
And now I hide and bury my two eyes
With both my hands and disappear for shame.

XIX.

The delicate Mystery of God.

"The deep of wonders no man penetrates."
What if that deep has penetrated man!
If He should be the all, the Apocalypse!
"And on what star alone dwells all the Truth?
And in what man?" — The earth is but a star, ...
A star is but a word of the long speech
That has gone forth out of the mouth of God
And still is going. See, hear, how it speaks!
Thou seest that breath stream yonder like white frost, —
They call it Milky Way in mortal speech;
And every flower that the child only plucks, —
And the lamb plucks to pieces, — to the heart
Of him whose thought has taught him to believe
In revelation, as impressively,
As softly, silently, and solemnly,
And audibly speaks forth the self-same word.
That which agrees with all things else is true;
Yet know thou, truth is not an empty show,
Truth is a real being, not a thought;
There is then but One Truth: the Universe!
God! God himself is Truth, and God is true;
Yet be thou also true and truthful, — godlike;
It is impossible to enunciate God!
Therefore has no one yet declared "the Truth."
Accord thou with the all, then art thou true.
To do the truth, — would be creating God.
Truth must be seen, heard, felt, loved, sought, explored!
Explore thou it! — For nothing else is life

Than to explore, more and more deeply know,
Behold, hear, love, and feel the all-present God.
"I am a mouth of Truth," say thus at most,
"I have a heart, I have a spirit and zeal
And every drop of blood to give the truth."
So saying thou speakest rightly. But to say,
"I am the Truth," that is a word from which
The very God himself might shrink abashed,
The modest one who fills the Universe,*—
Yet steals as gently, softly, secretly,
Into the bosom of a new-born child
As into the low violet, violet scent!
And then just breathes out thence as from his cup!

XX.

The Spectators of Nature.

Who is it that shall come, to witness here
Full-glowing summer's pomp and majesty?
Surely a monarch from the sun o'erhead,
A king of many stars, come down from Heaven,
A god with wife and children at his side,
And retinue of connoisseurs divine,—
To estimate and honor such a work!
Who will, who shall, then, haply, buy the earth,
That she so stands oppressed with finery!
For, sure, no dead one from the giant age
Of earth, no one of her dead heroes all,
Of her dead men, were worthy that the earth
Should loose him from the grave,—to see this pomp!—
The very best would not deserve an hour

* "God fills the Universe, silently and without noise."—SOUTH. TR.

The sweet life in the lap of beauty here
As pleasure paid for pains of past exploits!
For how industriously have storm and winds,
Like tireless and strong-chested servants, worked
Till they were breathless, sweeping the green hall
Of earth, till each old leaf was hustled off,
Huddled away in pit or stream or pond;
How have the clouds in fetching water toiled,
To speed the growth of all the thousand flowers!
And dropped soft drops to lay each speck of dust!
How oft have thunder-clouds at morn and eve
And night filled all the fields with fragrant steam!
How long invisible spirit-hands have wrought
Day after day in sunshine, and by night
In the bright moonshine, and in darkness too
Beneath the silent veil of mist, to hang
Green leaves on each least twig of every tree!
And now the golden fruits among the leaves!
How richly decked the mountains to their crowns!
How have they waked the chafers, summoned up
The merry birds with silver voices all,
Yea, driven them into these magic grounds;
And even sent away each little cloud,
Like children, that the spacious hall of heaven
May shine unstained in azure-brilliancy,—
And see, in azure-brilliancy it shines!
Pure as a drop of water, gleams the Sun,
And all has now been ready days and days!—
And *no one* comes convoyed from yonder heaven,—
On wingéd steeds comes riding through the air,—
To see here all the summer-majesty!
And we are plainly left here all alone,
All by ourselves!—There 's no one more to come!

What rises yonder is but a white cloud, —
Disguised as a great goddess to the eye.
Yet breezes waft e'en now the lovely head
Off from her shoulder! And the head sails off!
The goddess sails away! and melts to fleece!
Then lost in musing I cast down my eyes!
Then my blest spirit, explaining, says at last:
"Expect no longer gods from yonder height!
Expect no longer any other guests!
All have long since arrived. The nightingales,
The roses and the lilies and the pinks,
The stork, the crane, the swallow, and the thrush,
The starling, too, and all the summer-birds,
The fields all full of glad and quivering stalks,
The lands and all the woodlands full of beasts,
The waters full of dumb, enormous brutes,
And the invisible ones, — the innumerable
In every drop of water, grain of dust!
The ancient guest — now almost host — of earth
Is present: man, who comes and comes again
As child, — O only see them there at play,
How lively, how ecstatic is their joy!
Ye all are the true guests here, all of you!
The master's works, — they are themselves the guests,
Are his spectators and his hearers. They,
They are the blest and honored ones for whom,
And through whom, He has made these wonders all
So beautiful, themselves so beautiful!
Ay, see yet more! Nay, mark but this one thing:
Creation's works are after all His works,
They are his living ones: his beauteous life,
His very traits of character, his soul!
The only merit therefore is: existence;

The greatest wisdom, simple life itself;
Whoever lives fulfils a godlike task,
A heavenly one, with art divine, and clear
Intelligence! and then and only then
Richly and wholly, when his heart is set
Purely to do, not scrutinize his work.
Behold the happy mother-swallow there:
She leads her children out to-day. Five children
At once! out of five quiet little eggs;
And forth now fly the fledglings from the nest
Following their parents to inspect the hall
With their own eyes, wherein they have just waked,
Not wonder-struck, not secretly surprised,
Only already tired with their short flight,
They now sit down. The sun shines down on them,
The mother sings to them, the father brings
The food he has picked up, and feeds them with it,
And twitters. Lo! These are the summer's guests!
They spring forth from the earth and from the heavens
Freely as tears of joy gush from thy eyes!
For joy most deeply touches human hearts, —
Yet look around, — not human hearts alone!"

XXI.

The Swallow's Message.

Thou hear'st the swallow in the hush of night
As in her nest she whispers to her young.
By many a human mother thou hast known
Already, what the swallow-mother says:
"Be quiet, little darling, I am by,
I take good care of thee, I bring thee food,

I stay with thee, my darling child, be still."
Thus has the swallow spoke these hundred years, —
Thus has the swallow spoke these thousand years, —
Thou art not listening up the swallow's breast,
Thou 'rt listening to the cry of Nature's soul!
Thou hearest in this song the eternal word, —
Hear'st in this mother the eternal woman,
Awe-struck to feel so near the Mighty One!
She has come down into the passing times!
And she twines round thee in sublime embrace,
She draws thee up to the primeval breast,
Thou livest in her pure felicity.
Thou are not a mere name, O man, inscribed
On the sarcophagus of Nature! Not
A half-formed sculpture! Round, original, free,
Thou liv'st the life of Nature. Thou art she,
And she is thou, and thy word is her word,
And what thou feelest, that she feels and is.
Thou speakest nothing *after* her, she speaks
In thee; yet canst thou say: I, I say this!
For without thee the mighty one were not,
Were null, were naught, and with her thou art all.

XXII.

Man's Pride humbled.

Self-analyzed, and laid out piece by piece, —
As on a carpet, broad and beautiful,
Worked full of myriad animals and flowers,
All full of living, calmly busy works,
And yet bound fast together by the woof, —
Such Nature is! and basks in endless suns.

Each of her individual traits makes out
A separate being; yea, a separate being, —
A new and different world seems brought to life.
Now man's peculiar character and charm
Is kindness. This it is distinguishes
Him from the trees, the flowers, and even from all
The animals, from sun and moon and stars,
Yet without giving him the right to feel
That he is *better* than the very stone.
For nothing can be better than divine;
And what exists, is Nature's very self.
And each, as Nature, is a perfect thing,
Else were the universe a monstrous crime,
An outrage multiplied a thousand times.
Now dream, the judgment-day at last has come, —
A May-field where *one* Lord in judgment sits,
And hear now what the deaf, blind creatures say:
Lord, I, — I was on earth a thistle-bush,
And I have borne a thistle-bush's lot:
For that I justly now claim my reward!
— And I, Lord, I have been a dromedary,
And sorely fared, as dromedaries do:
And justly now claim my reward therefor!
— And I, Lord, I have been a stupid hake,
And must henceforth discourse with angels' tongues!
— And I, lo! I was actually a frog, —
And so must now become a god at least!
And like a choir of maniacs all cry out:
"For whoso was a least one, he of all,
Deserves henceforth to be a highest one!"
On such a claim comes man, in turn, and says:
— And I have been a man, have loved and lived
Happy ofttimes, for the most part unhappy

For very love and kindness; yet, O Lord!
The frog himself demands — to be a god!
But I have been a man and I have loved, —
How I have loved thee, thou dost know full well!
— And thus in stern reproof the Eternal Love:
Verily, hast thou? Art thou all thou sayst?
And have you all? And were you all such? All!
I have so done, so been. What shall I be,
But be! abide! Be and abide in me.
He rises from the golden judgment-seat,
And all have learned from Him a thoughtful mind.

XXIII.

Against Witchcraft.

How shall the spyglass help thee in a dream,
That like the deep flower-gardens of the sea,
The dreamy shapes shall thus be clearly seen?
In sleep's delirium the speaking trumpet
Carry thy voice to Minos on his throne?
Or the ear-trumpet help thee hear the stars?
— They shall not even help thee truly dream,
No more shall thy dark shadow-webs of dream,
Woven by daylight, in the noonday sun,
And those delirious words for living ones!
"Thou *shalt* not practise witchcraft!" Then thou *canst.*
Thou shalt not deal in charms! For the great Master
Has charmed thee now as much as seemed him good!
The gracious apparitions of the earth,
Wife, child, are wonders quite enough for thee;
The realm of sunshine is the place for man,
The *house of life* and not its workshop, — that

Is thy delirium, sleep in open day,
And even the sun meanwhile is quenched for thee!
Thy very body falls meanwhile to dust!
When sober, too, thou canst believe on God!
But drunkards believe only in their wine.

XXIV.

The Voyage of Night.

Now thou embarkest in the skiff of night,
Leaving a land thou ne'er shalt see again:
The day that softly died! and wondrously,
By merely a black veil drawn over it,
'T is buried in the light and fleeting air;
And yet it is as surely buried, there,
As is the loveliest youth men laid in earth;
The motley thread of Day is all reeled up
By his great Mother Sun, who spun him, too,
On that fast-swelling, and e'en now so full
Cocoon, the Earth. And thou now sailest on,
Wafted along so softly, tranquilly,
Through a blue, dusky, glimmering grotto full
Of little lamps, that shine so soft and fair,
The very largest of them dazzles not
Thine eye (light-veiled beneath the sheltering lid),
With its pure gold, its ruby, and pale-green.
Like dew of heaven they hang there in the sky
And play soft colors and mild brilliancy.
And on the broad expanse of hovering,
Of busy, twinkling drops, that child of light,
*The great white rainbow,** in the grotto rests;

* The Milky Way.

The drops send forth no song, — they live all still,
Crowded and swarming with invisible beings,
Yet full as every drop is full of ether.
Through all the grotto scarce a whisper stirs,
Or a fresh breath! scarcely at times there darts
Far into secret depths a golden gleam,
And trails its lovely fire behind its path.
So through long times, how long, thou knowest not,
Through far, far, trackless space thou sailest on.
Meanwhile come swimming, as from blessed shores,
To meet and greet thee new and wondrous flowers,
Signs of new land approaching, purple streaks
And auburn gold in mists of fragrance veiled,
And growing ever clearer and more clear,
The grotto lights *itself* by slow degrees,
Transfigured wondrously before thine eyes!
It grows itself, to a wide exit-gate!
It grows, itself, to a new land for thee!
And deeply blest thou sweepest on to meet
The coast, and ere thou thoughtest, there it lies;
Clear, stirring, morning-red, and morning-fair,
Like an enchanted garden full of roses! —
It is the unmistakably present shore,
Never before beheld, of the new day!
Thou disembarkest now and enterest,
As if it were thine own familiar house, —
A realm, divinely new, of heaven-wide space!

. . . . .

But men say of the wonders of the sail
Through this enchanted grotto: "Yesterday
I went to bed, and woke again this morning."

XXV.

The Way to cure Implacableness.

The way to cure implacability
Is: never feel offended in thy heart!
Easy enough, if thou art a true man,
Nay, simply far from hard, presumptuous pride.
Nor shalt thou ever forgive any man,
Not the least thing; the greatest least of all!
He is a haughty fool who will forgive.
Thou seemest scarce to see the heavenly law
Which but thy foe, thy murderer, overlook.
And now wert *thou* this law, — the law is love, —
And art thou it, — who e'er can harm thy love?
The loving spirit is far beyond offence!
It comes as pity, kindness, solace, help!
As in the cloud that hurled the thunderbolt,
Thou recognizest still a heavenly hand,
So recognize thou the divine in man,
The presence, essence of the indwelling God,
Which he was surely, is, and still remains.
I pray, see clearly: He who will forgive,
Must be offended! And, to be offended,
Who must he be? — more pitiable far
Than is the faulty one; be thou not he!
Be not the man through whom the offence shall come,
And be not an offended man; for God's sake
Be thou no pardoner, — one who will forgive,
And lives with men in the delusive dream
Of pardoning and procuring pardon thus
From Some One, — who 's offended with himself!
A loving heart can never take offence,

Never from others who are men ; still less,
Assuredly, from that which is not man,
With *that* he lives in everlasting peace.
The clear and loving soul commit a sin ?
It sins not, never shall, and never can ?
Only where clearness and pure love are not,
There man is led astray in passion's mist,
Urged on to steal a fleeting show of good ;
And *whom* dost thou, when thou forgiv'st, forgive ?
Lo, thou forgivest only a poor soul !
The Devil, I would say, if such there were.
And *what* dost thou forgive, when thou forgiv'st ?
A soul's *disaster*, and a soul's *disgrace !*
That shalt thou not for all the good of earth ;
And who art thou thyself, when thou forgiv'st ?
The Devil, I would say, if thou wilt be ;
Accept no pardon, — and thou needest none,
Thou shamest him ! And do not *thou* forgive,
'T is to commit a sin, the greatest sin
Of all : the sin 'gainst love and blessedness
Both in thy breast and the wide universe.
If I should hear of men : "They are offended," . . . .
"Cannot be reconciled to wife and son," . . . .
"But now they have forgiven their enemies," . . . .
Then would I say with right : They 're not yet men.
Or heard I of a God : "He is offended,
"Cannot be reconciled to wife and son, ...
"The God has now forgiven his enemies,
And, for his friends, long since forgave them all," . . . .
Hardly were he a man like thee and me,
And sure could never be a God of men :
For God is Love, Reason, and Blessedness,
Who in his wrath would do despite to *these ?*

Not thou, not I, and surely no true man.
O what delusion still oppresses men,
Drags down to dust their life and better heart,
Which yearns to feel magnanimously like God,
And must so feel, since God within them lives!
Who feels himself offended will revenge
Far sooner, haply, than forgive the offence,
Just as the boy, reluctantly lets go,
And sullenly, from his hands the captive bird.
And therefore say I to thee for thy good,
And for the good, repose and peace of men:
"Ne'er feel thyself offended in thy heart,
For thou canst never love thy so-called *foe*,—
Thy *enemy* implies thy *enmity*,—
But easily and heartily a man;
For in him dwells the gracious spirit of God.
Behold then,— know no foe, but only man!
And where it seems to thee *offence* draws nigh,
'T is only a loud call: *Help here a man*
To insight, reason, tolerance, and love!
And now make haste with zeal to succor him!"

XXVI.

The Moral of Card-house-building.

When thou didst build card-houses, as a child,
Thou didst not dare to breathe! how patiently,
With all a child's devout simplicity,
Presence of mind and earnest faithfulness,
Thy stiff and weary arms went through the work!
Or was a rose-bush given thee to tend,
How oft 't was sprinkled, watched how carefully!

So all that thou beholdest round about
Has grown and prospered only by the care,
Diligence, earnestness, persistency,
Which chose and used the means each end required.
And shall thy inner man, then, rear itself?
Like a wild plant, thy soul grow of itself,
Thy disposition, mind, and character?
No star, no grain of sun-dust jars another,
The mountains stand there calmly side by side,
The forest-trees, the lambs within the fold;
Yet sooner all wild beasts shall dwell together
Harmoniously, when hunger drives them mad,
The lions, crocodiles, and giant snakes,
The tigers, lynxes, panthers, and hyenas,
Than in thy brain the thoughts dwell peacefully;
Tame, order, curb them with an iron rein!
Be lord and master of thy bosom-thoughts,
Then art thou master of thy passions, then,
Then only art thou sure of thy pure bliss.
Lo! in the mighty herd of human folk
Do not, exactly, differing bodies dwell,
They all in almost equal bodies dwell;
But differing minds impelling different ways
Into sea-waves resolve humanity,
And yet the waves *one* ruling wind compels.
Hast thou then trained thyself to be a man,
Then hast thou made far more than kingdoms thine
With thine own spirit's treasures for the spoils,
With power and empire over all the world;
Even o'er death and life, distress and pain;
Then hast thou done more than all masters have
With brass and stone, with colors, and with tones;
Hast wrought within thyself a godlike work

That lives! that moves! divinely thinks and feels!
Hast made the universe to be for thee
A living fount of beauty, love, and truth!
And filled with its rich powers and influences,
Thou growest up its noble son, — a man.

XXVII.

Fear of Thunder.

It thunders; godlike thunder! speak yet more!
It lightens; ravishing lightning! flash yet more!
No other sound so vibrates through the breast
As thunder's roar, the child's-talk of the clouds.
O would but once Heaven speak a very word!
And when I long have dwelt at home on earth,
Long in the crowd of men forgot myself,
And dream, I in a city live with king
And beggars, human faces, forms, and speech,
In a poor, narrow circle spellbound thus . . . .
Once more it thunders, and the ancient sound
Out of the hoary eld, electrically
Hurls me to earth, — and lo, I am at home,
At home, indeed, in our old house of gods!
Then do my children gather round me all.
A flash, — a crash! I tremble at the cloud
That hangs down black and lowering o'er our homes, —
"To feel thou 'rt in the power of a cloud!
The power of vapors, which the wind's breath drives,
How wretched!" Wretched? Didst thou speak the word
Contemptuously, despising, as a fool,
The all-amazing unveiled majesty, ...
The veil itself! Lord, hear not what the fool

Hath said! O Lord and Master, they despise
Thy robe, Thy flaming garment they despise,
Self-living robe, because Thou touchest it,
Because it touches Thee, charged with Thy power!
This now they scorn, — the pictures on it too!
— Godlike as they themselves are, all Thy spirits,
How much so e'er they after Thee have wrought,
Shaped, and created; images and thoughts,
Man fashioning man and works so worthy man, —
Though they have wrought so much which Thou hadst planned,
Yet has not the divinest of them all
Created after Thee a grain of sand!
Not one will ever after Thee create
A drop of water, no, nor air enough
To give a fly one breath, not even that!
Say nothing of those full and swelling veins
Of blood, wherein each droplet is a star,
A light, a lustre! and far less say aught
Of the whole giant frame! the termite-pile
Of ether-waves! the golden giant shell
Full of clear liquid pearls! Alas, Thy house,
The snail-house formed out of their own life-sap,
Thy likeness, by Thyself delineated,
Thy property, yea, property of soul, —
This they despise, the pictures on it, too!
The robe of beauty incorruptible
And indestructible that wraps Thee round,
Conceals, reveals, contains Thy deity,
Just as the human body forms the man,
Who *is* man only while in flesh. The flesh,
The incarnation of the Eternal Love,
Yea *that*, O Lord and Master, they despise!

And O were this unsearchable existence
Thy body, ah, hadst Thou a body, too,
And were it still diviner than Thy soul, —
Then would their petty thought divorce itself
From Thee forever, just because their soul
A body wears, which crumbles into dust!

XXVIII.

Goodness is simple Being.

Goodness is nothing more than simple being;
All other being is but going-to-be,
Or going astray from being, going to waste.
Be not, O good man, proud, thou merely *art*,
And as the rose may bloom out suddenly,
Each who is going-to-be may straightway *be*.

XXIX.

Praying to the Great Physician.

When, to the mere physician, thou dost dare
To utter words like these: "Ah, do, I pray,
All that thou canst to save this sufferer!
Neglect no means! Fail not to visit him!
The apothecary's shop is well supplied
With medicines? the attendants are not drunk?
In thy prescriptions pray make no mistakes!
The remedies thou orderest, best of men,
Will certainly not harm him? Thou art sure?"
The doctor might unblamed make coarse reply!
And wilt thou pray to God in words like these?

And if thou dost, believ'st thou in a God?
Whoso believes in God shows reverence
By hope, and offers him a silent prayer!
There is but *one* prayer! — 't is a pious mind.
And mark, a pious mind has godlike joy,
'T is joy in God and in his godliness.
Thus all things point the heart of man to joy!
True joy, however, is the hardest work
Of man, the hardest and most serious too. *
Give not the name of joy to levity,
To idle mirth and self-forgetfulness!
They that are noisy now erelong will weep
In silence. No! the mother of true joy
Is thoughtfulness, — the eye of God in man, —
That sees all clearly and loves all things clear.

XXX.

Man's Ability and Responsibility.

Thy hand hath made and sent me forth, and now,
O Father, here I stand beneath Thy clouds,
Confronted yonder with Thy beauteous heaven,
Thy great sun mildly beaming down on me,
Right in the midst of all Thy miracles,
Here on thy festally attired earth!
Each mystery of Thy artistic soul,
All the half-veiled, half-manifest loveliness
Of the divine creations, great and small,
Which Thou in the full glow of fervid love
Hast shaped, my eye unlocks to me, my ear,

* "Res severa est verum gaudium." — Motto of a Music Hall in Berlin. Tr.

My spirit, of Thy lofty spirit born!
And bliss-bewildered scarce I comprehend
Yet that Thou art, that I am, and how blest!
That I do feel Thee in my glowing breast,
That I do love Thee in my swelling soul,
That I am still before Thee here, a man,
And set so high, — o'er all Thy children round,
The little flowers, each holding in its eye
The speck of dew, — more than clouds, rock and stream,
More than the sun there in the heavenly blue,
Through Thy clear image in the human star,
Through the heart's fiery glow that gleams from Thine,
Through thought's enrapturing flow that streams from Thine!
And O, what hast Thou not conferred on me!
Intrusted to me! till I dread to think
That a man's hand should hold the gifts of God:
Thou hast even over spirits given me power,
Who as my servants are assigned to me, —
Power o'er Thy best children's destinies;
Not the rose only which my hand may pluck,
The flowers my foot may tread on at its will, —
I can destroy at pleasure man himself,
And if I will, can send him from the earth!
The soul that loves me I can so afflict
That it with inward grief shall silently
Transform the fair and heavenly frame to dust,
And weeping, flee for refuge to Thy breast;
Whole cities even can I with the torch
Of Thine own holy fire annihilate,
Poison the well-springs for their little ones,
And none shall hinder, — none shall know of it
But Thou and I! Yea, I can sacrifice

Myself, and burst these walls before the time!
And Thou, Thou must, howe'er reluctantly,
Open to me the grave, unlock to me
The halls of death, full of all blessedness,
And even the cup of immortality
Reach out to me, — though with averted face!
But ah, I sink, I wither at the thought
That Thou couldst ever turn Thy face from me!
O turn Thou towards me! Ever turn on me
Thy pure, Thy heavenly-beauteous countenance!
And whatsoe'er on earth, whate'er 'mong men
Resembles Thee, — forgive the blind, blind word, —
The dimmest, distant shadow of Thyself,
That will I reverence! love, as loving thee:
Whether Thou comest as a little child,
Whether Thou comest as a lovely maid,
Whether Thou comest with the silver hair
Of the old man, or the blind beggar's staff,
Or comest Thou in the mother swallow's form,
Feeding her little fledglings in the nest,
Or as the lark that soars and sings aloft,
The mottled pigeon that so busily
Picks up the golden corn, I must not let
My shadow scare her from her quiet work!
Or comest Thou in my own children's form, —
I 'll bear them in my hands as tenderly
As if I held Thyself, so small, so dear!
Or takest Thou the gushing rain-stream's form,
As from the clouds it falls in dancing drops,
What time Thou thunderest high overhead,
And flashest rosy lightning far abroad, —
I will scoop out a little trench wherein
The holy water from the clouds may run

Gayly where Thou hast sent it! — Hear this too:
If in my own form Thou shalt clothe Thyself,
In my own mind and thought shalt be with me,
I will revere myself, will so revere
My body, as a shape of holy dust,
Of holy bones from Thy prime matter made,
My soul, as light from Thy primeval light,
That honoring Thee shall all my glory be,
That my rejoicing shall Thy gladness be,
That to be Thine shall be my endless life!

XXXI.

The Secret of Equanimity towards Men.

"How painfully must thou have schooled thy heart
To look on all calmly and equably,
To talk with beggars as respectfully
As with the emperor composedly,
To greet with pleasure every one who comes,
As if he had come down from the blue heaven,
And when he goes, never to say, nor yet
To think, an evil word behind his back,
But with a heartfelt blessing follow him
To God's great palace whereinto he went!
But this I deem the hardest thing of all
That thou, as frankly as before a child,
As frankly as a child before thyself,
Disclosest and confidest — say I? Nay —
But simply utterest, communicatest
Thy every wish, thy every thought and work,
Without disgrace, wrong, danger, or a blush
For men as for thyself; melodiously,

Aye, chiming as a lark's voice with the spring,
Or as a bell with all creation's peal.
And wilt thou not divulge thy secret now?
Thou seest the man in every man, seest man
In the universe, the universe in man;
To thee lives only Nature; childish stuff
From the old times when man knew not himself,
Honor 'mong fools, — place and prerogative —
Precedence, pomp — and all the mummery, —
All *that* to thee is empty nothingness,
All wasted to a shadowy, spectral life,
To think of it, with anger knits thy brow;
Thou seest man naked, in the nakedness
Of all his inborn beauty, every man
Thou seest in his first and final worth;
And all he might have been and was to be,
By virtue of his mind and of his heart,
In a just spirit thou ascribest to him!
And if he has not, is not, such great things,
Thou blushest for the world, and pity then
Exalts into a glow thy reverence.
Who could before the sun — a color hide?
And who could wish, before the Thinking one,
The Thinker in the Ether and in man,
To hide so much as but one flying thought?"
To think on God, — 't is that creates thee man.

THE LAYMAN'S BREVIARY.

AUGUST.

AUGUST.

I. God's Universe is its own History.
II. Christ's Meekness rebukes Christians.
III. The light and easy Yoke.
IV. Treat Humanity as a Child.
V. Human History:—The Chaff and the Wheat.
VI. Dawn,—its Wonders and Glories.
VII. The Blessedness of Obedience.
VIII. Trust the Heart of Man.
IX. Let thy Giving, like God's, not oppress.
X. Man's Regeneration shall redound to all Creatures.
XI. The End of Life is to live.
XII. Be no Tyrant in thy little World.
XIII. Persecution begets Pride.
XIV. Charity believeth all Things.
XV. Contemplate calmly the Mutability of Things.
XVI. Think soberly of Thyself and All.
XVII. Mother Nature's Love is new to each Child.
XVIII. Man's Want of Respect for Man, Nature, God.
XIX. True Praise reveals to Man the God in him.
XX. Swearing profanes the Lord's Day every Day.
XXI. Nature glorified in Family Love.
XXII. One bad Habit like a Fly.
XXIII. Everything beautiful in his Time.
XXIV. Stand divinely in thy Lot.
XXV. Each Creature's Life dear to him.
XXVI. Transformation of the Caterpillar and of Man.
XXVII. Sorrow for Death turned to Joy.
XXVIII. Virtue not virtuous till easy.
XXIX. Comparison kills Things.
XXX. Time's Ruins exalt a right Soul.
XXXI. True Worth asks no Appraiser.

AUGUST.

I.

God's Universe is its own History.

THE history of the world, the Universe,
None writes; who lives it, he has not the time,
For life he never gets to history;
Nor could he find a soul to write it to,
One who could understand him or his work,
Its plan, performance, glorious success;
What he has done himself, he knows himself,
He sees it clear and constant as the sun;
For what he does is evermore the same:
Himself! — the ever-equal, highest love
With ever-equal, highest might of joy.
To live himself, — *that* none can do but God, —
God has no history, nor the Universe;
And wondrously sublime would sound the leaves
From the great log-book of the starry fleet: —
"The stars are moving duly on their course;
There is not one, that has not joyfully
With passionate love fulfilled his holy task,
No solitary one! of the great fleet
No ship is missing, — not a streamer lost,
No rudder broken, — all is safe and sound,
We have not had a drop of water spoil,
We have not lost a particle of earth,

Each breath of ether holds its freshness yet,
The deep, blue flood is free from danger still,
We all sail safely o'er the silent sea,
In peace and comfort, in exulting joy,
As if spell-drawn into the stillness here!
Only to some does *this* seem singular;
They guess and guess,—but cannot guess it out.
That we on all the stars bear round with us
A great black pall outflying as a flag,
And yet are all in health!"
—"And wishing health
Remain as in our previous report."
"*Postscript:*—the wind is fresh. The night is fair,
As in each other's sight we sail the deep,
Each with his light in silence on his breast!
And myriad lights reflected on the sea!
Yet sealed in mystery the orders lie
In which our mission's end and aim are wrapped.
Attentively and patiently we wait
The signals on the passage, bidding: Break
The seals, let go the anchors now, and land!
Yet still and still and still no shore appears,
No bird, no green twig, floating, welcomes us."
So would it sound at morn and so at eve,—
The morn and eve of new millenia,—
So would it sound again upon the morn
Of the fair day of long millenia!
That which is greatest has no history;
That which is small is history,—and is small!

II.

Christ's Meekness rebukes Christians.

The Testament says: — "Jesus spake: Ye know,
The princes of the world, they exercise
Authority; the great ones rule by force, —
So shall it not be among you! But he
Who will be great and mighty among you
Shall be your servant." — May not now a man
Well ask, supported by such words as these:
"Are ye still heathen? Worldly, — heathenish?"
No, indeed? "Are you Christians?" — Be so, then!
That word "among you" cries to every man!

. . . . .

"If any man shall smite thee on thy cheek,
Turn thou to him the other cheek." That word
Is said, indeed, to each one who receives —
But for the shame and betterment of him,
Chiefly and properly, who gives — the blows!
That one's misdeed avails not to annul
The meekness of the others, but their meekness
Disarms, destroys the others' evil mind;
And surely: when they are themselves *the meek.*

III.

The light and easy Yoke.

The Koran says: "God willeth that his law
Should be made light to men, for man is weak."
But hearken thou and understand: Does gold
Feel itself heavy? Is the falcon's plume

Light to itself? 'T is merely to itself.
The law of God is *thy* law; otherwise
It could not be thy *law*. Be thou a law
Unto thyself, and then thy life shall be
Light as an eagle's pathway through the skies.

IV.

Treat Humanity as a Child.

Thou punishest not in children children's faults!
Haste, loudness, running, falling, laughing, weeping,
Breaking things, overjoy in novelties,
Fondness for morning sleep, improvidence,—
For these are faults that childhood brings with it,
And these are faults that children all outgrow;
So day by day they vanish quietly
As flies and other autumn insects do,
Never to reappear.—And wilt thou then
Visit thy wrath upon humanity,
That poor sick child, ailing these thousand years,
Because amidst its many troubles all,
It has not put away yet all its faults?
Humanity's must still be children's faults,
—For it appears like children, ever young,—
And such are faults that childhood brings with it,
And such are faults that children all outgrow;
So day by day they vanish quietly
As flies and other autumn insects do,
Never to reappear.—Wilt thou now use
Hardness and hate, mistrust, rage, yea, revenge,
To punish others, punishing thyself,—
Invoking against heavenly ones the spirit

Of hell, instead of onc good angel, one,—
Where patience, nay, a hint, were quite enough!
For better being is there none than man!
But of all men the father is the best.

V.

Human History:—the Chaff and the Wheat.

The God in mortal flesh, the God in small,
Man, with his day and night, and fall and spring,
With infancy and youth, old age and death,
With ever changing impulses and thoughts,
Man, moral man, alone has history,
He becomes history, a silent word
In the unwearied utterance of the race;
Each noble deed is done, is in itself
Complete, and nobly it completes the man:
—Not Heaven itself can thereunto add aught,—
Man fully ends his work, for his life ends:
—Not Heaven itself can thereunto add aught,—
Life ends each day, each hour, ends momently
With changing moods, with each new coming thought,
With the clear survey and the better light.
For mark, man does not live his very self,
He lives another being; another lives
In him, from him, through him,—as through a veil,
A hand invisible reaches down to earth:
Brings him, brings to him; takes from him, takes him,
And all things round about him takes and brings.
Thus does man grow to history for men,
Who grow themselves to history, because
They creep across the earth, a little race,

Accomplishing forever little things,
And done with them, when they have just begun,
Just stirred the hand, and scarcely moved the lips,
The little life enjoying in the great,
Like children. So a boy will hold the reins
And proudly think he drives his father, he
Holding meanwhile the reins behind his head,
Slyly, — that so the child may drive with joy!

. . . . .

The sun has perfect right to disown day!
The more thou namest days, the more does he
Disown them, conscious only to himself
Of shining and of light. Dost thou disown
The history of the world? — Not without right;
Only the human heart has always lived,
The constant, never-swerving, changeless one,
At no time long befooled or led astray;
Are only folly, error, — history, then!
For is, now, all that ever came to pass,
The history of the human heart! Those crimes,
And murders, and those horrid midnight deeds
Of men made mad by greed of gold or lands,
Are those, forsooth, the deeds which man has done?
Not men, but monsters, single criminals,
Standing apart, alone in time and space;
A train of senseless deeds, is history.
Far other work the human heart, the people,
Has thought, done, lived, in the full glow of life,
In the still circle of its fruitfulness, —
What has been laid up and showed up, to us,
That were the history of a maniac!
Alas, not history; for it is no whole,
It has no sequence, — all the mess of stuff

Is but the refuse, chaff of the great harvest,
Whose heavy ears were heaped up silently, —
The leavings of the banquet of the gods,
Fragments of potsherds, broken words caught up
From the street brawl of drunk and angry men,
Marking the steady victory of the good,
Who, if they suffered, — perished without help, —
Did steadfastly the old eternal good;
Who, after, as before, the idle stir,
All sat around life's table tranquilly,
Enjoyed their heart and nature's equal gifts.

Take, then, good heed, O man, that thou and thine
Never become mere history, empty words!
Then were you happy, being truly men.
" 'Gainst bad men thou must arm thyself with steel."
Does that make happy? Ask, I pray, the world!
And ask'st thou: When shall fraud and fury end?
Noble and base together shall, good soul.
Now then still call what happens, History.*

VI.

Dawn, — its Wonders and Glories.

O ruddy dawn! thou beauteous holy glow,
Still, golden well-spring of the sea of haze
That floods the vales, the mountains, and the skies,
Streams into every hut, envelops it
In blazing purple, fills each little room
With splendor, from the ceiling to the floor,

* Geschichte (history) is related to geschehen, (*was geschieht*, — what happens., We have no such correspondence in English. — Tr.

Suffusing all the lightly waking ones
And cradled infants with such loveliness,
That they, as by enchantment, seem arrayed
In Heaven's own delicate and rosy veil,
Adorned with godlike beauty for God's day:
That even the heavy axe, the hoe, and spade,
The senseless tools and implements of day
Wherewith men occupy their little life,
Seem to them heavenly, light, and gladsome now,
When they, as gracefully as living friends,
Bathed in the same celestial radiance,
As if refreshed to do a new day's work,
Willing and modest in the corner stand!
O dawn! unutterable coming forth
Of the unutterable: the new-born day;
No meteor thou, that with a sudden flash
Darting through heaven, in thunder disappears!
No apparition thou! Thou art immortal
As sun and moon and all divine things else!
Though dying every morning, still each morn
Thou reappearest yet more beautiful,
Adorning heaven again and yet again
With hues and glories never seen before,—
Making the ocean to the seaman's eyes
And to the dolphin one vast purple flood;
Tingeing the sea-mew's wings with molten gold,
With gold the small sails of the nautilus,
Turning the lark's wings in the air to flames,
So that the young lark dares not trust herself
To such a conflagration of the clouds!
In the great, rich, and gorgeous hall of earth,
Full of all kinds of wonders, old and new,
Thou art the friendliest of the precious things,

And still shalt be, so long as pilgrims come,
So long as earth and as the heavens shall stand!
Man journeys to the mountains that spout fire,
The thunder and the spray of cataracts,
And deems the little journey well repaid.
But the fair journey to the realm of dawn,
The journey to the watch-tower of this earth,
Where thou beholdest fiery dew-drops fall,
Where thine own form becomes a sparkling ruby,
Where the white roses sparkling rubies are,
Wherein the snow of blossoms turns to gold,
To gold the towers and all the works of men,
Wherein the soul within thee grows to hope
And hope to the most fervent ecstasy, —
With *that* fair pilgrimage, enchanting dawn,
Thou blessest the Great Spirit afar off,
Who to behold thee a few mornings only
Is glad to let himself be born a child
And buried an old man; shall he not rest
Forever in thy purple, in thy gold!
Ah, dawn! — as over children's graves we lean,
And our dear dead, — over old sacred stones, —
There most of all art thou heart-thrilling, — Ah!
Incomprehensible, to me too, me.

VII.

The Blessedness of Obedience.

Obedient shalt thou be to God alone,
And him who asks of thee the works of God,
That which is always right and always good.
But yield a cheerful, glad obedience

To life and death, to fortune and to fate!
Obedience alone can make thee blest:
And through the good which then thou followest
It makes thee so! Art thou obedient now,
Then art thou praiseworthy; but art thou so
With discontent, reluctance, even tears,
Hast thou then plucked the fruit of what is good?
Thou hast but painfully climbed up the tree,
And fallen down again among the thorns!
Naught is more blessed to the proudest man
Than pure obedience! blind obedience,
Yea, the most thoughtless, inconsiderate,
Resting upon another's godliness,
On equal, positive, and holy laws,
Which, given invisibly, hold visible sway,
Offering infallibly the good man life,
Threatening infallibly the bad with death.
Well, — there is one bliss, then, laid up for man:
Obedience to Nature! who stands fast,
Guarding and executing her own law
With more than iron inflexibility,
With still, inviolable truth, and seems
Blessed herself, reposing on herself,
Like a kind shepherdess stretched out at length
In the green pasture, while the feeding flock
Roams far and wide, secure from every foe!
So rest thou, too, O Man! Is that so hard,
To sink thy doubts and questions and unrest
In a serene and godly confidence!
Just to believe in this bright, endless day!
Not to dread thunder, not to hear it growl,
Till somewhere in the sky a cloud has risen.
But look and see, — no cloud will ever come!

Into this pure blue heaven there never shall
A giant stalk! nor ever with strange voice
Shall a strange law challenge the universe!
And now this ancient, gladsome law of His
Thou canst to-day believe, to-day embrace!
Canst at this moment wed thyself thereto,
And have Heaven's treasures all poured out on thee,
Peace and security and joy and bliss,
The sleep of childhood and a child's glad waking.
But above all, — employment in a work
Sure to be crowned with heavenly success!
Which, as thou growest more perfect, grows with thee.
'T is easy to obey the will of Heaven!
With gods to share the strife, the victory,
To feel gods round about thee, at thy side,
And, if thou fall'st, to fall victorious,
And from the battle-field by gods to be
Borne weeping.
                    Hard, indeed, it is to yield
Obedience to men. Impossible,
To robbers, tyrants, murderers, and liars;
Impossible not to wake through gloomy nights,
Not to interrogate one's boding soul,
To plant one's self defiant on his strength,
With fear and trembling, even with bitter tears:
To feel, the heart must lean on self alone,
Take petty measures for its own defence,
Instead of joining with a mighty host
Of noble men nobly and innocently
To carry human powers to height divine,
And to behold, astonished, all the brave
Achievements of a simple, childlike soul,
Which, undeceived, knows only to obey!

To make obedience possible, — be thy work
With thine own children and the sons of men,
For 't is the work which Nature has herself
With clear example set before each man.

VIII.

Trust the Heart of Man.

Thou tremblest at the childlike confidence
The sons of men repose in sons of men;
O tremble not! The instinct of mankind,
The human race with its instinctive sense,
Stands like a mountain, fixed immovably,
There where a proper faith impels it not:
Faith that the end is good it seeks to reach.
Thou 'lt sooner move a mountain from its base
To take ten thousand steps than stir a man
To go a way he does not choose, to do,
To will, nay think that which to him seems bad.
So truly does the human heart abhor,
Because the human heart so warmly loves:
Its inner, unseen, future being, *that*
It holds by, as the sick man clings by night
To *this:* to-morrow's sun shall surely come!
You cannot stir a disobedient man,
He is a dead man; and a dead man is
Heavy as lead, while one wounded to death,
Upheld and led by others, helps himself!
And millions of the disobedient
Are millions of the dead, and heavier
Than all the lead on earth. A word, a word,
Faith in a single word alone it needs,

And all these dead start to their feet, walk, fly!
Thou thinkest, surely these dry bones do live!
For to obey is what all angels long
To do, and even the Devil longs to obey.

IX.

Let thy Giving, like God's, not oppress.

One foe alone is left to man on earth,
The greatest enemy, — his first and last!
All things on earth stand so in dread of man,
That the wood-pigeon, field-lark, forest-roe,
Long since fled from him, and the flowers and trees
All would have fled from him, if they had not
With their one foot been rooted in the Earth!
Soon will the crocodile, the elephant,
The anaconda, even the very whale,
Fly from him, as the nimble lightning darts
Down o'er his house, hurrying to hide itself.
The thunder and the rain-fall and the storm,
The scorching sunbeam, and the winter snow
Well screened he passes by contentedly;
No more on earth nor yet in Heaven there lives
His enemy, all things are kind to him
And bless him; he has forced their blessing from them
Just as he has the tiger's spotted skin!
The great sea-turtle's house, the ox's horns,
The sago's marrow, and the cork-tree's coat.
And now so free of soul, so proud, so strong,
He feels but one to be his highest foe, —
The proud, rich, mighty, gracious man, he only
Afflicts him by his very graciousness,

And wounds his soul more bitterly than death!
The way of giving makes it an offence!
To whom one gives, not *what*, honors the gift.
And now I say, — it is thy brother, man!
Born like thyself of woman, — it is man.
And this old feud one word brings to an end:
"Each is God's child, and God gives gifts, to him," —
And "What thou giv'st to man, thou giv'st to God."
Do good by stealth, then! Scarcely press the hand!
God also gives to man so honorably,
So modestly, he lets him seem to earn
By his brow's sweat the harvest. He bestows!
Whoso is godly, feels for man like God.

X.

Man's Regeneration shall redound to all Creatures.

Each man has in himself his greatest foe,
And finds no peace, till reconciled with him.
And when each man becomes now his own friend,
Once learns the way and feels that he is such,
He knows no longer any foe on earth,
Not even his own heaven-mirrored image, man, —
And now at length there lives a man on earth, —
And to this happy man one day shall come
The birds all flying back again from heaven,
The forest roe shall come back with her young,
The fish shall come to him around his ship,
And even the fox from *his* truth shall learn truth;
The fables, and the legends of old time
Shall have a truth they never had before
Through love, grace, honor, strength, and liberty.

Thus shall the word inborn in every man,
The old primeval word: *Love God*, be given
Through mediation of regenerate men, —
Even to the lamb, roe, horse, and very ox,
Who even now rests on the Sabbath day, —
And without war, — without high penal courts:
Given to the iron and hemp, and to the flowers,
The forests and the mountains and the seas,
Through the pure heart of man, till peace at last, —
Poured from the fountain of the universe, —
Flows back again through him on all the world.

XI.

The End of Life is to live.

"Why does man come on earth," — thou askest? Man
Comes not on earth! For he is simply here.
"Why does the spirit become man then?" To live!
Surely; for no particular purpose, sure.
The lovely world of childhood closes soon,
Youth flies away, and never more returns,
With every morning dies the dream, the night;
With every evening sun the day is buried;
Love consecrates to youth alone the virgin,
The universe; its charm soon fades for man;
Not always can the best be doing good,
To find the opportunity to do
A good deed is like lighting on a treasure;
The fire of joy burns dim in daily cares;
Man is not even conscious all the time
Of having eyes and ears; how should he then
Glow always with the sense of fairer gifts!

Thou sayest well, then : — Man is here to live.
Probably so ; for naught else certainly :
To live what life 's lot is to every man.
Pity thou not the generations past,
As if dragged hither from a godlike height!
The lightning, twenty thousand years ago,
Shot down out of the heavens into the sea
With just as eager flashes as to-day, —
So did God's life into humanity ;
The flames burned never brighter, in all time,
The very smallest spark was bright and hot ;
Never more vile, inwardly miserable,
Unmindful of its temple than to-day,
Never unloving, was the inborn spirit ;
What it illumines, that is bright ; if now
It lights itself, the universe, man's heart,
Then is there one light only ! But one love !
As life itself has palpably disclosed.
The miner has his table of gold ore,
Which is no more, more golden, coined in small.
To live continually a full, rich life, —
Not foolishly the spirit hither comes,
And here has made its home thousands of years ;
Thus he who now is poor is still a man,
He who now suffers is a spirit still.
For none can fail to know the whole of life,
Though he have much of this, little of that,
Though from few things he draws the joy of life,
The heart's full treasure is enough for each,
Humanity and the fair universe.
Then live out rightfully thy life of man,
And as an old man seek the silent tomb, —
Thou hast fulfilled the spirit's word and work !

XII.

Be no Tyrant in thy little World.

And though seven angels flew down out of heaven,
And though seven devils came up from the earth,
And kissed each other, and kissed thee, and swore :
"A tyrant wants an empire's broad domain,"
Believe them not! 'T were happy for the world,
If thou couldst so believe, for then there were
One tyrant only in the whole wide realm!
But now in the wide realm no tyrant is;
There is no tyranny save that of love
And reverence. And do all know any one?
Does any one know all? Only by few
Is each one in his little circle loved;
On hearts closed up against him none can work,
On hearts laid bare to him he works with ease,
And lays on them with ease a heavy load,
To make them weep! ay, even bleed to death!
Be thou no tyrant then in thine own house,
Be not a tyrant to the hearts that love thee,
And hope more from thee than from all the world.
Tranquillity in the heart and in the house,
Liberty in the house and in the heart,
These are the goods man needs, which he himself,
All by himself, has fearful power to mar,
Destroy! Were there not tyrants in the house,
Thousands of tyrants in as many houses,
Tyrants of millions of affectionate hearts,
Then were there peace and freedom in the world,
As well as elsewhere; bliss as nowhere else;
Then would the will of others harm thee not,

Each, his own master, then would reverence
Freely and lovingly the loving gods,
Who came down on the earth to visit him,
And spread within his house a heavenly feast.

XIII.

Persecution begets Pride.

When, now, the people say ill things of thee,
Believe hard things of thee, deride and doubt
Whether thou dost what 's manly, — nay, even right;
How all such doubts stir up and nerve the soul!
How clearly, sweetly, thou rememberest
Thy purposes from childhood to this day!
How proudly all the various knowledge gained,
All the good spirits, faithful friends to thee!
How calmly glows thy bosom in the flame,
Richly as flowers in tempests breathe perfume!
Maligners lift thy heart more than is right!
Then see that thou hast good repute with men
That thou mayst be ashamed, modest and still.

XIV.

Charity believeth all Things.

Sternly refuse to hear of men's disgrace!
It is ungodly; therefore, 't is unmanly.
Naught damps thy courage more than knowing evil,
Fills thee with shame that thou too art a man,
And chills thy ardor for a man's free strife.
A pure heart, a pure conscience, but above
All other things a pure clean consciousness

That thinks each being as perfect and as pure
As if of crystal, pure as yonder sky,—
Sustains thee in the region of the gods,
Clear above clouds and tempests and all fear.
And say not, that thou need'st to know mankind,
That thou mayst be a man and wisely work.
For say not that thou *then* dost know mankind,
When thou know'st ill of them,—which they repent.
Man,—yes, he fails, yet he no failure is!
Then only know'st thou man, when thou believ'st
The highest of him, and demand'st the hardest,
And in all cases where thou makest not
That high demand, counting him earthly, there
Only, with scorn he lets thy thought come true!
Thus gods themselves grow like our thought of them!
That was a pure thought in Mahomet, when
He willed Christ only should be judge of men,
That he for punishment should know all sins!
And God, to be God, pardons every fault,
And draws to his heart in silence, man, his child.
Be then, like God, O judge, physician, priest!

XV.

Contemplate calmly the Mutability of Things.

Will ever men write thus,—*post Christum natum:*
"Eleven millions, eighteen hundred thirty"?
Of such long periods the astronomers doubt.
What was not always will not always be;
This word in sight,—look out upon the earth.
What has not always been, abideth not.
And once even man himself was not, they say.

Time was when there were yet no priests nor kings,
Physicians, court-house, temple, golgotha, —
All these humanity has brought with it.
What was not always will not always be ;
Once only have there been Egyptian kings,
What was not always, that abideth not.
Once only have there been Hellenic priests,
What was not always, must one day go by
With us, with all, to-day, to-morrow, ever,
Yea, evermore. Then prize thou not too high,
What was not always, what is only now!
To holy Nature 't is of more account
That her mere rose-bushes should flourish still,
That even her race of flies should not die out,
Nor her strawberry-plants be all extinct,
Than that there should be Pharaohs in Egypt,
Than that there should be marble gods in Greece,
Than that in Italy there should be painters,
Forever painting copies of *one* myth.
Far more important still, than that the rose
Should ever bloom, the race of flies live on,
And earth not lose the race of strawberry-plants,
Far more important is it in Nature's eyes,
That she should still keep man with all his dreams,
With all the *mutable* works his mind and hand
Are ever bringing forth to adorn his life ;
A tree, whose emblem is the orange-tree,
That while it casts its blossoms shows new buds,
And bears perennially ripe, golden fruit, —
Like to herself, yea really a blossom
Of her! nay more, a green and swelling fruit, —
Which she, too, casts off, when it pleases her,
That which not always was, one day must fade.

XVI.

Think soberly of Thyself and All.

Stand firm and dignified upon this earth,
And let no kind of dizziness turn thy brain!
No dizziness before the holy past,
From which old temple ruins towering up
Look down reproachfully on these thy days,
As lingering rocks of landmarks washed away
Lift up their heads like ghosts out of the sea,
And greet the ship, the seaman of to-day, —
To-day 's as old as any yesterday.
Stand firm and dignified upon this earth!
Look up undizzied at the dark abyss
Of the unending grotto of the stars;
The Milky Way, the Nebula of suns,
Take not for clouds born of thy dizzy sight;
Let not the sun's effulgence smite thee down, —
Earth is contemporary with the stars;
And thou, thou art a man upon this earth.
Nor let the great men daze and dizzy thee,
Who, by the tales the dwarfs spin out, have wrought
Monstrous exploits with bones of other men;
Who, with the chisel, with the beaver's hair,
With spirit-might have just produced themselves.
See clearly each thing's essence. A great man
Is but a bundle of minutiæ.
Nor let thy head be turned before the men
Who sit in purple robes in golden chairs, —
The green turf is the highest throne for man,
High, godlike, lifting him by right divine
O'er starry seas and mountain-peaks of day.

Stand firm and dignified upon this earth,
And let no kind of dizziness have power
To turn thy head! Not even at the thought
That thou, beside being grass, art also man!

XVII.

Mother Nature's Love is new to each Child.

Nature sees through thee, knows thee, through and
through,
And seeing through thee, therefore loves she thee,
Loves her own love in thee; and loving thee,
Therefore respects thee, and in thee herself.
Behold now: never could a human mother,
In all her human poverty, respect
A child of hers so chastely, sacredly,
As Nature from the first doth honor thee.
The beam of light is new, and heavenly-pure
That greets thee as a child; the nectar draught
Given thee to breathe, each mouthful of pure air
Is fresh-prepared in that great laboratory
Of spirits for thyself, an effluence
From newest heavens; each beaker, nay, each drop
Of water is prepared and cooled for thee
In secret caverns, — and the strawberry
And the sweet cherry which thy childish fingers
Bore to thy little mouth, not one of these,
These treasures man e'er tasted before thee;
They have been made, compounded, wove for thee!
The little glossy goblets of thy grapes
Only for thee have they poured out the must
She brought to thee fresh from the Maker's hand,

From secret depths of ecstasy, for thee,
For thee alone prepared, the maid, to be
Thy consort;—and the children, only thine,
That none on earth had ever owned before,
That none on earth will ever own henceforth,
So long as Heaven endures!—the cloud itself
That sails so swiftly by, will never shade
Another,—for behold it falls in rain!
The breeze will never cool another brow,—
For lo! e'en now it dies in yonder brake!
That rainbow no man ever more will see,
For even now its hues fade on thy sight!
The lark will sing this song to none again,—
For from the clouds she drops and it is hushed!
An only song which thou alone hast heard,
Thus all is thine uniquely as thyself is.
Yea, know thou that the hand is always new
With which thou takest nature's every gift;
With ever new and ever changing hand
Thou givest *his* gift to the beggar; ah,
And his hand has e'en now grown older too!
Night after night Heaven sends fresh dreams to thee,
Day after day new senses and new will,
New and original force, thoughts, mind and life;
A life unique, peculiar, all thine own,
Thou livest forth from the eternal fount,
Entwined with Him more closely than the child
Is with its mother in the mother's lap!
Like a great thunder-cloud far-stretching, full
Of might and majesty and fruitfulness,
Broods over thee God's presence ever near,
And through the delicate network of thy frame
Passing the tissue of the finest flower,—

The heavenly influence flows down into thee,
With blissful, ever new-creating might,
Like streams of fragrance pouring into flowers,
That stand benumbed and breathe benumbing scents!
And thou — forget not thus to breathe around
Rich perfume of pure thought and of still love,
Still — as the thunder-cloud that charges thee!

XVIII.

Man's Want of Respect for Man, Nature, God.

Want of respect; disrespect, yea, contempt,
That is the mother hive of all the faults
That plague each individual and then all.
Look sharply once into the heart of man,
And see what no one e'er exposed to thee,
Hear, what at home in silence is suppressed;
Each scarce respects himself, and if his life
Should be a failure, 't were not much, he thinks,
Not much were lost in him, or even in all —
For after outward things the world still strives,
To outward things alone his mind was turned,
Yea trained, and therefore is the deep, dumb soul,
That dwells in each one sadly in the right;
It deems, and each one deems, a neighbor may
Perchance be useful still for this or that;
For all the rest he knows, he feels contempt, —
And so in the wide circle each one does;
What but a dismally cold world can rise,
If it must spring forth out of *such* men's brain!
And saving wife and children they esteem
Scarcely twelve human beings out of all

That earth in her whole course has e'er produced;
And only in some favored hours do these
Float by them, still as shadowy images,
Stirring them scarcely more than moon or stars! —
But now the better son of earth shall scarce
Step from his house, before with thoughtful mind
And feeling heart and studious eye he notes
The grass and flowers beneath his feet, and proves
The shadow, looking upward to the sun
That paints it on the carpet of the lawn!
— And soon he recognizes, too, the heart
Of the shadow, which in his own bosom beats,
With his own heart all other human hearts,
And with the hearts of men the heart of God!

XIX.

True Praise reveals to Man the God in him.

There lies before thee the old silver coin,
The inscription blurred, the image quite a blank,
And only a vague reverence now it stirs.
But now the assayer heats it on the coals, —
And from the surface blurred and blank, behold!
The old inscription rises and stands forth
And glowing speaks the words it spoke of old.
The godlike image gleams out in the fire
Sublimely fair; its eye looks up at thee,
The forehead kindles, the lip burns to speak,
And even the hair seems in a gentle blaze.
So he who praises thee does with thy heart!
The warmth of praise rekindles all thy faults,
Each word distinctly speaks to thee again,

Thou hearest them come up as from a shaft!
Whatever in the coinage of thy life
Miscarried, where the silver was alloyed,
Where levity despised devoted work,
All *that* thou feelest, glowing with the praise!
A modest man praise drives into himself,
Till, lost in thought of self, he haply weeps!
And glows all through like the old silver coin!
Yet in the fire the godlike image too,
In its old beauty, has he seen again;
Its lustrous eye has turned on him its glance,
Hinting and signaling to him anew
All the exalted and ennobling ends
For which in word and work he ever strove,
And to his death will never cease to strive, —
A modest man praise drives into himself,
Till, lost in thought of self, — he haply weeps!
And glows all through like the old silver coin!

XX.

Swearing profanes the Lord's Day every Day.

"Thou swearest? — know'st thou not it is to-day
Sunday and church day, too, when hundreds pray?"
O rather in thy secret soul know this,
As base to all thy feeling let it lie,
And sound as constant keynote of thy words:
To-day, to-day and always is "sun-day,"
Bright with ten thousand suns and "a high day,
A holy festival of all that live."
Now are a thousand souls born into life,
Now are a thousand men right at thy side,

Transfigured, — they stand up, unseen by thee
In this one mighty sanctuary, in this
"House of the Lord," true angels of the church.
What means "good standing"? — standing up 'gainst
sin!
Stand well, then, soul! Let thoughts and feelings be
Worthy thy place! pure words, soft speech, be thine!
Hast thou not seen how modest and how still,
How reverent, children stand beside the dead,
Step softly round the coffin and speak low,
As if God lay therein! If God did lie
A coffined corpse, thou would'st not rage and curse,
With frantic gestures, 'gainst thy brother man!
But now God lives and moves above, beneath;
He hears, he sees, sees thee and hears thy words!
And thou wilt have less reverence than the child!

XXI.

Nature glorified in family Love.

It pains me oft to see the faithfulness
Of parents, who beneath the open heaven —
In the clear radiance of the beaming sun
Journeying along above their ancient earth —
Rule in the house, the children all their thought,
Forgetting in the sweet and narrow round
Their interest in the broad humanity.
The mother sews a garment for the girl;
The father bleaches linen for the boy,
Proud of the little one now grown so big,
That he will soon go forth now from the house,
Into the strange world, who to-day is still

At school with little sister! — They 're alone,
And stillness reigns in garden and in house
Round the good, faithful, life-enjoying pair.
And I have need of all my self-control,
To keep the tears from starting to my eyes.
What now consoles me, so that I can look
With pleasure on so narrow, pleased a life? —
In every race of creatures Nature lives
Full and complete within and round about;
The Eternal Love resides in every pair;
Nor for its children all could even that love
Itself provide more conscientiously,
More beautifully than by placing them
Beneath a roof and in a mother's care!
So in the little cot here love now lives,
Robing herself with sunbeams of the heavens,
Making her steps soft with green carpeting,
Wooing a little runnel through the flowers,
Shading with vines her window gracefully,
And finding pleasure in her life, her rule
In such a sweet familiar privacy, —
Taking in all these transitory forms
A forward step into futurity's
Great hall, into the earth's eternal spring.
Now come with glee brother and sister home,
The mother holds the garment up, all made!
The father, meanwhile, shaking down ripe pears
That shine like wax, — like gold, — like God's own work
For children, and the children read thereon, —
Clear as a script the blind man's touch might spell: —
The father's old love in the newest fruit.
It is not true that Paradise is lost, —
'T is just begun, — it comes when children come!
And in the garden, lo, the Father walks!

XXII.

One bad Habit like a Fly.

I liken a bad habit to a fly.
Thou chasest it away at intervals
A hundred times; still it comes back again
And plagues thee worse and worse. But if thou wilt
Be rid of it forever, — ward it off
With ceaseless and unwearied blows awhile,
Even when it seems not to be there, — meanwhile
It sits in snug concealment on thy neck;
Thence also scare it! It will stay away.
No holding fast to *him*, — it wisely thinks!

XXIII.

Everything beautiful in his Time.

Misfortune and good fortune are things past,
Else are they things that have not yet arrived,
And what is past, is done irrevocably, —
It is a form of Nature now to man,
And only by a beauteous, holy law
It came to pass, and Nature welcomed it!
Dissatisfaction with the thing that 's done,
This is what makes men miserable! content
With what is done, this is men's happiness.
What now is wise in passing through this world?
To know what Nature brings to best account,
To make of it a life, yea, festival,
As children do with snow, which, fluttering down
Silently, buries all their pleasant days.

And never hold thy life a finished thing!
Then fortune, good or bad, is not yet come,
Then life has not yet happened; 't is to be!
Man has material yet for bliss and life
Till the last hour, even death itself is such,
Which in a godlike way pronounces good,
And blesses what is done! For sure 't was good,
True, human, heavenly in God's beauteous world,
And in the good heart long since beautiful.

XXIV.

Stand divinely in thy Lot.

Deem not that *this* is human happiness,
Serene, sublime, unchanging happiness,
To know no pain, enjoying changelessly
On earth the cloudless favor of the gods.
No, — but to take one's share of weal and woe,
— The extract both of bitter and of sweet,
From the whole lump of sorrow and of joy,
The lot appointed to all human kind,
Whereof each woe may fall to any one,
And every good may fall to any one,
Yet but a measured part can light on each,
— One's griefs with heavenly sweetness to endure,
One's bliss with heavenly sweetness to enjoy,
Building all up into a human shape:
The heart yet young and the old heart no less,
The tears, the smiles, the yearnings of our lot,
The flight of men, the love of near and dear,
The throng of living, death of loving ones,
One's own encroaching age, approaching death.

And *this*, then, deem thou human happiness,
Serene, sublime, unchanging happiness!
To live with all one's heart right in the days,
An intimate inmate of their joy and woe,
And then, when one draws breath again and thinks,
Thinks of himself, thinks of his lot, his heart,
And of the power that shapes his life for him,
Then to stand clearly up before one's spirit,
And see: who 't is that suffers and enjoys:
A man! And who then lives man's life: a god!
And see: what life he lives: the life of God!

XXV.

Each Creature's Life dear to him.

Life soon becomes so dear to every one,
By habit, indispensable! And yet
It is to each one ever a new scene,
To woodland roe and flower-haunting bee,
So new, unheard-of, never felt before!
That thou, as man, thy life so lovest here,
Is but a proof that every form of being,
Every condition, — wheresoe'er it be, —
Has quite peculiar worth and preciousness,
Else men would never love this life so much;
Nor woodland roe, nor flower-haunting bee,
Nor other creature, would so love its type.
Each finds as worthy to be loved and lived
Existence here, as being is to God;
And each is happy as a God therein;
Well, then, I say, fear not thou to live on!
Fear not thou to live elsewhere, anywhere!

The very swallow flies with swallow's wings,
And gives up her sweet life (which is not death). —
Intoxicated and infatuated
By Nature's self, instinctively she flies,
And fain would be a swallow evermore,
Not knowing *who*, as swallow, lives in her.
And smiling, man beholds the swallow's flight,
And yet he smiles not at his own fond love.
— Such is the common glow, the general thrill,
The sympathetic, ever-busy might
Of the bright consciousness of this vast whole, —
Solid, yet pliant as the power of gold:
Breathed o'er an image, to be gold, at last,
Through thousand transformations always gold!

XXVI.

Transformation of the Caterpillar and of Man.

Now the gay colored caterpillars spin
Their web and winding-sheet around themselves,
And by the evening sun's great golden lamp,
Take, in the holy banquet hall of earth,
One more last meal, — and now of their green leaves,
Will they from this time forth in this their world,
Not eat again, and of this purple dew
Not sip again, until they drink it new
In quite another, — and to them new world,
And yet the same, wherein the butterfly
Knows not the worm, nor yet doth the worm know
The butterfly, the green, the purple dew,
The sun, the golden table of the earth,
That still abides, while they alone are changed.

Out of this worm now grows a chrysalis, —
And yet this being, man accounts as naught,
Whereas of godlike Nature 't is a type,
The mother of all creatures, only one,
Who is all mothers, — universal wife: —
Of him, that dearest little merry spouse,
The gay-dressed, fiery-tempered humming-bird,
Of the great whale, and of the elephant,
Of the blind worm down in the darksome earth,
And of the flower-dust in the air no less!
"Well, of the chrysalis a butterfly
Comes, and lays eggs again, and then these eggs
Soon grow to worms," — and think'st thou that is all?
What were an egg, that should possess such power,
Far beyond that of all the elements!
No! Nature throws herself into this egg,
With her creative and her shaping force,
She swells it with her most mysterious,
Divinest essence! She despises not
And never will, — "to be a caterpillar!"
"To be a summer-apple, — swan, — or worm!"
And could'st thou only search the blade of grass,
Thou would'st not find the blade of grass, but *her*
With all her force bound by the sweetest spell
To the short round of summer's circling hours;
And so 't is not the serpent's egg becomes
The serpent, nor the aster's egg, the still,
Brown seed grain, that becomes the aster, nor
Does the ostrich's egg become the ostrich!
No father — mother — can become their child.
But with the first deep stir of yearning love
Nature becomes: what in her life comes forth.
And all that she is, is alike, is holy.

'T is of her blood, it *is* her blood, her life;
'T is of her soul, it *is* her soul, her love.
And were it now thy lot to be a snail,
With ever so beautiful stripes, purple and gold,—
Or were thy lot to be a carnation pink,
With ever so beautiful, tender, fiery spots,
How would'st thou shudder, how thy sickening heart
Would sink within thee, just as if the Shah
Of Persia were condemned to be a rose,—
Ay, even a drop of the essential oil
Of rose,—an ostrich or a nightingale,—
And yet he is but dust! an element,
Soul, Nature, and remains but soul and life,
Whate'er he was as man, in form and speech.
And more than Nature,—nothing, no man, is.
Whate'er her hand creates, each blade of grass,
Shows her whole art; in every single thing
That lives, is all her love; nay, she herself,
Is all, and so possesses all that is,
And even her spirit, that is she herself,
And she is it; not a dead grain of sand,
Living apart from Nature, but would be
Her most terrific foe,—a second spirit!
A second God! But tremble not, O soul!
There is but only one. Yet One there is,
As truly as this worm here shrouds Himself;
And if He is, and without Him is naught,
Then fills He all with equal art and love.—
What could there be in the wide realm of things,
Thou would'st not freely be, become, remain;
What would'st not dare to be, or great or small,
Or naught, since all is equally divine,
Alike in make, material, skill, and love.

Art thou not glad to be — and always — man!
Therefore no being in the universe
Dreads death: a death, — his death, save only man,
Because he thinks to know death, — and yet scarce
Thinks *of* death for the joy he takes in man, ...
— In the Shah of Persia, — and of every hut, —
Man, image of his God, which once the earth
Yet knew not, and will one day know no more.

XXVII.

Sorrow for Death turned to Joy.

The one old sorrow oft comes over thee,
More clearly 't is renewed at each return, —
The sorrow that thou sharest with the sky,
The Spring-time, yes, thou sharest it with God,
On whom, as on the mirror of the world
It is cast back from everything that lives!
The sorrow that the pure, glad, heavenly soul
Here to the ancient earth must link itself,
And to the ancient Death. The Soul must mourn
The breath that sheds a blight upon the bloom
Of all her flowers: the dust that blinds her eyes
So that she cannot see her loved ones more;
The dust that seals their lips and chokes their breath!
The Beautiful must wed that which is dark,
Fleeting, yet what it needs to work withal!
That it may know itself, and may be known,
Now, through a thousand blooming forms, it lives.
On light and perishable canvas must
The artist paint the glorious, glowing shapes
That came to him from the pure spirit world:

The singer must breathe out into the air
The tender, touching tones that die at once,
And with them, too, breathes out his very soul,
Which, like light air, itself then floats away;
The good must hide his goodness in a loaf,
Must hide it in a gold piece, in a sheep,
Sent to the poor: the poor must recognize
The goodness in the sheep or in the bread,
And so the bread becomes — a holy bread,
The sheep becomes a consecrated sheep,
And the whole world, the body Love puts on,
And even the dust, the heavenly-carrier,
Herald of Beauty, mouth of all the gods, —
But ah, the tongue of gods is also dust!
And instantly after the finest deed,
Their very arm falls from its shoulder-blade,
And what was joined to dust, is turned to dust.
Rejoice, then, in the rainbow! Nay, in that
Rejoice not! in all beauteous hues rejoice
For the Sun's sake, whose magic called them forth,
Who evermore returns, forever bides:
The inner sun that beautifies the world.
So by and by shall things become to thee
Transparent, and the world a crystal sphere
Wherein serenely life and beauty sleep!

XXVIII.

Virtue not virtuous till easy.

Those are the easy and inferior virtues
Which thou canst exercise on evil men:
Patience, forgiveness, pity, helpfulness,

Respect, truth, tenderness, self-sacrifice, —
Thy very life, which they sometimes shall need.
They are the poor, and so they leave thee poor
In strength and act, poor in the genuine life.
The virtues, which begin with faulty men,
But cease with good ones, — these are few and small;
They fade, and silently must disappear
As good and happy beings multiply.
(If God — so please him — has not laid the base
Of this new world in sin and woe and tears,)
So long as thou still hearest virtue's name,
So long believe thou not that men are good.
What dost thou now with the good men, I pray,
Who meet thee, circle thee, innumerable,
Like noble trees hung full with juicy fruits?
What dost thou with thyself and of thyself?
What with mild Nature, the beneficent?
What with the flowers, that in their friendliness
Ne'er do thee wrong? What dost thou with the dead,
Who lie before thee in their coffined sleep,
Who cannot with a finger trouble thee,
Or one dark glance of envy? What with God?
Virtue must grow an easier task to thee,
O friend, O friend of man and friend of God;
He never knew her who finds virtue hard!
Make her thy joy, thy passion! And at last
Transfigured find her to her simple self!
A simple sense of being and of love!

XXIX.

Comparison kills Things.

Thought makes thee great; but Feeling makes thee rich,
It fills out greatness. Only after-thought
Dissolves and brings things to corruption soon!
Comparison is the death of things, and he
Dies with them who compares. Out from their soil
Thou pluck'st them like carnations in full bloom,
Thou tearest off the flowers and plantest them
In the hot sunshine, as a child sticks flowers
In his small garden, where they droop and die.
Thou tearest them from the world's all-consecrating
Embrace and its all-beautifying power,
Thou tak'st the water-lily from the pond,
Tearest the sun away from heaven, and fain
Wouldst scoop it up out of the water-pail.
Thou robbest the thing likened of its power,
The holy, inborn, self-subsistent power,
The power to be a part of Nature's self:
The eye God sees with and itself divine.
That which is self to thee, is godlike, whole;
What is no self is naught and good for naught.
But thou in the divine alone shalt stand
And live. Dwelling in love, to look with love,
To see things in one's own first blissfulness:
That is the wondrous mystery of man,
Key to his blessedness, his love and life.
Now, wilt thou love, adore, and taste of bliss,
Compare no thing! Take all things pure and whole!
So does the beggar take the very crust
From out thy hand as an entire gift,

As thy full love and the full love of God.
From God's hand take thou all divinely, too;
And wouldst thou spoil the rose which thou hast plucked,
Rob of her charms the fair bride thou hast won,
Ay, wouldst thou break thy faith with thine own wife,
From thine own children turn away thy heart,
Make the best man seem common in thy sight,
Steal merit from the artist, from the work
Its glory, from the stars their brilliancy,—
Thou hast but to compare them,—that is all!
Compare thou God,—the act deposes Him.

XXX.

Time's Ruins exalt a right Soul.

"I looked where once a hundred cities stood,—
I found but ashes in the place and stones;
Of all their glory naught but earth was left."
—Nothing but earth? But was not, then, the earth
Still there? heaped up in silence like green grave,—
And was she not, I pray, still bringing forth
The old eternal miracles, 'midst all
The fresh, spring influence she breathed around!
Look, then, my eye! A mighty spirit once
Swept through the world! Into this very mould
It entered and rose up as living gods,
Exalted spirits, men divinely fair;
It loved here: lived here; here long time abode,
Built houses, graves, and buried; but itself
Is not yet buried; like a hurricane
It swept the earth,—and took itself off, too!
And what it was can here no more be found

In Ilion's hills and mummy-wrappages!
Egypt to-day lies nowhere on the earth,
Nowhere in heaven to-day Judæa lies,
Carried aloft; nowhere in upper space
Jerusalem lies, nor evermore will lie,
Save there where heaps of rubbish mark its place;
Carthage and Corinth, Athens and old Rome,
They lie no more on earth, — no causeway leads
The traveller to *their* gates, that stand this day,
No pilgrim at *their* fountains slakes his thirst
That gush to-day, and in their havens rides
No ship to-day, from all the storms secure,
Under the old gray steersman's pilotage!
Thou strikest on these columns with thy hand, —
Yet dost not touch them! And these ruins here,
These stones, these crumbled fragments strewn around,
Are not memorials, witnesses, of earth,
And of its rocks; no, each one of these stones
Has been a holy bone of the great spirit
Of the creation that once swayed it here;
And is a nobler voucher than the moon
That here the spirit shaped itself a world.
And see, ay see! now comes the selfsame spirit
As a late pilgrim, wondering at himself
In these the ruins of his olden time;
And in the old time opening on him here,
He only sees his being running on
In one eternal course of changelessness, —
In grayest age so venerably old,
In holy Now so venerably young,
And dreams, in human shape, that his eyes weep
Ah, o'er the godlike beauty that has set, —
But only weeps at his immortal life,

The ever-touching, ever-beautiful!
And were there no gray hair in all the world,
No venerable weather-gray old walls, —
By what, then, would the spirit know its age,
As the tree's years are counted by its rings!
Yet when the flood-tide surges, spooms, and sweeps
Above the grave-mounds of old heroes dead,
When the last rain from out the latest clouds,
When stormy time on the old graves of kings
Devours and rattles, crumbles and destroys, —
That is not Death, that sweeps away the dead!
That is the holy stream of holy life,
Which with mild, kindly face, not rude and wild,
Draws that into its waves, which is no more!
So melt the frozen pictures of the ice
At spring's warm breath into the pond again!
So devotees into the furnace fling,
In which the master casts a great new bell,
To give it, and their names, a finer ring,
The silver beaker and the golden bowl,
To swell the molten metal's fiery flood!
Exulting in the work and sacrifice
Which they have furthered with their dearest wealth!
And now what superstition does, can man
Not do? The superstition that casts down
The beaker's offering into the bell-flood,
Does it not spring from the serenely great
Devotion of the sacrificing soul,
That, looking on with joy, sees ruins melt
In the eternal master's mighty forge!
Then see with joy thy temples crumble down;
For He who melts them honors thee; for thee
And for himself erecting a new work.

What was, thou understand'st not, else wert dead;
What is, thou understandest, as thyself,
Else wert thou not alive! Then let thyself
Sink into that which evermore springs forth,
Then art thou sunk and swallowed in thy life.

XXXI.

True Worth asks no Appraiser.

He who must see his purpose, work and worth
By the price-current of the world appraised,
Paid for, by men, and then, and not till then,
Can venture to appraise, himself, his work,
Worth, purpose, life, — ay, and the world itself,
He is a miserable man! He is
Still more, he is a fool for doing so!
What would men haply, of their own accord,
Give God in money for the glorious
Diurnal light and guidance of the Sun?
What money-price for a green-shaded walk
At blossom-time 'mid songs of nightingales?
Not much! For men have naught in shape of gold
But what their strength and industry have earned;
Who would pay largely for a blade of grass,
Or for a leaf? So fine a masterpiece,
A human artist well might want to die,
If cautiously some child should offer him
His long saved penny for the chestnut-blow!
And Michel Angelo would hang himself
Should some boor haply driving home his kine
On the fair evening *painted by himself*,
Scarce once look up, and then say only this:

"By the sun's look it will be foul to-morrow."
How then shall man ask for his handiwork,
For all his industry of days and nights,
Higher reward, than God for a God's work?
Or cherish in his heart more pride of worth,
Than God, the modest, in his heart divine?
And lo! the gard'ner-maiden sells thee now
A bunch of roses for a penny or two!
And eyes admiringly the beauteous flowers,
And feels the proper value of the works!
And gives it grudgingly! Thy sense of it
It was, that won from her the heavenly things,
Which have no knowledge of her, none of you,
To which there cleaves no stain or sign of earth!
And no less pure is thy heart's sense of them.
Mark thou: In all things man knows well to prize
Right highly the ineffable, divine
Value, 't is that he prizes in his bride,
His wife, the troop of children round his hearth;
Yet is this value, which no price can tell,
In godlike stillness understood, concealed!
And all the sweeter is its secret force.
Be then at ease about poor human souls!
But here 's another treasure claims thy thought:
The worth thy busy hands possess for thee,
The prosperous, though unambitious work,
The well-tilled field, the furrow cleanly cut,
The buxom tree, the vine well-trimmed and trained,
Whose hundred clusters speak its silent thanks, —
Thy little daughter's neatly braided hair,
The old man borne with reverence to the grave,
The true and timely word, the well-spent day,
And, as the harvest of a day's pure life,

The quiet evening hour, the dreamless sleep,
And every well-accomplished human work!
And yet a greater treasure claims thy thought:
The quiet sense of manhood, where not even
Modesty dwells, which in still self-content,
Self-fruitfulness, brings forth its manly fruits,
And sheds upon its day and its day's work
The illumination of a light which it
Sees not because it *is* the light, but which
Fills earth with beauty, and the heavens with brightness
As of a sunshine, and man's heart with bliss.
Who truly lives then needs no looking-glass
Of human praise, and will avoid all such;
Him no man needs to tell what he is worth,
And what the worth of that he does and makes;
For how he feels no one can say to him.

THE LAYMAN'S BREVIARY.

SEPTEMBER.

SEPTEMBER.

SEPTEMBER.

I.

The Cameo.

CAMEO ! that art one single solid mass,
Yet in so many layers of varied hue,
A type of man thou showest me : in the green
The child ! then in the rosy-red the youth ;
And in the heavenly blue here the old man !
Each beautiful, each kept in its own sphere,
Each bearing true similitude to each :
The old man still retaining the child's look,
The child, the youth already prophesying
That of the old man ; as if gradually
Waked up to separate being from *one* sleep ;
As the tall corn-stalk grows from out itself, —
And in the very blade I see the ear !
Yet more artistic still than thou is man,
For stone and work of art, One God hath made,
And still more beautifully from our breast
Form after form he summons forth to light !
The form of gladness and the form of love,
The form of wisdom and the form of death,
And all, yes all, out of one common ground,
As lily, aster, violet, and rose,
Blue, red, white, yellow, myriad-colored, all
Spring up together from the same dark earth !

II.

The Father consoled over his Child's Coffin.

Poor father! thou hast lost thy child, and now
As in a dream thou wanderest to and fro,
For now the lusty, loud, and lively boy
Lies dead, all silent in his coffin there;
Now nothing seems to thee impossible!
Not even that yon sun should fall from heaven,
That hill, vale, house, should disappear from thee,
The world sink into ruins burying thee.
One sight alone fills thy astonished eyes:
The heavenly apparition of the still
And solemn coffin, the festoons and wreaths,
And one so young laid dead among the flowers,
Illuminated by the sun's mute glow!
Thou smilest through thy tears to hear me say:
"The heavenly apparition of the coffin —"?
That broke in mutely on the festal day!
Ah! not enough I said, not rightly spoke!
The apparition! Nay, no apparition:
A wonder-work of Heaven the coffin is, —
The Deity himself this coffin made
When he contrived the world, and life and man!
The joiner only carried out his plan.
The earliest grave was dug by God himself,
The grave-diggers their lesson learned of him,
Else were the grave but an unmeaning pit.
Do thou take courage then and lay thy hand
Upon these flowers, this silent coffin-lid, —
Thou touchest there the holy soul of God!
And if the coffin is a work of God,

I pray thee, I conjure thy spirit now,
See even in the beautiful dead child
God's newest, venerably beauteous work, —
This very dead one also God hath made!
For without God not even a leaf could fade,
Who could have power to kill, save God alone!
And now if God's own proper self has done it,
Ay, 't is the very living God himself
Whose august greatness even in death appears,
Then weep for him the blessed, holy tears
God's apparition forces from thine eyes.
The mother has already bid her child
The last farewell, — lay in the coffin now
The rosy wreaths, and cover him softly up,
Not long can man endure the vision of God,
The play of lightning from the thunder-cloud.
To look upon the mother sorrow-worn,
The brothers and sisters bleeding, crushed, and dumb,
The pale and heavenly visage of the dead, —
Ah, it is unendurable! Let earth
The blessed, hide it! Then let us be men!
Set *over against* God, we are but dreams.

III.

How to bear little Troubles.

If thou canst not life's trifles understand
And string them with good sense upon a chain
That bears itself with ease, as in the air
Like to a chain of bees what time they swarm,
Or flight of cranes upon the eastern clouds,
Or a full wreath of flowers upon the sea, —

How wilt thou ever, like the blind old man,
Ill-regulated one! thy pile of sticks,
Not to say all the thousand little boughs,
Bear home with thee from the great woods of life!
Thou must feel things rest lightly on thy heart,
Lightly as on the pine her thousand needles,
Lightly as on the oak his heavy limbs.
Lightly as man carries his own two arms,
Or rose-bush bears all its rose-population,—
They must grow up out of thy very soul!
Then will great Nature bear them, as her stars,
And then, like *thy* stars, will they gladden thee!

IV.

Recovery from past Faults.

After each fault thou canst be pure again,
Wilt thou but feel them old, and feel thyself
Still young and good as thou still art to-day.
Thou art the fresh force, childlike purity,
Thou art thyself the very rage divine
Which with such heavenly might cast out of thee
That which was done and now is done away!
However deep and sore seems thy remorse,
So deep, though modest, is no less thy joy,
To feel that such a pure will lives in thee,
And such a strength, that thou, too, like the sun,
At every hour art new and art divine.
Now understand the word: "God pardons sin."

V.

All is born of Thought.

Thought is the very greatest power of all.
The mind of man bears up the heaviest load,
Enormous, gorgeous structures, — built of clouds ;
Breath is to man all that he feels, endures.
Praise and opinion are the strongest pillars
Of things, of men, and even of Gods themselves.
And things when once built up, are not torn down,
But thought down, laughed down, and so swept away !
What thou no more believest *is* no more.
Thought is the very greatest power of all,
And so not meaningless, but full of sense
Was the old word : The world is but — a thought.

VI.

Humanity bears its Lot with Divine Willingness.

Never believe men to be so befooled
As if they dragged along their painful road
Themselves, and with them many a needless thing,
Needed no more, by tyrannous custom's will,
Because a strong one a light luggage bears.
To think well of mankind is worth a word, —
Search intimately then and thou wilt find :
Naught in the world endures or can endure,
Not one day more, which man would not have be.
What, then, thou seest in the human race,
However oddly strange it seems to thee,
Yet hangs together by a vein, a hair,

With Nature and with man, the common heart
Of man, its hopes and its remembrances,
—And as there *are* whims,—say, too, with its whims!
But then this hair, albeit invisible,
While man yet chooses, is so utterly
Indissoluble that whole great temples hang,
Robes, mitres, crosses, golden coronets,
Hang by it: all the world of man, in short,
Hangs by a single hair! Yet by a hair.

VII.

Marriages made in Heaven.

Call thou no error trivial; the clear look
Through life and nature is a gladsome thing!
—And thinkst thou now, as youth, to choose thy bride,
The holy shape on earth to match thine own,
Out from the midst of all brave, beauteous maids
At pleasure? Lo, restricted choice is none!
Though hosts of women have already been,
Though hosts of women yet shall be on earth,
In these thy days there only live with thee
A certain number, sent into the world,
One blooming group of the long flowerage!
Thou canst not pluck a fruit from off the tree
Save that which bloomed and ripened there this year;
Thou canst not pluck thyself a rose, but that
To which in turn its time had come to blow;
There 's not *one* mother that can choose her child,
Whether a boy or girl: only a God
Lays on her bosom his child as her own,
As if he had taken her to be his wife,

And seeing the divine thing in her arms,
She seizes it with eagerness divine, —
Such bliss, — being a woman, — has she earned!
So hast thou only seized thy lovely bride!
Such wife hast thou deserved, — thou art a man!
Only the chosen one was pressed on thee
By thousand spirits: the primeval love
And beauty, by the master of all artists,
Whose every work turns out a master-piece,
Who crowds into its head, heart, body, soul,
The holy fulness, — all that they can hold:
Strength, love and beauty, goodness, blessedness!
Thus art thou not deluded, only blessed,
For thou hast God's beloved, — and thine own!

VIII.

Honor Woman, the Wife and the Mother.

In earth's old temple shines to-day still fresh
In lovely, legible and touching lines,
Gracefully wove with children's hair, the word:
"Woman is good, she is a wife, a child,
The daughter, ay, the metamorphosis,
Of Nature, woman's mighty prototype!
Of that great holy mother of us all,
In human form, the form resembling thine,
Who while thou liv'st, lives out her time with thee."
And even a blind man would say this who once
Sat as a child upon a mother's lap.
But thou must — *honor* her, as such a daughter
Of such a mother! must *believe* in her,
That she with perishable human hand

Will bless thee and can bless thee, like her mother,
Who ever faithful, friendly, bountiful,
Stands, aye, a visible helper at her side;
Love her thou must; then only will she feel
Assured that she can bless thee too. For only
The lover is it possible to bless,
Love only makes man capable of bliss,
Only the lover does a woman bless,
To see him crowned with self-earned happiness.
And if thou to thy wife dost show thyself
In man's true worth, wisdom and dignity,
Then wilt thou waken in her tender breast
All the good heavenly spirits, them alone!
Where blooms the spring, no bitter winter frowns,
And where love lives, there can no hate draw nigh.
But wheresoe'er thou see'st a woman vexed
By spirits that even in her bosom slept,—
There hast thou wickedly aroused them, man,
By doubts, by disrespect; there hast thou not
Loved her, hast not known how to honor her!
Whoso cannot love woman in the wife,
Can never love, nor yet respect a wife,
Although to be respected is her life.
Beauty is woman's robing, it is not
Her being; *that* is to be wife and mother,
Pledge of existence, fount of endless youth,
Nature,—the careful and the motherly,
In beauteous, primal presence clasping thee
And asking thee to clasp her to thy heart.—
His own faults only man does penance for,
In house and heart and in the world of men,
Even with Nature, the great stepmother!

IX.

Be Reasonable with the Unreasonable.

With you 't is easy dealing, men of sense;
Fools you both bear, and bear along with you.
But human reason only he can claim,
Who knows to deal with the irrational
Right humanly, with Nature's gentleness,
With peace and profit to himself and them!
And canst thou not do that, do they annoy thee,
Then blame thyself alone; thou art no man,
Thou art unreason! That deserves to suffer!
Be this a sign to thee, that thou hast gained
Reason, — God's blessedness, — ay, God himself, —
When not the world afflicts thee, nor thyself,
When in thyself and all things thou hast joy!

X.

Man's Work its own Reward.

"Thou say'st so much of duties, no, not duties, —
Of works which, as pure act, man must fulfil,
Yet sayest nothing of reward therefor!
Great as they are, hard their accomplishment!"
— A handsome life is the good man's reward;
In manhood manly action finds its goal.
For this is the wise ordinance of Nature,
That each shall find his cloudless happiness
In being wholly that she made him for;
For each existence is the highest duty.
And as each being is a bounded thing,

And made a being only by its bounds,
So in the human circle thou fulfil'st
Not every task to holy Nature set,
But only human tasks, enjoyest only
A human bliss, and that is all to men.
Thus is the task its own reward and thanks!
For whoso, penetrated by his life,
Strives with live truth to do the thing he is,
He has no time to ask about reward;
He could not even understand the thing,
'T would be to him a new existence. Such
Reward receives he for continuous being,
So God rewards him for eternal love.
And thus all brings, — begets its own reward!
The Universe, and every little life.

XI.

The Grave, seen in Divine Light.

A watchful eye to things above, below;
Oft glancing backward, forward, either side;
A fine, quick ear, turned inward, — man, so live!
An invalid, well-tended, lives much longer
Than thousands of uncared-for well ones, who
This morning made a mis-step suddenly,
And who, beneath his windows now at night
Are swept away into, — the common rut
Of erring travellers, — the nameless pit!
For "Grave" I call an enviable name,
Known in its heavenly significance
To few, as yet, among the human race,
Who still must needlessly bewail the grave,

Till one day tender tears fall for the dead;
To earn the grave, — that is the highest honor
Of man. None rises higher. No, not one, —
Even if a God would honor this our earth, —
So is it honored by pure ashes now!
The Grave 's a mark which, like the human heart,
At the right hour, and only then, is hit,
When ends all human time, and when all suns,
All earthly bliss, have vanished from its grasp.

XII.

The Beauty of Moderation.

Measure and Order work so wholesomely,
That even the bad, under their leadership,
Still holds out long, by shrewd self-management
Distributing his pleasures, intermitting
His faults, and dreaming: what he does is right.
The very form of virtue, how divine!
Of reason's shadow how divine the power,
It stamps even half-men, half-blessed ones!

XIII.

Sleep and Old Age.

Wherefore is sleep, thou askest, holy sleep,
Appointed to the living? Dead men sleep not,
They rest not. — Sleep, the holy, sayest thou? —
The isolating, self-existing sleep!
Wherefore is man? The isolated one,
The holy, — why the earthly night of man,

Night, full of stars, of dew, and fresh young force,—
The flowers sleep also, buds and blossoms sleep.
And ask'st thou not: why also is old age,
The holy, cloistered, far secluded state,
Half sleep of sense, and winter time complete
Of worn-out feelings! Lo, the old man there
Is like a slumberer; a slumberer
Is like a bucket full of precious wine,
Which one sets by in a cool, quiet place,
Hedged round with ice,—to freeze. And whatsoe'er
Man has within, poured into him by life,
The evil part all freezes out to ice,
All vulgar, common, bitter, foreign stuff,—
And in the centre is condensed the virtue
Of days,—of life, perchance a small amount:
A beaker full, yet fiery, pure and mild.
The early waking one that beaker drinks,
With that the aging man refreshes him,
The new-born man of that same beaker drinks,
That beaker shall one day the death-judge quaff,—
The pure, primeval self of man and all.

XIV.

Learn Calmness of Nature.

Repose and dignity give being grace!
Short is man's life in the comparison
With nature's life, the morning star's, the earth's,
Ay, even the raven's and the olive-tree's.
Still shorter than the life of man is that
The faithful dog and faithful swallow spend,
The silkworm's life, the spider's, and the bee's,

And each one's frame suffices for its life
Even to the breath; and each has lived enough,
When it has wholly filled its being out.
Who would be man needs only a man's life;
Then hurry not away indecently
The slightest work, the shortest winter day!
Take time to greet the passer in thy walks,
To say a friendly word to coming guests,
To spread thyself serenely through the hours,—
Repose and dignity lend grace to life.
Let joy prolong itself as on the air
A flute-tone; wander slowly through the garden
Of spring; beholding, listening everything,
The nightingale, as an imploring child;
Time for his pater-noster give the beggar,
And give thyself time for thy piteous word;
Yea, grant, that it may vindicate itself,
Sorrow itself its natural human course:
Smother not grief, nor give it too much room.
So only is the very poorest rich,
In that he spreads out so composedly
And cheerfully his coarse white tablecloth
Takes time for his dry bread and leaves no less
Each thirsty child time for the water-jug.
So the last lingering lark sings her last song
The last fair autumn day, composedly
And rapturously as she sang her first,
Then sinks with graceful calmness to the earth.
The cranes that early through the purple sky
Sail hence to warmer suns, in circling dance
High in the azure heaven, away they wheel,
Like happy guests bound homeward from the feast;
The wild geese on their journey pause awhile

To bathe themselves delighted in the lake.
Note kindly, then, how Nature manages,
So that, by having all contented guests,
She in her house may be herself content!
Scarcely she lures the violet by warm gales,
Yet, if it will come, well, so let it be!
She interrupts by coolness of spring nights
The bloom-days of the eager hyacinth,
She dashes not the bells from off the stalk,
When they dry up and all their beauty 's gone!
She tears not suddenly and rudely off
The sunny buttercup's empty golden head:
Nor turns the swallow in the night to clay;
She lets her with the swallow long rejoice
In the half-builded nest, and lets the young
Long with the parent swallow nightly sit.
She leaves the child a space of years to play
Many times over every childish game;
She lets the old man still enjoy his ease,
When long his occupation has been gone;
She hurls not the first rain-clouds on the year,
Nor drives the last, like servants old and worn,
Out of the year; gives time for every drop
To fall, and in its falling, time to grow,
And down below, exhaling, to refresh,
In diamond-death: to flash all-colored rays!
And when the sun already has gone down,
She lets the rainbow for the children still
Long linger, the old columns, too, themselves
Of holier fanes her earlier children built
She lets in sad and tender silence stand
When they have long been gone away from earth.
So lives she in destruction, even in death,

Serenely. Thou, from Nature learn thy life,
The calm she gives to all things that have worth,
And all has worth in her eyes, even thou!
Then spread out generously thy human life!
Calmness and dignity give being grace.

XV.

Man, the Immortal, alone can die.

To be immortal and to die, — that is
The life of all, of man, of everything
That has a living soul and teems with force.
The drop of rain dies also, in the sea:
The spark is in the rain-drop quenched and dies;
The fagot dies in the fire, and the rose
Dies in the ether; they are all transformed,
All in the universal feeling merge,
In the great sea of forces; what they were,
Joins the great chain of being: what they will be,
Unharmed themselves by such transfigurement,
Abiding in divine, eternal life.
I know one being only who can *die:*
'T is man! Earth's finest work, the one of all
Fitted to be her very heart and soul,
To feel what *he* is, what the universe,
What life: to be immortal and to die;
And therefore take thou note: not all can die;
Nor die alike; but those who are alike;
The more experienced, the more wise one was,
The better, and the richlier endowed
With love and beauty, to appreciate life,
To hold his loves uniquely high and dear, —

The more divinely has he power to die!
As great as is the difference of life,
So great, too, is the difference of death, —
Of death, the great heart-searcher and world-judge,
Who every day sends million angels out,
With beakers full of holy joy, to float
Round this old earth, that sun, and round the suns
Of star-worlds, to refresh each dying one,
And celebrates among his own that feast,
The feast of ripening and the harvest home,
At which, as on the holy altar, in
The Holicst place of the still universe,
Suns blaze for lamps, and ether sparkling glows!
The highest hour of all things is their end;
Lovely is life, lovely the road, — the bloom;
But the completed root, — that is the flower,
When it falls off and richly strews the seed.

XVI.

Death, Man's Angel-Friend.

Only one wish were mine, but one desire,
The highest and the holiest wish of man,
Which each one wears his life out to fulfil,
Which earth and heaven are glowing to secure!
O that the whole of human kind might die,
O might one single man succeed to die!
So many generations, like the heads
Of poppies full of countless seeds, have come,
Have gone, — gone to destruction, every one!
Scarce one, one man up to this day has died,
Scarce of the holiest one has even guessed

What dying is and death. All, all of them,
In frightful wars, or in a frightful peace,
In battle-din of life were snatched away,
Swept ignominiously into the pit.
And still the murder-peal and howl of bells
From dawn till night circles the broad round earth.
O that all bells were charmed to dumbness, bells
Of snow-drops, with their tongues grown stiff and mute!
For in the wail and woe I wellnigh sink;
No! I could wish all bells an angel voice,
To cry aloud into the ears of men,
From dawn to dark all over earth's wide round:
O shame, shame, shame, ye mortals, know ye not
The holy name of "mortals," — what it means!
He only who has truly lived can die!
Nothing is fairer, perfecter than death,
More heavenly, sweeter to the universe
Than is a noble death for noble men!
And once, one day, will death and dying mean:
That one has truly lived a human life,
Not merely taught, imagined and seen toil, —
And none can truly live a human life,
Till all can die with manly dignity
After a beauteous sweet consummate life.
Discern, then, that the goal of death — is life!
And therefore is it, death is laid on you
As the last, greatest, heaviest, and withal
Unspeakably rich treasure of mankind, —
And not as the last torment, the last fiend.

XVII.

Keep along with God's great Flock.

Go always with the one great flock, that, like
A holy water-stream o'erflows the lands,
Through the still night forever pressing on;
Which has no shepherd, for its multitude
Is all too great to have one here below;
Which needs no shepherd, since on every side
For it on earth here, cloud-fed pasture blooms,
For it above there, — heaven shines brightly down!
Go not ahead! useless it were for thee
That thou alone shouldst have enough of all
While the flock starved or there were one in want;
That were to thee the very greatest shame!
What all have, that alone can gladden thee.
Lag not behind! canst thou in earnest think
That all things glorious are not now in all
Growing in rich abundance for all time?
Who counts himself as wiser, — or, (mad thought)
As better than the very least of all, —
Better in soul and total nature than,
Before or since his deed, the murderer, —
Such has not known the priceless inborn wealth
Which each bears with him — as *himself* — through life.
Go not aside! proud and oppressed with shame,
As the rich man beside the beggar walks,
Lest thou shouldst fall into the ditch, or wolves
Tear thee, or gnash their teeth at thee. "Beware!"
"Stand on thy guard!" that is the single word
Of the whole flock. Let each one practise it,
Then the whole flock is well-defended, safe,

Inviolably holy as the sea!
And if one meeting thee should question thee
And shake his head and say: a wretched flock!
Then look thou straight into his eye and give him
The time of day; and as the day may be,
Say, "Yes, it rains to-day." "Last night the wolves
Howled frightfully." "To-day a lamb has strayed,
The dogs are bad, they chase this way and that!"
"To-day a mist fell." "The sun stings to-day."
"'T is drawing water there, — 't will soon be spring!
For see the birds already come in flocks!"
This only. If he still waits, — smile and say:
"We journey safely as the stars in heaven!
Their unseen shepherd is our shepherd too!
And here below our heaven is called: the Earth."

XVIII.

The City of the Gods is in Man's Being.

Magnificent! "The city of the Gods"
I fain would see! It actually stands;
But mystical and secret as a dream!
For lo! the head of every little child
Reveals a palace, one divinely built,
Reveals a new, original world just made,
Such world as never yet was seen by man,
Such world as never came to human ears.
The child's eye feasts upon the universe,
And whatsoever charms and pleases it
It draws into the mystic viewless dome;
Like bees the thoughts fly out from it for sweets,
And heavy-laden bring their treasures home;
They gather thoughts themselves, which they extract

From stars and from the clouds and from the flowers,
And like the blue sky, broad and glistering
Soon their own heavenly temple rears its arch,
And its own shining sun it hangs therein,
And its own beaming moon ; and days and nights,
Spring, summer, autumn, winter, in their pomp,
Move round therein with new, peculiar grace,
Real, and nowhere else to him exist.
A goddess, too, the master takes to him
And sends out infant gods before the door!
Of them each little childish head shines forth
A new, original, and glorious palace,
A new heaven, lighted with its proper sun,
Full of all treasures, all delight and bliss!
And so millions of houses come to be
Crowded with suns and moons and all things fair,
So a whole city of spirits comes to be!
Does this sound like a fable! But, dear soul,
Not greatly, not admiringly enough
Canst thou e'er think of "being," — of the master
Who founded this full city of the gods!
What were sublimer, rarer, blesseder
Than all men's daily, homely, common life!
What can be lovelier than to be a man!
What holier than the culture and the love,
That open to dim sense its heavenly house!

XIX.

The Mountain of Woes lifts Man to Heaven.

The wind snaps off thy beauteous blooming rose, —
And thou, for grief, forgettest all the buds ;
Then comes a storm and fells thy cherry-tree, —

And gone is all thy mourning for the rose!
Lo, the white cloud hurls down its rattling hail,
Beats down and crushes all thy field of wheat, —
And rose and cherry-tree are both forgot,
As quickly as the clouds o'ershadow thee!
Lo, from the cloud's black mantle darts a flash,
And ere thou thinkest of the thunder's crash,
Thy house already smokes, is wrapped in flames.
Now quickly is the wheat-field in its turn
Forgotten, like the rose and cherry-tree,
In the new glow of the new-startled soul.
The mother bears forth some one from the house,
She bears out some one dead — see — 't is thy boy
Whom that same flash has torn from her and thee:
Even her mute lips, alas, they tell it loud,
The paleness of the boy, his stiffened eye,
As in the gushing rain he lies before thee,
And lo! heaven's water drenches all his curls,
The slightly singed and blackened golden locks!
Just as the wheat-field drove out of thy thoughts
The cherry-tree, the cherry-tree the rose;
Naught else thou seest and feelest but the boy.
Then suddenly a flash from heaven strikes thee, —
The heavens are opened to thee suddenly,
Thyself art dead, — and standest before God,
Thou standest before God in holy awe,
And in the vision is thy beauteous boy
Forgotten also now, — and the whole world!
And should not then a thought on God have power,
O living man, to make thee, not indeed
Wholly forget earth's woes, but tranquilly,
Humanely, and divinely to discern
How woe and joy both lift thee up to Him?

XX.

Pride of Manhood.

Whate'er is strewed with poison and with gall,
Choose not to take, — *that* utterly refuse!
And better, nobler wilt thou find thyself
When the short moment's gloomy mood is past.
That is the chasteness which beseems a man,
The chastity of thought, of sentiment.
Hast thou not longed for justness, search thyself:
Hast only longed for it, — then watch and wait,
And bide thy time; the mitigated sense
Mildly and humanly will bring it thee!
Mildly and humanly receive thou it!
And were it office, honors, freedom, love,
Yea, were 't the bliss of life, ev'n life itself, —
And if a god could thrust thee into life,
That thou shouldst there appear indecently,
Not unbecoming thee it were to turn
Even upon him with a resentful look!
The chastity of thought, of sentiment,
Guard jealously! With men its name is — Pride!
And pride of manhood graces every man.

XXI.

The Cry of Humanity, God's Voice.

[1 Samuel xii. 6 - 17.]

High on the rainbow stands a sprite and cries
Aloud with cloudy voice; Give ear, O men!
Ho, all men! Hear and see! Behold, it rains!

And if you hear, you laugh the fool to scorn;
Because he tells a truth you know yourselves.
But if perchance in the still dusk of eve
A poor man says with timid, tremulous voice,
Scarce audible, "O help, — I am a man," —
Laugh not at him! for thou too art a man,
And that he speaks is truth for thee to do;
And if he says it in broad day, with firm,
Courageous voice, full of sweet confidence, —
And if, now, all men say the same to thee:
"Stand by us, man!" has it less meaning then?
O laugh them not to scorn! they all are men;
And day and night, do thou, with men and God,
Truly remember them with hand and mouth,
With thought and deed, ay, dreaming and asleep;
For what the soul takes with it into sleep,
That it holds dear! That shall abide with it.

XXII.

A manly Life Man's main Business.

Man's main work is existence in the whole,
And all details therein are mere by-work;
The best and fairest are, though they should last
Half his life long. In the great whole of life
God has assigned to man the holiest task,
To which no deed, no work can e'er come up.
For see! how grand, immense a thing it is
To have been born a man! a weighty office,
To weep through all the tears of human woe,
To glow through all the thrills of human joy,
An inexpressible office too, to die.

It takes the whole of life to make *one* deed,
As it was *one* thought in the master's mind.
The weaver in his weaving does mere — by-work;
The fisher in his fishing merely by-work,
The doctor in his cures; even to the father
Is rearing children by-work; to the mother
Bearing of children is, and to the king
His kingdom, it is only by-work; though,
As each man's is to him, a serious task.
Then what, with narrow and mistaking mind,
Thou hast been used to call thy main-work, *that*
Call thou henceforward by-work. And the by-work
Henceforth call main-work, — labor, faithful toil,
True loving, seeking wisdom, cheerfulness.
So are there few all unsuccessful men,
So are there very few unhappy ones,
And even these only in small degree!
With such a firm and golden truth has God
Divided unto all their proper goods,
As if He had chained them to the golden well!
Lamed in his wing, the stork no more indeed
Migrates, nor comes back home, yet evermore
Dwells in his element, there builds his nest,
And has his wife and children with him too;
The mussel, though diseased, still forms the pearl;
The bear, though blind, still finds his honeycomb,
And man can never wholly, finally
Stray from the circle of humanity,
Can never be so utterly unmanned
As utterly to lose the fruit of life;
And none can e'er achieve such loftiness
As to be worth more than a simple child, —
The pure and universal lot of man!

XXIII.

Creation never finished.

A mighty word sounds through the heavenly halls,
And weeks and days, and sun and moon and earth,
They all speak out the word of gladdening life :
" The worth is in the work, not what is wrought:
What 's doing, *that* has life ! What 's done is dead ! "
So man believes : Creation is not done,
Else were it dead. It lives and works and lasts ;
Creation then is not ; but a creating,
A ceaseless working without finishing,
Is all we see ; the world is one great workshop,
Wherein all hammers are alive, all tongs,
The bellows, fire, water, anvils, all,
And with the One Great Master live and work
The little artists ; but *their* works they make
Complete, and when their work is done they die ;
They turn to dust, — they and the world, forgot.
But He — the mighty master — *never ends*,
And nothing that He does is ever done ;
Millions of years He 's been at work, and lo !
He has not finished yet a single flower,
No violet, not a rose, nor clover-leaf,
No palm, nor ivy creeping on the ground !
Nor moon, nor blade of grass, nor lightning-bug !
Year after year, He busily works on,
He busily works on in making man ;
And when He has divinely wrought Himself,
Into his works, inspired them with his soul,
Meekly transformed Himself into the saints
So as to be all, and know all Himself,

His works all sweetly help Him to create;
Each violet helps Him make a violet,
Each olive-tree helps make an olive-tree,
The jilly-flower helps make the jilly-flower,
Man likewise lends his aid in making man,
Each creature helps its own development,
The mussel and the trees — ay, and the sea!
For even the very workshop helps complete
The workshop, make it new, and keep it clean,
As if 't were opened the first time this morn.
So each helps faithfully create the other!
The sea helps form the clouds; the wind, the rain;
The rain, the grass; the grass, the lamb; and so
He never ends, Himself; the laboratory
Itself is never done; the aster fair,
The evening-red, nor evening of the year,
The grape! nor man, nor yet the joy of man;
And in the endless evolutions, He
Evolves Himself, too, everlastingly,
And calmly, thoughtfully he says Himself:
"The worth is in the work, not the thing wrought;
What 's doing, is alive; what 's done, is dead. —
This mighty word rings through the halls of heaven."

XXIV.

The Child's World and the Man's.

Sweetly the child takes the whole world as his,
One whole; and indistinguishably great
All rests with him in chaos of still love:
The sun in heaven, his parents and the flowers;
And magically, though in miniature,

He seems a very god in the blest power
Of feeling the whole universe as one;
And everything he has, he calls it: thine,
Because his mother told him: "That is thine!"
The boy thinks: He alone is all the world;
And gambolling, as in a mother's lap,
He drinks the world's blood through a thousand veins
To ripen in the kingdom of the sun.
The youth mysteriously breaks in twain,
When the fair maiden stands before his eyes;
He feels what he, as man, as human, needs;
The woman — and exulting leads her home.
And in the house, the children prattling round,
The double image by degrees fades out —
He becomes she — she becomes he — and now
Husband and wife together make one man.
And wondrously, yet naturally, touched,
Man feels himself once more now all alone,
Yet he is whole! That gives him lofty calm,
For all the thousands are no more than he!
Only in number. And he stands on earth
As host in a great house alive with joy,
And as he looks around he boldly counts
As guests the very clouds! the sun! the stars!
His children — trees and flowers — and even his dog!
For he, too, is a father, is a world,
He and his wife! and now, as with the child,
So with these two, all rests in orderly
In clear, pure love, like offspring of their own!
In open, visible presence, like the sun.

XXV.

How many Elements are there?

How many elements are there? — "Hundreds!" — Nay!
Too few! Are there not spirit-elements?
Perhaps none else, and nothing said of them!
Forms, types, masks elemental, are there not?
Wilt thou not reckon man among them too?
The snail? Yes, and her house! and every tile
Upon her little house! The elephant
Is as indissoluble — as the rose,
And long, yet long time will the humming-bird,
The bee, and the bee's honey, and the sun
And the fly's egg defy analysis,
Till one day there will be no element,
But only elements; numbers, but no number.
The poppy-head consists of — million grains,
And if this prove a falsehood — man is lost!
Man, — who himself believes that he is man.

XXVI.

The Child's bleeding Finger.

The boy has gashed his finger with a knife,
And, stained with blood, runs to his father now:
"Ah! — Father! — is there blood, then, in my body?
And am I, — only so, how shall I say,
Do I not live, — I know not what to say, —
O father! tell it to thy darling child:
For ah, I faint with fear, — the blood runs out,
Must I now die? Ah, is death coming now?"
And smiling, says the father to the boy:

Thou young "old head," and must I tell it thee, —
Thou liv'st not "only so" as nothing, canst not
Live without hand and body, world and blood:
Thou liv'st in blood! yet pure and all unharmed
By this red juice wrung from the elements!
Thou hast been told of God, how He himself,
Even He, lives in this body of the world,
As a clear spirit, uttering words of love
Loud to His children, as I do to thee;
He lives in blood, so pure, so all untouched
By this red juice wrung from the elements!
And as it trickles down so from thy hand, —
Think thou upon it! Think upon thy life,
Think then upon the world, think upon God,
Who lives in thee, — in thee as in His blood!
And thou too livest in His heart, dear boy!
I pray thee, honor now the wiped-off blood,
Go, and beneath thy rose-bush bury it;
It is God's body, and the body of love,
And roses thou shalt see bloom up from it!

XXVII.

Old Things made new.

Each man must brave the wilderness of life,
Long fasting, shyly tasting as in dream
The bread of men, and the good gifts of earth,
Loosing his own heart, the great inner wings,
Like the young eagle in a still amaze;
Each one must climb the temple's pinnacle,
The kingdoms and the glories of the world
To prove, and bring his spirit back unstained;

Even to the dwellings of the dead must thou
Go down alive and mount to heaven again.
When thou hast oft and sorely been in doubt,
Ay, in despair, when thou hast left the world
To the world's self, and to thyself art left,
What is and what takes place canst calmly see,
Having resigned thyself to death and life, —
As if thy dear heart had died out of thee,
And with pale cheek and silent, silent step,
Old spring returns to thy indifferent eyes,
Risen anew from out his earthly grave, —
Then, not till then thou art! The universe
Then wakes for thee, then thou begin'st to live
And liv'st a glorious and a godlike life
In the old seed-house of the spirit-world, —
Thou hear'st perchance a voice from hoary eld:
The work that thrills thee so with awe and dread
Which thou hast with such human-childish eyes
Gazed on, should be to thee a radiant work,
A work of beauty, fair and light and gay
To thee, as thy old, joyous, godlike soul.
For naught is serious which is transitory,
Death least of all, and places of the dead;
Naught has significance save to the mind,
That like a rock withstands the sea of time,
That rests on its own anchors, buoyantly,
Even as a ship on the sun-bright expanse
Of the deep, dreadful, and wide-weltering sea.
Whoso rules not himself, a lord of life,
He cannot live, he is not living yet!
He whirs about here under the blue dome
Of heaven, as bats do in the pyramid, —
Thou hast both heard them whir, and whirred thyself.

XXVIII.

Take all Things as natural.

Shall naught till that dread morning's thunder-peal
Rolling, awake the sleepers from their tombs?
Must first the noonday sun to blackness turn,
Does not e'en now the sunlight sing and say:
"Is it not still all human, everything
Which thou conceivest in thy heart and thoughts,
Of goodness, God, and immortality?
Does it not turn to human, all, in thee?
Dost thou not just take home to thee thine own,
As the child plucks the house-flowers for himself?
Cease of the superhuman to discourse;
To man is nothing superhuman, naught,
For hope, presentiment, faith are human too,
Ay, dreaming, sleeping, dying. How could ev'n
A man so much as die, were 't not that death
Is human, too, man's property! Thou 'rt spirit,
Be spirit! Whatsoe'er is such, — has all."

XXIX.

Discontent is Despite to God.

Enter with me the realm of thought, and dream:
"Into this life a God doth usher thee,"
He lets thee first of all survey the world,
Shows thee beforehand all the million graves
Of them who left the earth ere thou wast born!
He lets thee hear their moans of sorrow all
Float in the wind, — lets thee see all their tears

Swoll'n to an ocean, all their works as dust,
Till thy soul trembles, and thy hair stands up, —
And thou, — in rage, thou smit'st him in the face!
He says to thee: yon sun in heaven must sink!
The life of man consists of day and night!
He says to thee: Yon flowers must fade and die,
Thou must thyself lean on the staff one day
A gray old man, and sink into the grave, —
And then, with rage thou smit'st him in the face!
He says to thee: While thou dost live this life,
Will cold and heat oppress thee, pain, and want,
Thy friend will turn to be thy bitter foe,
To speak the truth will cost thee worldly peace.
Thy children, once grown up and come of age,
Will go from thee to wander through the world,
Thy handsome wife grow haggard with old age;
By thousands men will waste each other's lives,
The highest insult man inflicts on man, —
And thou with rage smitest him in the face,
As if he told thee lies, ay, terrible truth!
And art thou in advance so violent,
Thou wilt refuse to enter *into* life,
And liv'st thou in the midst of this fair world,
And thinkest still such wilful thoughts as these,
Then wilt thou, impious, fain go *out* of life;
Thou wilt endure with hate the human lot,
Thou wilt not live, wilt tease thyself to death!
The malcontent smites God upon the face!
Therefore: to be content with *that*, to win
By one's own might a happy lot from *that*,
In which thy life peculiarly consists, —
That is the power, wellnigh omnipotent,
That knows and wills and does that which is man.

And so does the great people of mankind,
That troubles itself more for bread than death.

XXX.

Love those round thee, and so All.

What wilt thou, man, with the great swarm of men?
Thou unit, with the thousand duplicates?
What can the single drop do with the sea,
What shall the grain of sand with mountain-chains!
For that so many thousand legions all
Round thee are men, rejoicing in the sun,
Rejoicing in the earth and this fair life,
That, ah! makes mad thy heart with ecstasy,
And helplessly thou liftest up thy arms,
As if a friend should fly to thy embrace,
As if thou to thy heart shouldst clasp a bride,
And in thy frenzy, lo! thou tak'st wild steps!
No! stay, stay quietly in thine own place,
Thou canst not make thy way to every home,
Away o'er all the seas, to all the isles!
The sun himself cannot come down to all,
Come down to every board round which men sit, —
Can but shine on them, each one's shadow cast,
Rise in the morn on each and bring his day,
Go down for each at night, and leave him sleep,
And wilt thou have more power, then, than the sun,
That moves in such close limits, that in heaven
With its bright eye is yet itself stone blind,
Shines, and sees not! But thou, — thou hast a heart!
Thine eye is watchful over all thy loves;
And thy warm love broods like the clucking hen,

Above them all, — with thy so narrow wings!
Nor canst thou reach into the distances,
To be there, act there, make thy voice there heard!
They live unknown to thee and silent all!
Thou liv'st unknown and silent to them all!
And all of them can never come to thee,
More than the sea can to the water-drop.
Yet one man and another of the sea
Of men comes on the flood-tide to the shore,
A wave, to thee the dweller on the strand,
And as an envoy of the people, thou
Receive him, as thy guest in a glad home!
And what the cellar, what the coffer holds,
That spare not, save not for a greater day!
The greatest day is when a man comes to thee.
And if he comes from o'er the ocean sick,
Outcast, and ragged, nurse him, clothe his limbs,
Do him such honor as the land is wont,
And give thy penny to him for the road,
Love's penny and the blessing of the heart.
At every dawn ascend thy mount and pray
For a good day to all humanity;
At every dusk ascend thy mount and pray
For a good night to all humanity.
And whatsoe'er thou wishest for all, all,
Refuse not to thine own! not to thyself!
No, with collected, wakeful, active powers,
Provide it for thyself and those thou lov'st!
For: "I too am a man," the universe says;
And say thou after it: "I too am a man."
Let each one say so! That it may be true,
What good men wish to their dear ones afar!

THE LAYMAN'S BREVIARY.

OCTOBER.

OCTOBER.

OCTOBER.

I.

The Cochineal Worm's Roof-Shield.

BRIGHT purple roof of the gay-colored earth,
Covering her autumn with a holy calm,
The crimson-tipped young harvest, and the buds,
Eyes of the trees, that in another spring
Will open to the light, — fair heavenly shield,
Soul-touching sight! How like is, after all,
The great of God to the small things of earth!
And ah, how like the littleness of life
To the great things of immortality!
And so I liken thee, thou purple roof,
To the mother of the silken purple worms,*
The marriage scarce complete, the husband died.
But she survived him haply by a month;
Upon one spot she sits and never stirs
Till she has duly brought her children forth.
The more of them she has produced to light,
The thinner she herself, poor mother, grows,
Until at last she dries up to a crust;
And under this still dwells her little tribe
A goodly season, safe and prosperous,
As underneath a beauteous holy shield, —

* The Cochineal worm.

Maternal love grown into house-like shape!
And so art thou, purple-red evening-heaven,
That coverest autumn now with holy calm,
Maternal love grown into house-like shape,
Beneath whose roof we tarry yet awhile,
The crimson-tipped young harvest, and the buds,
Eyes of the trees, which in another spring
Will open to the light, — but thou art gone.

II.

All Seasons and Beings are linked together.

Now when the trees in autumn leafless stand,
The sun shines down upon the bare, brown earth,
Earth, — not appointed to unfruitfulness,
And utter ruin, — and the falling leaves
Show, on the twigs, cosily nested there,
The little, new, expectant, next year's buds, —
There, — undeniably, inseparably,
Surviving all the faded, vanished life, —
There, with their sacred and eternal claim
To life, earth, sunshine, and the human heart.
Ah, then, athwart the light of the cold sun
Gleams the new spring-time, and the heart of man
Lives in the future! lives with thee, and feels
Immortal youth, O nature, in thy breath,
In thy prophetic soul, eternal mother!
Naught stands alone. Naught can alone abide.
What is, needs each thing else to help it be;
What lives, needs each thing else to help it live;
The sun goes not without the great star-clock,
Nor burns without the sea of ether-oil.

The earth shows not upon her dial-plate
One buttercup without the starry clock.
So shall these dry rose-bushes at my side
No more bear leaves again, — no blade of grass
Lift itself up again without the help
Of the whole universe, the magic power
Dwelling in farthest depths, which has till now
Called to the earth with ceaseless, noiseless force!
And thou, O man, wilt lean on self alone?
Stand by thyself without one other man,
Or without all men? without all the world?
Here bow thyself! Confess aloud and glad:
Yes, I do need the dew, that falls by night,
The sweep of clouds, the fanning of the breeze,
For each fresh respiration; even to see
My hand, say nothing of the mother bearing
Her infant in her arms among the flowers;
Yes, I need man, ay, and the beggar, too,
And every child that meets me in my walk,
The very bird that darts by overhead!
The tempest's uproar and the silent flash,
(For the All needs it indispensably,)
Yea, I have need of death, I need the grave
For life! for youth! and for accomplishment! —
More than, for blooming, the dry apple-tree
Needs the artistic, delicate, seeing fingers
Of the still sprites, whose labor shapes the spring, —
For I do need the spirits, as a spirit!
And I have need to love, as being love!
And to be loved, as the reward of life.
'T is the reward God yearns for, to be loved.
Whoever says: "Thou art!" he says: "I love thee!"
Who says: "I love thee!" only says: "Thou art.

Thou art to me!" Learn love then, thousand-fold,
By insight deep; "What thou art not — is all!"

III.

Patience of Nature and Man.

Now all the flowers are dying! All returns
With silent speed to whence it lately came,
And now, more sharply, and more sadly far
Than once spring's blooming twigs, — pale autumn points
With myriad withered flower-stalks up to Heaven:
To ether, of all things the bourne and grave;
And ah! this silence wellnigh breaks my heart,
The supernatural hush of the blue grave,
The silence of these withered flower-heads,
That patient perish, as they patient lived.
O, truly! We are better than the flowers,
Yet happier are the flowers than are we men,
Yea, ev'n the leaves that rustle at our feet,
They know no fear, no, only human hearts.
So lovely even the show of patience is,
That thou dost praise the flowers — that they endure.
Endurance is not patience! with pure heart,
With heavenly soul to bear the lot of earth,
Feeling one's self, living above it all,
As high above the clouds the sun shines on, —
That, — that is patience! with guilt-conscious heart
To appear patient, is but punishment.
With lightsome joy to accept mistaken things
— Serpents for fishes — is sheer senselessness.
Only the best wear patience as a crown
Fair as a lunar rainbow, and as rare!

IV.

No Evil in the Universe.

Badness thou know'st not! 'T is impossible
In this, God's world, — world of outspoken love.
Only the pitiable, *that* thou knowest
Well, yea, right well, the sunlight's blinding glare,
The misstep of precipitancy. Yes,
I know the yonder side of every heart, —
The home of other men I recognize, —
That which to thee and other men seems hate,
Robbery, murder, villany, and crime,
On this side, — looked at on the other side
That of the living and the loving One,
Is only favor, honor, truth and love, —
In its *own* way, upon the scale of man,
As he, oft darkened, comprehends the world,
Sees darkly and defends his home, his heart,
And thirsts to do that which to him is good.
And will thou call what must be, evil, then?
Works, — without which the spider or the wasp,
No, not the tiger or the crocodile,
Nor the hyena, can prolong its life, —
Works, without which they would not be the creatures
Tormenting and tormented as thou deem'st,
Which now they are, as thou wouldst not be man,
Didst thou not act the part of man to them.
And if to swallow down the tiger costs
The anaconda but a little rage,
Forgive her for it, — thou oft art hungry, too,
And appetite must be strong to eat the skin!
Yet all the thousand-fold, thousand-year-old

Carnage in watery seas and seas of air
On all the stars, in forests, on the earth,
To the clear human sense it is no more
Than if a violet sipped a drop of dew,
Than if a man before his table sat
And prayed: Thy servant, Lord, will eat, — will live!
For from the moment when it once is born,
To eat: is every creature's daily birth,
And without eating — if we view the thing
Externally — creation, life, is not,
And without love creative, is no God.
And eating is the world's one mighty want,
The great necessity, the holy law;
And suns and constellations evermore
Swallow whole streams of life-sustaining drink,
In every drop a living multitude,
Even spirits must they take into themselves.
See now, upon my window-pane the wasp
Seizes the gold-fly fast; and gradually
Devours the fly alive; the carcass leaves
All hollow, — and if even the gold-fly
Could chant a miserere, pray and cry
All through King David's psalms in wailing tone,
She would not, — for she feels not human woe,
The pain and grief of finely kneaded man,
She sucks, while dying, honey from my hand,
She has no sense of death, — *she is but bread;*
And as, to man, a hundred thousand creatures
Have been but bread, so is he bread in turn,
One day, to them; as he has acted death,
So nature in the lion, now, to him
Is death. Naught else! And is there misery here,
And is there pain, — no evil is there here!

And now, if this contents thee, worthy soul,
That in the universe no evil is,
This workmanship of pure and perfect love,
Nor in each little work, — live calmly then,
Released from dreams of terrors haunting thee!
For if a wasp should ever eat a fly
Out of pure malice, then would rightfully
The very heavens at once in ruins sink!
Our God is not: arch-crocodile, arch-tiger,
As oft thy fancy shapes the dreadful ones, —
The very crocodile is childlike, lives
As child beside the pike who, with his prey
In his teeth, swims all day with him in the pool!
And first be they, — on God *then* pronounce sentence,
And call him Ahriman and call him Devil.

V.

Rule thy Tongue at Earth's Banquet Table.

A well-spread table is a pleasant rack,
By wine and lickerish viands amiably
To draw out from the fool his secret thoughts,
And make him lie about himself and others.
Who can keep silence there, is well advanced!
A travelled one, who only hears and learns.
To all men verily the earth is just
A well-spread table and a pleasant rack;
The host, too, has withdrawn himself from sight;
Now, whatsoe'er enchants them, whatsoe'er
Oppresses them, that must they put in words,
All they have seen, heard, learned, and done must they
Set forth agreeably. If there were left

One shy one, from his heart a handsome wife
Were sure to coax out the last mystery
Till he stands empty as the bottles there,
Yet glad: that he has talked himself all out!
Who help them out in this, they are the poets,
Who for the duller ones take up the word,
As elder brothers and sisters do for children.
Who can keep silent then is far ahead!
A travelled one, who only hears and learns.

VI.

Neither Life nor Death, a Dream.

That is the greatest falsehood this world tells:
That "death is like a sleep and like a dream."
How long are dead men dead? say, till to-morrow?
If living on faintly resembled dream,
'T were better for thee, then, not to live on,
Than, all dissolved, from every virtue loosed
And decency, willingly do and bear
Things most revolting, as a dreamer must,
In the dream-fancies of his soul a wretch
A wicked man and slave of wicked men,—
Whose waking thought and deed were free and noble!
Believe thou gladly: spirit is will! believe:
The true will is to choose the purest things.
Therefore, no sleep, no dream is death; and therefore
Death also is no dream, no sleep,—it is
In this fair universe much less a thing
For spirits than sinking into element!
The true man is true spirit. To the spirit,
The one sole substantive in all the world,

All other words are only adjectives!
Good luck and bad are adjectives; birth and death;
Yea, even love is but an adjective.

VII.

Be Content with the Present.

O see, the flowering time of pinks is past,
And no more fragrance will these pinks exhale
So long as heaven shall stand. Thou thought'st, perchance,
They would for one day and all days to come
Bloom on for thee, as thy admiring eyes
Beheld them blow in such magnificence!
And then thou didst neglect them, — for a day,
Day after day, — till now they are no more,
And thou art shocked! So be thou never shocked
At human life! O see, I pray, the eyes
Of friends and loved ones blooming all for thee
So tenderly, so sweely! Think, they too
Do only in their season bloom for thee,
And in their season they, too, fade away
And die, — and thou hast only visited,
Only neglected them. Neglected them, —
The sweet ones? Ah, unique is every shape;
Each figure that has ever issued forth
From holy Nature! . . . . while so many come,
Daily, by thousands, crowding on each other,
That cheats thee with a show of permanent life
In them who with thee tread the common earth
And look to-day upon the sun with thee.
The soft light of the sun, — nay, your own light
Fades softly, — imperceptibly, — and thou

Canst no more speak a syllable to thy friend!
A word, a pressure of the hand, a look
From him were dearer now than a whole sun!
Less possible than flame from ashes now!
I only beg, then, not demand of thee:
Clearly discern the present! 't is thine own,
Thy only time, — prize it accordingly!
Let what thou hast, abide before thy eyes,
And to thy heart come homeward, — like thy blood!

VIII.

The Soul's instinctive Thirst for Purity.

I look with wonder on the human soul,
That yearns to be as pure as polished steel,
As crystal clear, — seen through and seeing through;
And every slightest stain is a sore load, —
It is not pure! and so remorse and shame,
Not only in the sun's eye, torture it, —
Before the very child, before the flowers!
It needed that, to be, and to abide,
And to be ever growing, God's own like.
The maiden conscious of no other fault, —
She weeps now merely for three summer shoots,
Just as in prison he grown sober, weeps,
Who slew one yesterday in a drunken brawl.
And that so much high soul and heavenly fire,
In all men's bosoms round about the earth,
Breathes out, burns out, in shape of fear and dread,
That makes the thought upon our human kind,
Good souls, — so sweet and precious to the good.
And even he who had no task on earth,

Would have a world beam out to make him think,
Would have a world bloom out to make him feel.
I tell thee this, thou sick, thou suffering one,
Thou aged man, thou captive! Strike *this* thought
As in thy prison thou wouldst strike a light, —
All shall be heavenly-light and cheerful there.

IX.

Reverence in the Living the future Dead.

Revere the living; stand in awe of them,
Nor from the eye of childhood wring a tear!
They may one day, and soon, before thine eyes
Become dead men, and whatsoe'er of harm
Thou, dazed by day, hast ever done to them, —
That hast thou done to poor, poor, poor dead men,
Yes, — or hast done to lofty, lofty souls,
Yea, — or hast done to God, to God himself!
But to thyself, for certain, to thyself,
And on thyself the deed comes rushing back,
And earth now with her open eye — the grave —
Stares at thee for it, — the sun's eye glares at thee,
Yea, though the dead against thee close his eye
Still as a little child whom thou wouldst kiss, —
The sight of him shall pierce and rend thy heart!
The blow thou gavest to the poor sick dog,
Will wake remorse in thee, — when he is dead,
Will wake remorse in thee, — when thou art dead.
O not from childhood's eye wring thou a tear!
Revere the living; stand in awe of them!

X.

Humanity the Roof of Man.

Why do the tiles themselves form so secure
A covering to the roof? Is 't not because
Each one so closely nestles to the rest,
And streams of rain glide off as from a shield!
But if man e'er so little parts from man,
How shall humanity securely dwell?
That is their shield, that is their house and roof,
Their host, their guest, their very One in all.

XI.

Man's Dress becomes a second Skin.

The dress of man soon grows to be his skin,
Ay, and its color eats into — his soul,
Be it or black, or purple, or blood-red.
And what, by day, he carries in his hand,
Sceptre or sword or yardstick, thereupon
He dreams by night, just as the beggar's dreams
Are off his staff. At last, even in broad day,
Man walks and talks out loudly in his dreams,
And ceases henceforth to be only man,
Unless, perchance, he ever dreams — of man.
Reflect, then: whoso has a dignity,
He mostly parts with that first dignity
Which Nature gave him, as a naked child.
Then let him think of her and hug to himself, —
What he, as fool, endowed himself withal;
For wert thou born beneath a torrid sun,
Even there thy skin would dye itself again.

XII.

The Magnetic Mountain of the Divinity.

"What mighty thing is this *divinity*,
Wherefrom and whereinto thou spin'st thyself and man,
Whose — macroscope alone discloses it?"
I know not. Yet 't is certain for all that,
And well may have, perchance, great love and woe,
Pleasure and pain and toil within itself,
If to its play of power all is not light;
Even blessedness in overmeasure, light.
Divinity means — all things possible;
'T is one, hence with itself forever one,
Steadfast, more firm than any anchor is,
And all the stars securely hold by it,
And so, then, may, I think, even little man!
And were he only iron, not a magnet,
Still he belongs — to the magnetic mountain!
'T would still attract him, — as it once repelled him
Into this life, — in angel-armor clad!

XIII.

The Spirit has and sees eternal Youth.

The morn seems far more beauteous than the day,
And yet is only young day's holy hush!
The new-born child appears a holier thing
Than the great full-grown child, whose name is man,
Who clanks in armor, marries, builds, — grows old!
Youth seems a gladder period than life,
And yet is but its inner coming forth,
Its inner growth, schooling and finishing,

Related, as the cook to the full feast,
And as the bride-bed to the perfect bride.
And therefore, when thou dost survey and judge
All things around thee, then forget thou not
Their origin, their going and outgoing.
The acorn is not meaner than the oak
As thou may'st see, when it strews acorns round,
How it bore acorns only, as its best!
That only which things leave behind them, all,
That is their touchstone, evidence and pith;
— Their worth is, like a mill-stone, proved by use.
End and beginning meet again at last,
Old age and childhood meet again at last,
Man ends, as he began, with sleep,* — and sleep
Comes out of waking and is lost therein.
And naught in heaven resembles morning red
So to the finest flame, — as evening's red,
Which tranquilly at last completes the morn;
And all things end again, as they began.

XIV.

Living in God.

For worthy living open thou the heavens!
Open the heart of God and — live in it.
Thou livest in thy house, thy house again
Lies in the country, and the country lies
On earth, and earth lies in the lap of heaven,
It swims therein, reposes in God's world, —
And God's world rests *deep in the heart of God.*
Live worthily, O man, thou liv'st in God,

* "Our little life is rounded with a sleep." — SHAKESPEARE.

God lives in thee, He lives in all the heavens,
He lives here on the earth, lives in thy land,
He lives within thy house, He lives in thee!
For worthy living open thou the heavens!
Open the heart of God, and live in Him!

XV.

Reason the Guide, the Way, and the Goal.

What man is he, who, journeying by night,
Will throw his guide into the ditch, put out
His torch, and think he now can better tread
The easy way that leads him to his home?
That man is *man*, who scorns experience
Nor follows reason's light, the lamp of life.
That man wants reason who spurns reason's eyes.
She shows the way, urges him on therein;
Reason, — that *is* life's road; — as Plato once,
Kind to a band of strangers, journeying
With him, unrecognized by them, to see
Plato in Athens, — led them to himself!
Do all thou needest to become a man;
Yet that is small! for man 's a simple thing;
Yet that is glorious! for man is much,
Is much already, — long ago was most;
The simple things are great, — so is man's soul!
Simple and beautiful, one with itself;
Quick-acting, even in all the small unrest,
That comes to it in the train of little things,
Which only man, in simple wholeness clear,
Has to take thought of and take knowledge of,
To see and say and do, — upon the earth.

Thou never wilt be happy yet, O man,
Till thou shalt cease to dissipate thyself
Capriciously, till thou shalt gather up
The powers of thy body and thy soul!
Till thou art simple and harmonious,
Simple in thought and feeling, love and life:
Simplicity itself with one whole heart.
Union, simplification, melting down
Of good things, which are hardly separate goods,
That is humanity's task and every man's,
Renunciation of what sunders men,
And solidarity, — a mighty power
In each one! and in all! what mighty power
And greatness! Inner peace! Tranquillity!
The tranquil man alone does rightly all
That must be done! the right! *The tranquil man*
Alone has little labor, — but much reason.
Reason 's the road, then, to tranquillity!

XVI.

On giving Advice.

Give no one "good advice." Take good advice
From no one. He subjects his soul to thee, —
And thou thy wish to him; you bind each other
Instead of freeing. Goodness must be free.
No man can mount up by another's stairs:
Many as are the houses, so the steps.
Who gives advice forces his steps on thee,
Nay, worse than that: his wisdom, yea, his life!
Advise and be advised to what is good!
The word is deep: Take counsel to do good!

Give thou the tune, and take it, from the sound
Of Heaven's music, strike upon that bell;
Therein unfolds itself the proper soul,
Like to a rose beneath the dew of heaven,
And out of the original fulness comes,
Original and beautiful and thine: —
The free deed, offspring fair of the free breast.
Counsel to good alone ne'er errs nor leaves
Remorse; wilt thou advise the rose to bloom, —
Then canst thou find, and God himself could find,
In this extreme stress and emergency
No better counsel and no surer way,
Than just to let it have the sun's warm light,
To give it water, and keep far away
The caterpillar from the tender leaf.
But man, — as if he were a marble block,
Thou wilt regard, rolling him to the place,
That seems to thee to suit the marble block.
Not more opaque the marble block itself,
Than a man's breast to thee and thine to him.

XVII.

Knowledge after Death.

When thou art one day dead and now art borne
Out of thy house, out of thy body borne,
Borne forth from out the friendly throng of men,
And, — and thou surely still shalt know the lot
Of loved ones left behind thee on the earth, —
Shalt thou not know the earth then? know a star?
Nay, and have power to know each star in heaven?
Shalt thou not know mankind, then, and its fate?
And who then must thou be, whom men call dead?

XVIII.

Bear with Thyself.

Remember not thy faults with bitterness,
Vengeful against thyself; 't were punishing
One who then was not yet, — thy better self!
Thou wilt chastise thyself, *that* proves thee better;
To-day thou liv'st, they are no more *thy* faults.
Remember not thy faults with pleasure, — then
They are, then thou repeatest them to-day.
Ungodly is remorse, that petrifies!
That thrusts thee down among the spirits of hell!
For in thee, dwelling in sweet secrecy
And blissful purity forevermore,
A spirit lives in holy silentness,
Far nobler, purer than will ever was,
That spirit is man. As such a spirit man
Should feel himself! Such ever should he be!
Thou should'st be man again and yet again,
After each night, as after each misstep,
After each day, as after each good deed.
That thou hast erred, should teach thee this one thing:
Thou may'st to-day, too, err in other things.
Then think not: how shall I to-morrow feel?
What good to-morrow do? What wrong commit?
The hour that cometh brings to man his task;
The foeman brings to the brave man his might;
Let only the next step be always right!
The next deed only always be well done!
Only remember always to do good,
Then in a godlike way thou shunnest evil.

XIX.

Grieve for Him who wrongs Thee.

Thou good soul, thou that sheddest bitterest tears
Over a foul wrong done thee by a friend,
Loved fondly, be thou tranquil! for thyself
Be glad! though, ah, for the beloved one not, —
Misfortune has o'ertaken thee! Another's
Misfortune! Yea, his blindness! his delusion!
So think, and now thy deepest grief is gone,
Is swiftly turned to courage and glad zeal
Not for thy cure, — no, his, the sufferer's,
Who has, alas! done thee such grievous wrong,
And, if he knew it, would so grieve for it!
And now thou nobly stiflest thine own grief, —
— Light earthly sorrow, conquered easily, —
Thou 'rt kind to him, and lo! he weeps and sobs. —
Is this the bad the world contains, O man,
Then will I never ask a better good!

XX.

True Virtue not Mercenary.

If for good works thou askest a reward,
Then sink'st thou to a servant. Be the master,
Reward the good, acknowledge it, in silence.
"The honest servant, who says naught, asks much."
Still, he repays most nobly, who in silence
Hides the good deed. Reward not then thyself, —
Say, haply there is one thou serv'st with joy,
'T will comfort much thy neighbor, comfort much

The poor to know: where to find help in need.
Does not one owe thee thanks whom thou hast served?
Dost thou not owe him thanks, that thou couldst serve
him?
Say, is the crop a debtor to the clouds
That rain upon it? Is the farmer, then,
The debtor? How then shall he pay his debt?
The harvest needs the rain; the farmer needs
The bread to live by: does it call for thanks
That some one is just saved from perishing?
And that he prospers and the giver too?
"In Heaven is no account-book, nor on earth,
Wherein is registered what each one owes,
Throughout the Universe, to all and each:
Neither how much the lily owes the dew,
Nor what the bee must pay the clover-bloom,
Nor what the clover owes the husbandman,
Nor what 's the debt the cluster owes the vine,
Nor how much the vine-dresser owes the vine,
Nor what the stork, as debtor to his wife,
Owes for his children and what she owes him,
Nor what the wide world over, man owes man!"
Only the blind would open such a book
Of reckoning with his very mother's sons,
With his own children, yea, his very father!
Lo, no one of the creatures will be paid
For its own proper work; the spider not
For wages spins, nor sings the lark her song.
As blooming to the tree, and to the dew
Its nightly fall, so let well-doing be
To thee, dear man! For wilt thou, then, be worse
Than yonder field, which for its crop of wheat
Desires no other thanks than, — a new crop?

Or than the Sun, who for his day demands
No other favor than — to rise again,
And does arise again — unconsciously?
O what pure, holy magnanimity
In Nature! What a blest activity,
Endless and tireless, through the Universe, —
Where one to another, and the whole to all
Pours out help, fellowship, yea, all its power
And love, and even its own fair being's joy,
With hearty faith, fulness, and still content,
In payment of an old, enormous debt,
Yet without even thinking once withal
Whether a particle is paid thereby, —
Until thy soul sinks at the sight with shame!
O be thou not ashamed! — Do thou the like! —
Know not, O man, even that thou doest *good;*
For sooner do thou evil *consciously!*
That shows thee noble! Whoso knows and thinks;
"Now I do good!" knows naught of God, nor yet
Of natures godlike in their purity;
Be still and know God lives in thee. Be good!
Then only do, what 't is thy nature to,
Just as it is the cloud's to scatter rain,
Just as it is the sun's to shine down warm;
The good man's doing is simply doing good.
So sleep does good to weary ones; and lo,
The sleeper knows it not! — nor yet does *sleep*
Know what it does! — be thou like sleep, O man.

XXI.

The Tranquillity of living God's Life.

Good soul, canst thou not suffer, innocent, —
Thou canst do nothing! canst not even breathe,
Be young, old, gray. — "But how shall that be learned?"
First think, for ten years' space: I 'm in the wrong:
Then wilt thou see, how oft thou truly art!
Each creature's proper being gladly own,
The Universe's, even to the finger-tips
Of every child! even to the tips of leaves,
Not to say, even to every human soul;
Then giv'st thou each its rights and tak'st thine own
By doing right, at peace within, — with all:
Not, to bear calmly and submissively
Each pain and hardship, is thy happiness!
'T is not the power to bear that makes thee happy:
Not patience and endurance make man good;
No, thou art truly happy that each pain
And every hardship is a *part of life*
For thee, and in itself a mighty boon:
It is to thee a pure, rich, noble stuff,
Not merely, as through crystal, to behold
The fair world through, and mourn it and thyself;
No, see it in its image *there!* This pain,
Itself is, like a rose, the work of God,
A masterpiece of the great Universe,
Of beauty full, and fragrance, for thy soul.
I know no pain, no hardship, that is not
A joy to man, a life, ay, sweetest life, —
When it gleams through him that God lives his life
And he lives God's; that all is seen and lived

Gladly, divinely, by the spirit of God,
Yea, that by Him all was divinely made,
That all 's divinely like which comes from God.
Naught hinders, nay, within thee and around
All things admonish thee, to be like God,
In cloudless contemplation and good will.
Himself within thee summons thee to know Him!
If He has power equal to his great house,
And thou hast power to fill thine only, that
Is a relation, but no difference;
God is not different, not distinct from man;
They are allied together, are both one;
Are like each other as thousand eyes and one,
Like as this light here of thy little lamp
Is to the light of yonder farthest star!
Thou mayest live as tranquilly as God,
Who watches thee, and does it silently:
Thou mayest die as tranquilly as God,
Who 's with thee then, and bears it silently.

XXII.

Accept all God's Creatures as they are.

Pacing the garden grounds, thou dost not wish
Thy almond-tree might be a cherry-tree,
The rose a jessamine, the vine transformed
Into an ivy-plant, the mignonette
To grass, — the grass in turn to mignonette.
Thou art, perforce, more modest; dost refrain
From using magic, for thou hast it not;
Thou art content with each thing as it is,
Thou givest each the care befitting it,

Hopest to see it blossom, waitest for
Its fruit, and when it comes, enjoyest it,
Each in its several way refreshing thee.
The lion in the woods thou would'st not change,
Nor make the wolf a fox, the stag a hare;
Nor make the carp that swims the sea an eel,
For he, too, comes what time thou wishest him.
Thou art, perforce, more modest, dost refrain
From using magic, for thou hast it not.
Only around thee in the human race
Wilt thou work miracles and first transform
Thy neighbor, so as then to deal with him,—
To deal with him, the utmost thou canst do!
To do without him,—that were loss and shame!
The art of intercourse is not to shape
Thy fellow-men anew to suit thy mind,
Thy wishes, oftentimes thy very whims.
That never amateur will wish to do,
Even if he could; his only pleasure is
To show in *life* his artist's-taste and art,
Intelligence,—and love, too,—lovingly;
Just as with pictures and with statuary,
He for his own advantage wisely shuns
To change the light their master placed them in.
"God is a Master,"—think thou tranquilly.
Then let all pass for good, just as they are,
Else hast thou foes in them and not allies;
Rejoice in what is good of them; hold up
This good upon the swift stream of the day
And of all days, fulfil the words they speak,
Just as a friend fulfils a drunken man's:
Lay underneath their works a noble will;
Hold converse with thy old familiar friend,

As if Saint John came for a little while
To visit thee; speak with the traveller
As an old friend whom thou wilt see no more, —
So shalt thou shun, methinks, hard words and blows!
Yet car'st thou not for hate and spite of men,
And holdest thou this art, perchance, as cheap?
The art of life is, sure, the highest art;
Thou liv'st not, if thou canst not live with others;
Thou liv'st not, if they cannot live with thee;
Ye live not, save with reason and with love,
And friendship is there none, without this art;
Nor yet society, nor marriage, even,
No mother's home, no mother land, no peace,
Only deception and half war, — as reigns
Between the beasts and their protector, — man!

XXIII.

Seek Goodness not Goods.

Tell me: is man the creature of an hour?
A short, bright, pleasing hour? Is man no more
Than just a splendid firework of life,
That shoots up, smokes, and vanishes in night,
In sorrow's and starvation's bitter pangs?
Nay, is he good for naught but to do good?
Most men strive only, all the days of youth,
For mere bright-blazing, short-lived rapture, found
In intercourse with men and things. Behold
Their pains, their shifts, their penances and griefs!
A real good must last thee all thy life,
Always remain the same and show the same,
Beheld at evening, morning, late in age,

Contemplated in sorrow and in joy.
And shall I name to thee what are thy goods?
I say, then: every good! I leave out none:
Gained in its proper season and enjoyed
With a clear eye upon the whole of life;
No one, one thing whatever, man can do,
Is sin, that to the future can be linked,
And to the future is linked honestly,
So that he feels himself melted and blent
In with his work and with his act, and lives
Therewith in gladness and security.
He rightly does, who treasures up life's goods,
Who thereby becomes He, a proper man.
Not so, who spends himself upon the goods,
Alas! he ne'er shall find himself again,
Never possess those goods, nor yet himself.
For only they possess, who rightly earn.

XXIV.

A pure Youth, — a happy Manhood.

If thou hast dazzled, as a child, thine eyes,
Thou 'st robbed thyself already of the joy
Of seeing wife, child, grandchild, of thine own.
If thou hast loved this maiden here, if thou,
As with a wedded wife, hast lived with her,
And then hast taken another to thy wife,
Thou hast beforehand broke thy marriage vows,
And faithless to thyself, hast robbed thyself
Beforehand of the one, pure sentiment,
The holy, cleanly one of human life, —
The joy of mingling with a whole, full soul

In all the mother's and the children's joy,
Never disturbed by old, dishonest thoughts,
That in life's holy feast will often rise
To haunt thy soul like an old creditor,
Who, warning thee of debts thou hast not paid,
And never canst pay, still tormenteth thee
And never will let go his hold of thee.
Then from the tree of life, O strike not off
The very buds, like a wild, idle boy;
Thou strikest off the blossoms and the fruits;
Nor ever sin thou in advance, O man,
Against the child, against the grain of seed;
Thou tramplest on the harvest, on the man!
Do not the tempting thing, the pleasant thing,
The thing thou lov'st, — not the right thing itself,
At a false hour, for what thou doest so,
Becomes a crime against futurity;
So dost thou pawn, yea, sell away from thee
The very heaven for a few empty nuts.
The genuine right is but the future's seed,
A flower that blooms to deck the wreath of life,
Which a pure soul, perennially glad,
In every coming, present hour shall pluck
To set it in the place it fitly fills.
But flowers that have no stalks, — and such are sins, —
These, whoso plucks them, scatters to the winds.

XXV.

Woman the Judge and Mirror of the Times.

That fishes all are dumb, provokes thee not?
Nor art thou vexed, whatever they suppress!

If women talk, — that is their nature too,
And gladly hear whatever they reveal.
Women reveal, no doubt, all that they are, —
'T is the great revelation of mankind.
Not, how they bear with patience what they must,
No, but what good is everywhere to be.
History itself is silent, — women hold
The great assize, a daily, oral one,
Held before God, in house and yard and land;
The right, pronounced, is right once recognized,
It is fulfilled. Right is the heart of souls.
Women, then, curious about everything,
Specially called to search out everything,
— Because their pent-up life requires it, —
They, knowing all things, summon from the depths
Of man's dark bosom to the light of day
Things just and unjust, evil things and good,
And judge inexorably all mankind,
All of the male kind, kings and queens they judge,
The laws, the very harvest and the year.
Each lamb, each apple in the gathering time,
And hen and egg and feather, all are judged,
Each new-born child, the coffin of the dead,
The dead himself and even death itself,
And earth and life. Inexorably, too,
They judge themselves, — but only one another;
That each may thus be good. For all the joy
And weal of human folk on women hangs.
And even to God 't is gain, that they are wise.
But woman, being silent, does great wrong.
And no one judges better than a wife,
She of the tenderest feelings, whose fine scales
A grain of dust shall move; whose sensitive

And shrinking heart is with light deeds weighed down
As with a load, and guesses and adjusts
All with a motherly presentiment
Of holy Nature's laws and ways divine.
For Nature's very daughters women are,
The mother who has sent them in her stead
To rule and manage in the human house:
None has more ground than woman has, to judge,
To loose and bind. For all that heroes do
On battle-fields, whatever conquerors
Leave undisturbed in peace, whatever seed
Men sow in council, city, land, and field,
What even the smallest boy is set to do,
That in the house, and by the silent hearth,
Women must expiate, if 't was ill done,
Burn up with inward fire, just as the flame
Consumes the wax, from which the torch was rolled.
So burn they, shining with the wax of life;
And in a woman's bright and cheerful face
Thou readest that good times are in the land!
Good husband and good children in the house;
Abundance in the fields; hope of good years,
And industry! no sick folk anywhere!
No naked child! no poor that pine for food!
The dial-plate shows only sunny hours,
But woman's face shows the whole horoscope,
And that not of the outward heavens alone,
But the position, course, and flight of spirits,
The inner one, — their world, — the moral sky. —
One wish, the crown of wishes, then were mine:
"Might every female countenance on earth,
To the last hovel — be a cheerful one:
To all things might her lips but whisper: Yes!"
Then were the golden age! Be that thy sign.

XXVI.

Man's Mind must be his Kingdom.

The highest goods thou must — insure thyself, —
Thou must beget them daily, momently,
From thee as father they must all proceed :
Love, goodness, gladness, happiness, and health ;
Yea, and the word holds good of beauty, too,
And freedom, of all goods foundation-stone.
What thou *art* not, that none can give to thee!
And whatsoe'er thou *art*, all *that* thou *hast*,
Of that none will, none can deprive thee, none !
So wilt thou oft hear foolish men crave much, —
When the brave word has long been teaching them :
"Be just and fear not"; that is liberty.
But now these hard, hard questions ask thyself:
Art thou, then, well in body and in soul ?
Art thou so full of love ? Art thou so good ?
Art thou so fair to look on, and so free,
That thy good things are more than wish and want,
Mere fear of others and the highest fear,
Fear of thyself ! Fear of the God in thee :
Purely and greatly to be all things great !
And live with manly vigor through and through !
That task still frightens hearts that hug the day.
Men speak great words and yet live petty lives,
Content with little, — even as children are
Who love to give their dolls high-sounding names,
And keep the very highest for themselves,
Projecting true life on a distant scale.
O Lord, when thou commandest, there they stand :
The spring-time, man, and through him, all good things !

Whoso owns no command, — he is a slave,
He who commands himself alone is free.

XXVII.

Earth preaches Generosity to Man.

Each forces us to give, magnanimously!
What treasures, precious and irrevocable,
We needs must lavish carelessly, let go,
As if so many hairs from a child's head,
Or so much dust blown from a traveller's cloak;
And man will laugh and call his neighbor fool,
If he laments for years and days and hours,
For youth and spring, not for the flowers, O no,
But only for the autumn's withered leaves.
For here he must needs be so generous,
As he is farther on! Possesses more!
But now on all that earth takes not from him,
That from which one day she takes *him* away,
Upon his clod of earth, on which he dwells,
Upon the trees that round his garden stand,
The gold he clutches and the very bread
Upon his table, on his old worn spade, —
On these his heart is set! He watches these
With jealous, grasping, avaricious eyes,
Because he thinks: Earth did not give me these,
No; these I gave myself! These mean to me
My skin and hair, hand, strength, and sun and moon,
These cost me all my thinking and my heart, —
These are the little fruits of the great mess!
So speaks *he* truth, — so must the miser speak;
So speak'st *thou* false, — man must no miser be,
Earth bids us calmly be magnanimous.

XXVIII.

The Man who in gaining the World loses Himself.

He who in battling for the goods of life,
Singes a hair of 's head, contracts a mote
In 's eye, a stain upon his soul, perchance
Scares health away from him, — the drawer-up
Of gladness out of the long stream of life, —
Is like the child who, having safely borne
A basket full of pearls o'er hollow ground
Through woods, where robbers, storms, and lightnings lurked, —
Now loses them, in eager quest of flowers ;
Is like the man, who set to steer a ship,
Freighted with jewels, to a distant port,
Day after day, for an amusement, bores
Through the ship's bottom, and one sunny day
With ship and treasure suddenly goes down.

XXIX.

Clearness of Perception brings Content.

'T is true thy spirit lives a wakeful life,
And with clear, steadfast eye looks down on all
The great eternal powers, relations, works
Which silently encompass thee as part,
Thyself, of Nature's elemental powers,
And make thy life the image of a vale,
Shut in by old, mysterious, quiet rocks ;
And, as if watching clouds, thou givest heed
To what comes up to thee from their dark lap ;

Thou hearest in thy breast the spirit's voice,
Thou hearkenest to fulfil its lightest whisper
— For in low tones the heavenly ones do speak, —
Thou steppest not aside through heedlessness ;
For just where human weakness needs a guide,
These troops of watchful genii fly to thee
And for a moment fling a gleam of light
Upon thy path. And so thou passest by.
Scarce anything can meet thee unforeseen ;
Against the ill that threatens from afar,
Or passes harmless by, thou takest thought
For help, prevention, yea, and even cure ;
If it surprise thee, then alarm — makes bold.
Nor looking into life, around on men,
Does aught in human lot seem strange to thee,
Thou tremblest not at parting, sickness, death ;
Calmly thou seest how the gods hold sway !
Yea, if the earth should yawn before thy feet,
And vomit lightning, thunder, fire, and smoke,
Quickly would that strong word come to thy aid :
"This, too, have men already suffered once,
And stood it out, — long have they been at rest,
And thou thyself hast looked upon their place."
To win, to find, to meet, and to possess,
Delights thee in the whirl of mortal life,
For lo ! they win, they find now heavenly things :
This one a bride ! That mother there a child !
A son, a wanderer comes back home again
To his old father ! Spare this human trait :
The housewife's batch of bread has turned out well !
The flax has prospered ! The old orchard-tree
Will bear once more whole baskets full of fruit !
The children are for winter warmly clad,

The first wee tooth shines in the infant's mouth!
Even such small joys thy heart can understand,
And privily thou seekest some dark nook,
And weepest a short moment, with dry eyes.
So liv'st thou glad for men and for thyself.
And yet, and yet, and yet thou still art foolish,
Unreasonable, unwise, unjust, and hard:
Impatiently thou chidest — the impatience
Of men and women, parents and their children!
Punishest wrath with wrath! Thou seekest peace
Through force, through war! not in the sure mild way.
Then go and learn once more the lore of life!
Thou 'st learned it ill! vainly! disgracefully!
Thou art not yet so good as the blind dog
Who barks when he has listened earnestly,
And ceases, when he knows the house-friend's step,
The children's; and his blind eyes sparkle then,
To see their faces, as he heard their feet!

XXX.

Sincerity.

Sincerity is honesty in speech.
The soul is truthful, that is full of truth,
And from the heart's abundance the mouth speaks.*
Pass not the very dog like a dumb man;
The lamb is glad, too, when thou greetest him,
And even the bird, so overjoyed is he
With human greeting, that he seems like one
Intoxicated, flying from his trees

* In German, *Redlichkeit* and *Reden* are related. The verbal turn could not be retained in English. — Tr.

This way and that, in utter ecstasy,
Yet as not knowing what to make of it!
If thou say'st nothing to the erring one, —
If thou say'st nothing to the suffering one, —
Utterest no warning to the foolish one, —
Art thou sincere? If as thou passest by,
Thou showest not the children how their game
Was fraudulently played, art thou sincere?
Thou seem'st a dumb man and thou art a dunce,
Art a barbarian, one whom pride condemns
To wear a painful padlock on his lips,
As if the tongue should then no more offend;
It is unlovingness offends, not speech,
A well-meant word even the old man hears,
The man of old experience, graciously.
And though thou knowest e'er so little, still
Thou knowest in this case, what to make of it!
The lot of each man is a thing divine!
The word of man unveils a heaven to sight
Whereof earth knows not, nor the very sun!
And every man in his own matter speaks
From the clear heart-flow unsurpassably,
His own word each one utters perfectly;
Even where he stammers, where he is confused,
He shows the trulier his beating heart!
Then speak! Be open as a fountain is,
To which the birds at pleasure come and drink!
Be each a modest priest and teacher, friend
And kinsman of our fair humanity.
Naught more confusing, yea, more criminal,
No one thing in the affairs of human kind,
Than haste and overhurrying of their life, —
As if this life were not a most high feast, —

As if each day were not a special feast, —
And every hour the acme of the feast:
Worthy of dignity, repose, and grace,
— Which change e'en things of naught to things of weight, —
And here no change is needed, only sense.
But thou, dismiss not dryly, coldly thou
The holy hours! O dismiss not man
With mocking coldness! Go to walk with each
Even at the moment which is granted him,
Give thyself to him unreservedly,
Hide, hold back naught from him, — he is a man,
Lend him a docile ear, — thou art a man, —
Thou need'st not be his friend, nor he thy friend, —
Be thou but man to him, and he to thee,
So shall each hour become to thee a joy
Of life, a sweet refreshment to thy soul,
A recreation and a wisdom's-fount.
Know every man, and let each man know thee, —
And therefore — speak! O speak! speech melts the breast,
Inspires, — and inspiration worketh love, —
Then speak! Speech only shows sincerity!

XXXI.

The Yearning to see our Dead ones again.

The sun shines down so sweetly through the vale,
That sleeps in autumn's dreamy quietness,
The leafless trees stand there so quietly,
The clouds above are quiet. Children play,
Women are going with baskets to the woods,

And the world seems an old acquaintance now,
Familiar, — as the hand is to the side,
As eye and body, white cloud and blue heaven, —
The bells are humming faintly in the air!
Yonder a train of men bear forth one dead, —
Earth-spirits cry from trumpet throats of brass,
And with a shriek the picture rend in twain, —
Like heavy mist the dirge falls on the vale!*
Like night! Or comet's glare across the night.
This is no more the old accustomed earth,
These are no more the same familiar men
Who sing! These are no clouds poised overhead, —
This is the house of the magician, death,
Wide open, full of naked miracles,
Which living men look on with shuddering!
This is the open clock of the universe,
From which the beings strike out as the hours!
This is the laid-out body of the Lord,
With its death-wound forever bare to sight! . . . .
And now, soft-stealing toward the open grave,
On which the same old sun shines brightly in,
As if one took the bridal-chamber lamp
And hung it in a dismal cavern's gloom, —
A voice of sorrow murmurs in my ear:
"Might I but see the dead one yet once more!"
And startled by that word, I turn and ask:
Dear soul, I pray, *which* dead one dost thou mean?
The dead that slumbers in the coffin here?
Then let them lift for thee the coffin-lid,
And look thou, then, upon the dead one there!
"No — no! Not him. I covered him myself."

* See Mrs. Hemans's translation of Fouqué's dirge for the Queen of Prussia. — Tr.

What then? The weary, feeble, blind old man
In his last sinking years, him wilt thou see?
"No, nor yet him! I closed his aged eyes!"
Wilt thou, then, see the dead as man and father,
His children round him in his happy home?
"Him neither; for I am myself his son,
His friendly form stands clear before my sight."
As bridegroom happy, wilt thou see him then?
As youth in foreign countries,—and as child?
"All *that* he oft has told us lovingly,
And I am said to be his very image,
And this my boy, of what he was as child!"
Say in what form then wouldst thou have him come!
The whole of him: all that he was and did,—
So wilt thou have him; he shall live again
Or he shall simply live, though without thee
If he is only happy! Thou lov'st him so.
I say to thee: I am a conjurer,
And if thou mak'st a definite demand
How thou wilt have me bring thee back the dead,
I will prepare myself; then come to me,
And I assure thee it shall be fulfilled.—
Meanwhile the dead was silently interred
And each withdrew himself "for fitting thought—"
When he should once have overcome his grief.

Since then a holy year has now passed by,
And, smiling, I await his coming back!

THE LAYMAN'S BREVIARY.

NOVEMBER.

16

NOVEMBER.

I. Treat Man according to his Needs, not his Deserts.
II. Father and Child needful to each other's Manhood.
III. Nature hurries not to End her Work.
IV. Humanity on its great Voyage.
V. Live a wakeful, not a dreamy Life.
VI. Mother Nature's Autumn and the human Mother's.
VII. Farewell to the immortal Angels of Summer.
VIII. Childhood charms down even God.
IX. Contentment lies in a few representative Things.
X. The Riches of the Poor in Spirit.
XI. The immortal little People.
XII. Each secure in the great Unity of Being.
XIII. God is All in All.
XIV. Magnify thy Being as Man.
XV. Live and love as God.
XVI. Not a free Will but a good Will Man wants.
XVII. Power is Will and Will is Power.
XVIII. God disposes better than Man proposes.
XIX. Be not a Flaw-Finder in the Universe of Beauty.
XX. Be Good and so do Good.
XXI. Prayer the Transfiguration of Man.
XXII. Friendship and Philanthropy.
XXIII. Make Account of Spirit, not Person.
XXIV. Contemplation of our loved Ones asleep.
XXV. Man hugs his selfish Wishes in Death.
XXVI. Rest even in this fleeting Life.
XXVII. What is Death?
XXVIII. What can Man give God?
XXIX. Love abideth forever.
XXX. The great future Autumn of the Heavens.

NOVEMBER.

I.

Treat Man according to his Needs, not his Deserts.

O him whom men, fate, or the elements
Rob of his peace, thou lendest cheerful aid,
For thou hast seen how such things come about,
And robbers, sickness, lightning, — all are plain.
But whoso through unreason, violence,
Perverseness, awkwardness, an evil mind,
Spoils his own peace, repels thy heart from him,
Because thou seest not through the potent cause,
Because thou hatest it, thou wilt not take
Whate'er is done, and is, as an event
Of the interior world, the former world.
But who now is the more unhappy man,
And therefore the more pitiable too:
He who, through care, good sense, and honesty,
Forethought and human help, will soon rebuild
His house, his field, and his prosperity, —
Or he who, radically miserable
Through a bad mind, the web of his old days
Tangled and snarled, renounces human help.
Respect then the soul's blight, thou happy one,
And help the foolish as thou wouldst a child!
And help the bad, for none more poor than they,

Help! else art thou still worse, art not a man;
And whoso once had ample goods and now
Begs, — give to him, — for he has need of thee.
For to the man to whom unstintingly
God gives his own good spirit, wouldst thou then
Not give a morsel of the bread of God?
Man carves out virtue of far other wood.
O might the helping word be given to all
Who by whole tribes suffer for darkened souls,
Entangled in the sad snare of old time!

II.

Father and Child needful to each other's Manhood.

"A proper father let me be and grow,
In seeing thee, dear child, grow up to be
A proper man! without thee I cannot
Be such; nor canst thou be one without me."
So says the great Creator to the world,
So says a ruler rightly to his people,
So says a people rightly to its prince,
So says a father rightly to his son.

III.

Nature hurries not to end her Work.

Be not impatient! All will come to be,
That yearns toward being in thy teeming breast
And in men's hearts! All yet will ripen, all!
And unexpectedly, prepared by heaven,
As after a long winter, it will lie

Before thee, as upon thy table lies
The flowering stalk, or full-grown ear of grain,
Which Nature with enormous energies
Drew from the bosom of the universe;
A heavier treasure, far, more exquisite,
More slowly and laboriously wrought,—
Thousands of years secretly spent on it,—
Than by the miner is the finished gold,
Which, dug from rocky shafts not far to reach,
Where in stiff veins of ore the metal lay,—
Now shines before thee in the clear-cut coin.
O what innumerable glorious stars
Shall yet arise! What wilderness of suns!
What hosts of souls teeming with energies
Shall yet draw nigh, go down, and still create!
—And shall accomplish mighty wonders here!—
The welkin could not hold the mass of flowers,
The magic mountain of the future flowers,
That shall one day be scattered down like rain
Only on this earth's valleys! Verily,
The hosts of birds, of larks and nightingales,
The swarms of sweet and gracious singers all,
That yet shall flutter down as from the blue
Of the deep heavens above and warble here,—
Would darken all the air like broad-winged clouds!
Shut up within the boundless universe,
They still approach, but only secretly,—
Yet all shall one day be, yea, truly all!
—As all who ever lived and labored here,
As all of us, us who now work here, live.—
O what impatience well might seize upon
The spirit of the universe! And yet
How still he bides, in tranquil secrecy.

The well-springs only trickle softly forth,
The cloud falls earthward only drop by drop,
The mountains wear down only grain by grain, —
The battle of the Gods, the year's great fight,
He ends, ere sundown, in the afternoon.
He fills with seeds the heads of all the flowers,
But for the coming spring; they fall asleep
Like little old men, and their silver hair
The night wind snatches from them as in dream!
And in the late and lovely autumn days
He only forms on fruit-disburdened trees
The new, brown buds that swell in secrecy,
And checks their haste with cool of moonlit nights,
And wraps them round with veils of silver mist,
Like little children whom a mother's care
Screens from the light, that they may still sleep on.
Then moderate impatience! In its guise
Discern the noble yearning to fulfil
With the presentiment of perfect life
The task the master gives thee for to-day!

IV.

Humanity on its great Voyage.

Each one has still as far to go, as once
Columbus had, to reach America.
Only to-day the company on board
Demand not islands of the mariners,
Taverns upon the sea, and a short way, —
Only good passage in well-furnished ship,
And not a blockhead, nor still, stealthy foe,
For steersman. Burdens unavoidable

And hardships, each one gladly bears as means,
Yea, furtherers of his voyage to success.
Thus is the clear conviction of mankind:
That a long-cherished and deep-seated wish
Was a fine error, through a thousand fights
Only to be fulfilled conditionally—
The evidence: that many a fancied ill,
Explained, is parcel of their better life;
This, too, is an unutterable gain
To men, for peace and comfort, joy and luck:
With mind serene, with powers made strong in one,
To win by glorious conquest what abides
Like stars, when northern lights fade silently:
Freedom, to be, in soul and body, man!

V.

Live a wakeful, not a dreamy Life.

The fancy has its own peculiar woes,
From which reality protects us not.
When in our dreams we walk on piercing thorns,
It helps us nothing: that we sleep in shoes!
And when thou walk'st on roses in thy dreams,
Thou heedest not the snake approaching thee.
Only the waking ones can God release
From the night-horror of old, heavy dreams;
How mankind wrestles to be wide awake!
The genuine day is worth thy living in;
Truth is the most divine of poems, full
Of magic, depth, pomp, beauty, as none else.
Be always wakeful, then! Let neither woe
Oppress, nor joy beguile thee, into sleep!

For the pure sense of the true, great, whole life
More precious is than even thy greatest luck.

VI.

Mother Nature's Autumn and the human Mother's.

Like to a mother, who has just let go,
New-married, her last daughter from the house,
And for the first time since *her* wedding day,
Long years ago, sits down to rest again,
At last, at last, her life's work being done, —
So now in Autumn mother Nature takes
Rest from the labors of so great a work.
Thousands of little daughters, tender flowers,
She also has arrayed successively
In that fair raiment made for life-long wear
Each morning, and before they went to sleep
At night, has washed with dew each lovely face,
When they grew up, has richly furnished forth,
In radiant nights, beneath a silvery moon,
All silently for each a nuptial hour,
Then taken part in all the children's work;
Transformed the blossom-tree into a fruit-tree,
Encircled it with grandchildren — as fruits;
Let the snake hatch her eggs out in the sun
Till she could lead her children by herself,
Woven her year's dress for her, gay and new;
Painted the butterfly with blossom-dust,
Filled the vine-berry's cellar full of musk,
Traced the bean's delicate tints in its still house,
Forgotten on the weevil not a spot,
Nor smallest stroke on the dumb little fish.

And all her creatures bright and glad as ever!
In air and sea, in woodland and in field,
No one has asked, and each one has received!
O joy of the Great Mother of us all!
And now *to enter into her glad soul,*
Into her love's gracefully prospered work,
What other rapture is there passing that?
How shrinks to nothing what her great child, man,
Has done in all the circle of the earth;
For though unique, yet is he but *one* child—
Of the blest mother of whole myriads.
However many children Nature has,
Yet none, not even man, has other work
Than to behold her work, and being it,
Sweetly to search it out,—*that* all have done!
They were! And full of bliss they passed away;
And over all and after all still sits
The youthful mother unexhausted there.
But she, the human mother, whose last child
And youngest I have taken to be my wife,
Sits lonely there, looks after us and weeps,
She looks upon her weary, worn old hands,
And even while she looks, her form is changed!
She 's gone; she sitteth in the house of age,
Above her the eternal blue of heaven;
She bends down in her hand admiringly
The fruit-tree's leafless twig that glistens there
Full of brown buds, that shall, another spring,
Bloom and bear fruit. But she! alas, no more!
"Man is a bud upon the tree of life":
She, softly weeping, softly smiling, thinks.
Meanwhile around her swarm the year's late gnats,
Quick, quick! they seem to say, we yet will live!

She sits by flowers,—quick, quick, ere winter comes,
Will they, too, celebrate late nuptial rites,
And the full moon goes up in majesty,
To shine as lamp in Autumn's lonely hall.
Only the stream still murmurs as it did
In the old legend childhood held for true,
And clouds sail by as in the old legend, too.
Yon moon means nothing any more to her,
The autumn wind that finds no more a crop,
Scarcely a leaf, plays idly with her hair.
The calm is heavy to her busy heart—
She rises now, she sees a cluster yet
On the vine-trellis, feels a silent joy,
Looks round in silence on the heavens once more—
And on the earth—and now goes slowly back
With head bowed down, home to the empty house.

. . . . .

Such is the fate of man,—the mother's, too!

VII.

Farewell to the immortal Angels of Summer.

So then, farewell, ye blessed ones! farewell,
Ye who enlivened, filled, adorned this house,
Were blest, and made all round you blest, with love
And beauty, laden full with primal power,
Ye hosts, that with the autumn pass away!
'T is I that part—not you; for I remain,
Remain alone, and you go off in troops,
A godlike march of triumph home to God;
The flames returning to the ancient fire.
Ye did not make the Spring, ye *were* the Spring,

Yourselves! 'T was you, at last, that made the summer
True summer, the autumn yore; filled out
The holy time. Ye go now, and 't is filled
And sweetly filled, in myriads of hearts
That will retain fond memory of you all,
So long as they have memory of the earth
And of themselves, — so long as they are minds.
For therefore was the feast divine ordained,
And being well ordered has succeeded well,
And full of joy the ancient heaven laughs out.
For you accomplished is the greatest wish:
You cannot lose henceforward life nor love,
Nor power, nor spirit, nor the universe;
That which you have, you are! Inalienable
Is your possession, having what you are:
Being, — your being, therefore, aye, yourselves!
So farewell, then, ye blessed ones! farewell,
To meet again all through the universe!
To know and to be known, as love knows love,
Just as the gold-finer knows gold by gold;
But I am what ONE is in the universe,
And what the universe is in One and all;
That have I, and that all have equally;
Hence is it called the ALL, the "ALL to ALL."

VIII.

Childhood charms down even God.

How sweetly does the little child forget
His origin! Only instinctively
He still stares upward in a wandering maze
At the blue heavens with unexploring glance —

Until his mother kindly speaks to him
So tenderly, that now for the first time
He wakes to thought, he hears the human voice,
Looks up at her with slowly studying eyes
And knows her, gazing on the holy face!
And his first little tear-drop timidly
Steals up into the eye of heavenly blue!
His little lip trembles as if with age,
The little heart beats with a holy awe
At such a wonder, fills and overflows!
His breath stands still, his sight grows dim and fails,
And as for help his little mouth cries out,
When he with human beings finds himself;
And yet with human beings, after all;
For on his mother now his glad head rests.
Such are the child's ways, hast thou heeded them?
Then hast thou certainly and deeply felt:
"To look on the old dust, th' old human face,
On the old love and the old life once more,
So new, so young, so beautiful, and dear,
And clothed in such heart-thrilling loveliness,
To see again and love it everywhere, —
May well persuade the very spirit of Heaven
To appear as little child, upon the earth,
And vanish in the grave as blind old man, —
Else would he never fill a mother's lap!
Never the little nest of any lark!
Nor the poor chalice of a single flower!"
That is the witness of the zeal of love.

IX.

Contentment lies in a few representative Things.

For earth's acquaintance has the poorest man
Enough: wife, child, a house, and human lot;
More comes of evil; as a witness take
The rich who has too much. Too much is less,
Is little, naught, deadly, detestable;
Two suns reduce all colors to a blank,
Two suns would make one blind. Two lovely women
At once annihilate love, annihilate
The wife, all home affection. Ten best women
Are not a single wife to the one man.
Not from a hundred women could'st thou learn
With one to be acquainted; only one,
Thine own, can make thee rightly know the wife,
The hand, the lamb, the dog, the human heart,
The proper body, even the proper life;
Life-long must thou be learning life-long things:
The wife's life-long, unbroken, tireless
Fidelity, her undivided love.
Divided love the sister is of hate,
Nay worse: it is indifference, selfishness,
'T is idle lustfulness, love's suicide,
The cataract of men with beauty drunk,
The double sight of the disordered mind,
'T is the child's fishing for the moon in water,
The proper self-damnation and the sorest,
'T is the worst evil: poverty of love,
And impotence. No single work of God
So fair, so good, so lovely can be found,
That thou would'st not do with it as a child

Does with the rose he finds upon the street,
Scarce picks it up, and throws it down again.
Yet is each one of them a masterpiece
Of the great master, full of all the pith
And charmèd life of his entire art.
One starling, coral, violet, clover-leaf,
Differs but little from the multitude.
From each thou learn'st the nature of the whole,
That which thou learn'st from many is the power
Called art; skill, science, knowledge of the earth.
Yet art and science are not very life. —
'T is only on the spot that thou canst learn
What spring is; if thou travellest away
To search it out more perfectly, thou fall'st
This way on snow, and that on scorching heat.
A single flower before the poor man's house,
His apple-tree, his vine, his cherry-tree,
Is of itself a heaven-taught weather-man,
That points him out Spring, Summer, Autumn, Winter;
He sees no more than that on thousand trees!
Sees nothing, if he sees it not in one,
And sees but tokens of this universe,
Never itself, nor yet its very beings.
For Youth and Age, and Life and Death, and Love, —
Nay man himself, through his whole term of years, —
Are viewless as the light, never appear
Themselves; existence is their taking note,
Perceiving, and rapt wondering, no more, —
And with these treasures man, like one who bears
A little roll of pictures, disappears.
A little patch of sand, a little wand,
A mere forefinger, — and thou tracest, learnest
The path of constellations, and the forms

Of all things. That, by which thou wouldst be taught,
Must thou create and shape and educate,
Whate'er it be, thy children or thy wife ;
Must train thy friend himself, even as thou dost
The fruit-tree ; and beneath thy human hand,
Illumined by the human spirit's light,
All becomes human to thee, nay, divine,
Precious and dear to thee, and thy heart's own, —
To others useless, troublesome, destructive,
As that which others train up for themselves
Eludes thy effort to appropriate.
Look now on the much pitied poor and say,
If thou canst really still call them poor !
The way of earth leads not to wealth of gold !
In nature's course it leads sublimely safe
To wealth of soul, the feeling of the whole,
With the few goods man needs to live withal
In freedom his beloved and beauteous life.
The poor man must create life for himself,
Then is it life, 't is a possessor's grasp !
A slippery hold, and spendthrift's squandering
'T is to the rich, fancy's grandee, the proud
And discontented. Wheresoe'er thine eyes
Behold contentment, think : here dwells one poor
In goods, but rich in the true joys of life,
Having a cottage, wife, and children there,
An orchard tree or two, — and ah, withal,
Upon his window-sill a little flower.

X.

The Riches of the Poor in Spirit.

The mind that is wide open, wide awake,
Is poor on earth, yea, poorer than a child;
For all the things it knows and sees and loves,
How will it, can it, cares it to possess!
And like the sun it rides serene in heaven
Surveying all indeed, but craving naught
Save its own light and heat, and, round about,
A world to fling a glad reflection back;
And a life's destiny to rule over.
This is the mind called truly *poor in spirit*,
Not poor *of* spirit, love, large luminous vision.
Then tremble not, dear soul! but know thou this:
The more things leave thee, the more heavenly —
In compensation — they appear to thee!
The purelier, therefore, thou becomest man!

XI.

The immortal little People.

There is a human folk, forever small,
Living like jinns among and by themselves,
Unspeakably happy, knowing naught of death,
Nothing of care, of labor, and of toil;
That never had a loss, but still new gains;
To whom, day, night, all seasons of the year
Are but one time, nay one eternity,
The moving world a stationary house,
A hall of gods for naught but love and joy, —

There lives of children an immortal people,
That keeps its ranks forever new and full,
As often as, by constant living death,
It disappears in maiden and in youth,
As blossoms, swelling into fruits, are gone.
So faithfully does blessed Nature bide
Constant in her divine appearances!
The *buds* never die out upon the tree,
The lightnings never die out in the sky,
But in their realm become a standing light,
Just as the sun is a returning light
In Heaven, wherein he daily celebrates
His holy transubstantiation, making
By magic beings out of elements;
He holds each splendid transformation fast,
Repeats and varies it in ceaseless ways
With skill conspicuously inscrutable,
And every transit is a standing work,
The changes and the fullings of the moon,
Spring's rustling, and the flare of northern lights,
Migrating swallow, and arriving lark.
So also lives to Earth the children-folk
Of man, forever shouting out with joy,
Loving to parents and to parents dear.
And if, thou care-worn, sorrow-sated man,
If thou, poor man, thou weary lone old man,
Canst no more comprehend, *Why* life exists?
Why God exists? and why he never stays
His restless energy, by slow degrees
Letting the stream run out and dry away;
Why, then, God does not die, and so at last
Himself have rest and peace and be deep peace
And rest and stillness imperturbable;

Why, for the first time, then, in hoary eld,
He made the tear-stained, blood-besprinkled earth,
The long-lamented, tear-distilling stars,—
Like golden flowers taking root in water,—
Coagulate in the ethereal sea,
And drew them forth into the light, to bloom,
And after blooming-time to fade away
And sink dissolved in the vast sea of force,—
Look at the little tribe of children then!
Mark, only, *one* child's pleasure in the snow,
When the white flurry thickens all the heavens!
Note how his eyes will sparkle with delight
At the first snow-drop! How he gazes down,
Trembling with joy, when, kneeling in the grain,
He spies the lark's nest with its little ones.
Then wilt thou comprehend full easily
The great first Father, the child-loving one!

XII.

Each secure in the great Unity of Being.

Each being, thinkest thou, is what it is,
For itself only; for himself alone
The man a man; the woman for herself
Alone a woman; and the child a child;
So tree and stone and sun, fire, air, and water.
But lo! *the very spirit*, the rock itself,
Is not a being for itself alone:
All that,—and be it little, be it much,—
Whereby another thing exists, subsists,
Belongs to it; yea, whatsoe'er man needs
That he may be; may grow to a whole man,

More than *belongs* to him, — it constitutes him,
And he again is mystically it.
Thus man is also wife, yea, wife and child;
The wife is man, the child is father, mother;
Man is at once people and land, the sun
Is earth and moon and flower: the very flower
Is earth and moon and sun, and even man;
Man is both nature, too, and God; and God
Is child, no less, the sun, and nature's self.
My child, my darling child, the whole life-blood
Of the great world comes only from *one* heart,
And all goes back to that one heart again,
And every single drop needs all the rest,
And all the drops need every single one, —
Nature is only one great heart of God.
— Without all things, which are not thou, nor thine,
Is yet no life, no joy and even no grief,
That clearly understand; nay, even thy way to do
Is all blocked up, virtue is clogged and lamed;
The pleasant game of life is out, for thee
It never has begun. — Resign thyself
To Nature, all her beauty and her love,
With beauteous life will she compensate thee!
The freest, fairest property, the holiest
Possession of the lovingly possessed,
Is to belong to others! For all tears
And woes, for all the joys he finds in her,
And for his love to her, Nature gives man
All that she has most glorious, — herself!
All, therefore, that belongs to her is thine,
All that she is and all that others are.
Look upon all, as if 't were only thine,
As if the care of it were laid on thee;

And where the deed can *not* reach, there, be sure
Love can. Thou never more canst lose the thing
Thou once hast loved, more than thy love itself.
No God, no man, takes the least thing from thee;
And if what was thy love, becomes to thee
Invisible, sinks and is swallowed up
In Nature's holy deep, — then wilt thou not
Find fault with God, who on the heavenly road
Of Nature has promoted it; nor yet
Wilt thou accuse men, flowers, sun, moon, and stars
Of base desertion, nor have God himself
For an enormous, frightful giant-foe, —
For none but He could ever injure thee!
But verily, — He ne'er has done thee harm,
So thou hast not been harmed by any one,
And ever blest thy spirit bides, — like His!

XIII.

God is All in All.

Naught is but God, and *without* Him is naught!
He is alone; and all comes forth from Him
That comes; what goes, goes back into Himself,
And was not a breath's distance off from Him.
And has He changed His substance into dust
To lift that dust up to Himself again,
And, like a snow-ball, rolling it through time,
Make it at last as great as His own self?
How could there be a bridge to lead to God?
And where could one be found to tread it, — where?
And if one could, how should he cross to Him?
How could there be a ladder made of beings?

Then must there have been one, so long ago,
By three miles smaller than the universe;
Then must there surely have been one, long since,
Only three days short of eternity,
Three-lions-weaker than the only-strong.—
Just as, from the enormous vaulted roof
Of the majestic stalactitic cave,
The countless, ceaseless stony drops rain down
And with their silver-voices sing below,
So beams and gleams and flashes, streams and roars,
Down out of all the heavens, He who is *all*,
Becomes all, is all, and continues all,
And yet is naught but *He*. Naught is but God,
Naught is but He. Hallowéd be his name!
He is the Universe. No single thing
Is all; the Rose is not the Sun, nor man
The violet, nor the infant the old man;
Yet side by side with one another, all,
Multitudes,—multitudes,—uncountable,
All side by side together are divine,
The dust upon the wings of butterflies,
The purple sapling, the carnation-leaf,
The golden streak still left on the dead shell,
The very point in the egg,—the chicken's eye!
The thing that cannot name Him, knows Him well
In the heart-penetrating mystic thrill,
In deepest awe,—in being's holiest hush.
Naught is but God; in Him is all alike,—
Sand-grain and star,—hallowéd be His name!

XIV.

Magnify thy Being as Man.

How bold is man, forsooth, — to be so small!
How arrogant, to be so stupidly
Modest, as to accept from men: name, purpose,
Rank, standing, honor, and a different good,
A different humanity, — at the hands
Of human folly, human lot and need, —
From that which, loudly and majestically
High Heaven with silent eloquence proclaims,
When to the father's eye and heart it speaks
In the divine appearing of a child,
And says: "Give ear, to thee a child is born,
A man, a lofty spirit of the ether,
The world, the eld, — yea, an eternal son, —
Eternal father, too, — is born to thee!"
And see, no creature creeps into a mask,
So as to make himself less than he is;
The lion hides not in the ass's skin,
The ass lets not himself be called a dog,
The dog a mole, no, nor the mole a mouse;
They prize instinctively their native worth,
Nor suffer human names to change their life,
Because they know how they are called with God.
But men, men only, creep into the masks
Of stupid earthly show, put on the old coats
Of dull old servants in the dull old times,
And hotly wrestle to degrade themselves
In wearing all mean under-names of man,
Bestowed by fashion's fawning, flattering slaves;
But never once the one true name of "man."

Then wilt thou be, never pretend to be,
And wouldst thou last, be nothing — but a man.
The goose is more in her goose-dignity,
Than a vain woman who believes herself
Only the lady of a Mandarin;
The cock is more in his cock-dignity
Than yonder man, made blind with pride, who says:
Behold, behold, behold, a Priest of Fo!

XV.

Live and love as God.

Since, then, God's spirit lives in thee, as *thou*,
Art thou, O man, henceforward rid of God,
Of godly work, life, vision, feeling, thought?
Frightfully free art thou? Cut loose from God?
Without God, now that thou hast God *within?*
Must arrogance, vain-glorying, unbelief,
Presumption, fill thee, and the carnal mind?
Art thou, henceforth, released from goodness, then?
What? . . . . Hast thou not in virtue of partaking
God's being, taken it upon thee now
Right specially to do the works of God!
More by this knowledge hast thou pledged thyself
To what is good, than by a thousand oaths!
For thee, henceforth, is meant that noblest word:
What God would not do, do thou not, O man!
And all that God would, that do also thou.
Out of a consciousness of God alone
Comes godly living. From the heart of God
Alone love wells, a pure, perennial sense
And blessed vision of the Universe

And every smallest being it contains: —
Thou must love each of them as God would do, ...
Thou must help each of them, as God would do, ...
Must honor each of them, as God would do, ...
The faithfulest fulfilment of the task
Thy duty lays upon thee is, — thy being;
The task of proper being is: to be
The purest, feel thyself the fullest, love.
What, then, is blessedness? clear-sightedness!
So hast thou blessedness, when thou art God's,
When God is thine, when ye are wholly one,
As flower and petal, sun and ray are one,
And ray and light are one, and light and fire.
Thy living in a body, in the flesh,
No more compels thee to *be* flesh, than God,
Who in and through the body and the flesh
Of the vast whole is the God manifest,
Producing only a God's work, — His life!
Thou genuine man, God-penetrated one,
God-conscious, pupil of God's gentleness,
Conscious alone of pure humanity,
So be thou tranquil! — But this now I say,
Thou art a man! Thou only truly such:
A man to children, like an angel come
To love and teach them! . . . . to the virgin, man,
Pure, chaste, respectful, gladly granting each
The truest, fairest, and most loving life,
Just as if God himself had here on earth
A daughter, this beloved and only one! . . . .
Towards gold and all the treasures of the earth
A man, holding a faithful watchman's post,
Who has himself much greater property! . . . .
A man before the poor man, as if God

Lived here upon the earth a while as man,
And had not either coat or bread or staff! . . . .
Yea, even to the criminal a man,
As if God had his youngest brother here,
A blind man, who, going forth to find his way
To his physician, groped about in vain,
Wounding himself, and falling, every step! . . . .
Yea, to the hater, even, a loving man,
Who, like the silk-worm in his gloomy coil,
Still sleeps, till he shall wake and sunder it.
Thou art now in the fair, full Universe!
What need'st thou other doctrine, then, of life,
Where could'st thou find a nobler, truer one,
Worthier of God,—of truth,—and worthier
Of man, more fitted to inflame his soul
With zeal for all things godlike, to impart
Greatness, nobility, dignity, repose,
And peace and joy and full security,
In death and life serene felicity,
Than each has found who feels: "God lives in me!
Immediately, the all-immediate* One!"

XVI.

Not a free Will but a good Will Man wants.

Man must do good! In that his being lies;
That is, on earth here his distinguishing
Characteristic. The divinity
Of man is not the free, but the good will.
His free will is but error; while he errs,

* The Translator has given up the attempt to paraphrase this compound for the English reader.

So long, — no moment longer, — is he free;
When once he recognizes the divine,
It irresistibly constraineth him!
Rejoice in this and be exceeding glad!
For had man been but dowered with free will,
Then slavery had been his dowry too!
And if man is not of himself divine,
If the good will, like the free will itself,
Is only an endowment, given by birth,
Then he obeys only a foreign law,
Impressed upon him like a falling stone.
Yet dost thou note distinctly: *Gravity*
Resides with it, resides no less within
The smallest sand-grain of the crumbled rock;
So, too, art thou a pure beam from the fount
Of Good. *Goodness* is thy divinity.
To rid himself of the free will, that, that
Is the divine and earthly work of man,
And what releases thee from the free will
Is the clear out-look over earthly things
And heavenly things, it is the power of love. —

. . . . .

And now if man may call man to account,
(— And had I oft and heavily "transgressed"
As, erringly, thou dost baptize man's errors, —)
Reckon against me, — not that the free will,
No, — that a good will was not found in me!
For if a man should even have free will,
And not good will, how would a man e'er fail?
And having good will, — what can fail in him?

XVII.

Power is Will, and Will is Power.

Own thou original power to be free will
And pay respect to will as to free power,
Else is the universe the slave of slaves.
But every drop of water is a lord,
That neither red-hot iron, nor ocean's mass
Can tame, nor bend nor break his ancient force;
Each particle of dust is likewise free,
Free as a spirit is, and thinkest thou
That in the universe it serves as slave?
It works on there according to its force,
And wind and sea know not obedience,
Nor man, nor anything, nor all that is.
There 's not one power that strives to subjugate, —
Each will but be, and being is freedom, work.
And think'st thou, were a man once subjugated,
I 'd hide my head with horror in the grave!
Tyrants themselves are only clearing fires
And builders up of freedom. They first feel
Freely the power within them, — but they seek
To stretch it far o'er other powers, — and break
As breaks *one* wave on thousand rocks around,
And by the death-cry thus awaken men,
Who like old messengers in the still wood
Hear messages and carry them in sleep!

XVIII.

God disposes better than Man proposes.

I never saw a man who lived the life
His wishes and young dreams had painted him.
Most live with still and dogged sullenness, —
Yea, even like cast-a-ways by shipwreck, robbed
Of former goods, and left in some poor hut, —
In their rich mansion and environment!
From world and men on one side, and on the other
From his own mind, a mediate third results
To each, like the ship's pathway, which the dash
Of waves, helm, wind, and ocean-currents guide.
The steersman counts beforehand on them all,
Wisely makes all work with him, and so trims
His vessel that they all must speed his course.
The inexperienced boy cannot do this,
Swept on, at starting, by the holy stream,
And so he misses, every time, the mark
At which he aimed, and finds too, every time,
A land more beautiful, a richer zone,
Of which his novice-heart had never dreamed;
And this firm land, this sunny continent,
Is better than the land, — which nowhere was!
The earth and life are far more beautiful
Than ever entered into childhood's heart;
Not even the morn an old man's dream can catch,
For he who knew the future, were not man.
Who helps create it, he believes it! He
Is earth-born! He who recognizes it:
Each flying sun-glance, every passing cloud,
Each house and every rose the thicket hides,

And every smile and even every tear, —
Has sat in the great Council of the Gods;
Sits, as a child does at a father's feet,
Who, in the midst of turbulent elements,
Strode through the moony night with giant strength,
And with the morning tells him how he fared, —
While they repose beneath a fruit-tree, full
Of bees and blossoms in the broad, full sun!

XIX.

Be not a Flaw-finder in the Universe of Beauty.

Say that thou had'st a picture full of charms,
As large and fair and lustrous as the sky,
From which a paradise looked out on thee,
But on the golden frame of it there sat
Three flies, — Wouldst throw the picture in the fire?
Or say thou hadst a basket full of sweet
And luscious grapes, scarce three of them unripe,
Wouldst thou shake off the clusters to the swine?
Say that ten thousand virgins, perfect all
In beauty, hovered round thee, smiled on thee;
Yet seven had seven gray hairs in their heads,
Wouldst thou command the whole of them to hell?
That wouldst thou not. Yet dost thou something worse,
Not saying: "Man is good; the universe
Is lovely; life is worthy to be lived!"
What though a few, as among golden coins,
True gold indeed, yet seem not fully stamped,
And show thee not God's image bright and clear?
Yet if thou hast joy in the hushed-out joy
Of thousand tribes, which still from out their graves

Rises, and rings as echo down through time, —
If the ineffably high loveliness
Of earth and the great sky enraptures thee, —
And goodness of so many thousand good,
Methink'st thou couldst not, in thy ecstasy,
Thrilled by the heavenly music of the spheres,
With thy inspired, glowing vision, — sure
Thou couldst not note, — thou couldst not number then
The seven gray hairs, — but truly, faithfully,
Wouldst call the common face of man so fair!
And man so good! The fault lies in thine eye,
Perhaps, yea certainly, that thou dost not
Find even the bad man's soul to be divine,
Just as the surgeon's eye must needs confess
The very body of the criminal
A godlike work of God, — his masterpiece,
Though He had never built one more than this!
When cavilling makes happy, rich, and wise,
Then will I let my eyes be blinded, too,
And to my spirit say: "Hush, Satan, hush!"

XX.

Be Good and so do Good.

Findest thou any real difference
To lie 'twixt *being* good and *doing* good?
The leaf that shines and rustles on the tree,
Is that which thou, a human being, art,
Does that which human virtue does through thee,
Only in different and finer form!
With all thy doing, all thy knowing, thou
Wilt hardly match the lark's fidelity,

The spider's, as she weaves her wondrous web,
The wind's, that nightly sweeps along the sky,
That hurries on, inspired by God's own life,
And as it flies, fulfils his high behest.
O man! O good and pure and noble man,
Be thou so good, so noble and so pure
As not to lift thyself above thy soul!
For thy soul's pith and highest virtue is
Calmly and humanly to let thy life
Conform to that great universe around!
And not to contradict it! Only not
To be a discord in the harmony
Of heaven, in the great starry family,
And in the race of little earthly flowers!
O man, how godlike wilt thou be at length,
When thou art modest and a simple man,
In whom that pure, fair spirit loves to dwell,
Who fills the sky above and earth below, —
And thee no less, — with every beauteous shape;
And sure this sense of pure and primal life
Pervading round about thee all that moves,
Is blesseder than all thy doing is, —
'T is verily thy sense, thy *godlike* science!

XXI.

Prayer the Transfiguration of Man.

That which transpires with thee in prayer, — what thing
Thou dost in prayer, — that, sure, must be a prayer!
Thou utterest wakefully the name of God, —
And hast already *wrought a miracle*,
The first of miracles hath come on thee,

Shining like lightning, flooding thee with light;
The blazing morning sun, that stood just now
Up yonder in the heavens, — *has disappeared!*
Day is no more, nor night, — seized, seized, snatched up
By the still arm of power, thou lookest forth,
As over tranquillized autumnal fields,
O'er myriad sunken cities, far away
O'er dead and buried generations, long,
Long laid to rest, of this earth's men and flowers,
Away, over all graves, — and even thine:
And there is not *one* grave, for lo! God is!
On a sick-bed thou liest, suffering much, —
Thou utterest wakefully the name of God, —
And feel'st the freshness to thy bosom's core,
Which wafts thee health from all the universe, —
And art refreshed, for lo! thou feelest God!
Thou wast awake, the great, the private soul
Within thee felt itself, naught but itself,
But its own feeling! the pure, private spirit
With its own eyes looked through and through itself,
Deep as it could. And deeply as it gazed,
It saw all that, which was all, all its own.
O! a man's heart is broad as Heaven itself,
Has Heaven's own bliss! and, to arouse thyself,
To wake, to feel thyself awake, to feel
Who lives in thee, who is thyself and was,
From all eternity, and so remains, —
To make the universe thy home and bed,
Just as the swallow hies her to her nest,
Just as the drop of blood mounts to the heart,
That only is true prayer. But that *is* prayer!
And is then that a glory? or a shame?
Is that a misery? or is 't a joy?

Is it a prayer, or is 't a giving thanks?
Is it a refuge, or a subterfuge?
When thou dost will the godlike in thee, when
The will has once appeared to thee as deed,
And now appears in thee the greatest deed
And holiest: the most God-contented one,
Truly it is thy glory then, — thy prayer!
To honor, is the very highest honor;
Woe on the man who is ashamed to pray,
He is no man! He knows not what man is,
What he can do and what he ought to do, —
'T is the *transfiguration* of himself!
Of pain and woe and bliss and human life,
In its great, calm, serenely gladsome light!
And pain and woe and bliss and human life,
Yea, even a tear itself, can lead to that;
The stillest night, the light of a child's eye,
Is bright enough for that, and every clod
Of dust becomes a Tabor to thy sight.
What need of Moses and Elias † †,*
When God is with thee, in thee, round about thee,
Hid and loud-voiced, embracing and embraced!

XXII.

Friendship and Philanthropy.

Thou sigh'st: "I have no friend!" That saddens me,
Because it pains thee, — yet it gladdens me.
A friend is a *half* noble man, who gives
To one alone what he should give to all;

* This gap, so filled up, is in the original. Possibly the name of Jesus was understood. — Tr.

His time, his strength, his talents, and himself.
The mother is a friend of her first child,
Her only one; as, in the ancient times,
They who were *men*, became each other's *friends*.
Then comes a second child, a third, a fourth,
And lo! her eye watches with equal love
Over this second child, this third, this fourth, —
She loves them all, and now is truly mother!
And say thou hast a friend, and there lived one,
And there lived ten, a hundred, like to him
In everything, in body, soul, and grace,
Thou must be friend to all as to this one!
If now all men should seem to thee alike,
With faculties, ay, and their very faults,
Of superhumanly exalted worth,
And lovely as the near Divinity,
O must thou not then, — as the mother is
To all her children, — be to each a friend?
He is a friend to each, who honors each;
He honors each, who knows and recognizes
Each! Then at thy door only lies the blame,
If thou art not a common friend of men!
That all are not thy friends, the friends of all,
That is *their* fault, that is their sin alone,
Greatest of sins, the sin against pure love!
If, then, thou hast no friend, if to have none
I wish thee, — ah, what great thing wish I then,
For thee, — for all! Ah, — only human love!

XXIII.

Make Account of Spirit, not Person.

Timote della Vita da Urbino,
Thou painted'st the Madonna di San Sisto;
From an exceeding human modesty
Thou didst forbear to give the work thy name,
As if the features of God's blessed mother
Had feebly come to light beneath thy hand!
And now the caviller says, He did not dare
To trust himself, willing enough was he,
His work should bear the angelic Master's name!—
Thou wilt decide, good soul, the noble strife,
Thou who from genuine human feeling dost
Thy deeds of goodness in God's name, and yet
Doest thy godlike work in silent joy!
To will the good and to create the good,
'T is only fellow-feeling with the Lord,
'T is only fellow-working with the Lord,
The soul of all, the self-harmonious one.
Transparent seems the human soul through which
Thy soul of all shines; but that only is
Transparent, which is equal with the light,
Which *is* light; and wherever thou shalt see
A good man willing good and doing good,
Thou seest God's essence, not his image, there.
False, wretched, pitiable, abject is it
To expect from any creature in the world
Thy fortune, thy felicity, thy life,
To wait on him for freedom, truth, and right!
From whom expectest thou thy *Spirit*, then?
Art thou that spirit, full of its rich heaven,

What helper wilt thou look to among men?
And sure — thy *virtue* none bestows on thee.
Then quietly confront each heavenly power
And human might, and place thyself at once
Up at its side; smile when one says to thee:
"I am thy master! Follow!" For that Spirit
Who is as great as the whole universe,
He grudges not to each to be a spirit,
Like him, and is, from very greatness, still.
No word, no work, contains the truth entire;
The spirit needs the entire universe
Forever, to speak out, to manifest
Its being utterly, and as a work
Of beauty livingly unfold itself.
For that creation is a finished work,
Is but a fiction of the human mind,
Recounting all things future as things past,
Things that are seen, — because it looked on them.
O name me that one only creature, pray,
That only one, that was, is, and will be,
With which the great, great God has joined himself
So intimately, indistinguishably,
That, for the creature, thou canst see no more
The God, in which he has entirely hid,
Emptied, himself for all eternity,
And by him and behind him is as dead,
Yea, really dead. Tell me the creature's name!
And know'st thou none, — forever hold thy peace.
There 's none through whom life first has come to be,
Not through a man has man begun to be,
Man, the great, rich, fair vigor of the world;
Through no one's word has truth been first made true,
Or goodness good, or beauty beautiful.

Because there *was* a Beauty, Goodness, Truth,
The teachers ever came to utter it;
They have by it grown up to the true man,
The good, the beautiful; 't is not through them
The entire God, the entire truth, gets life.
One who reveals does not thereby create,
The Revelation is not yet the Truth,
The pouring from the cask is not the wine.
Art thou a spirit now? Or hast thou one?
Thou hast not one; for that which had a spirit,
Were higher, greater than the Greatest, Highest!
Thou *art* a spirit, then; and if a spirit,
Then art thou unbegotten and unborn,
Thou art from everlasting to everlasting.
There are not higher spirits and lower ones,
Immortal ones and mortal; there are not
Divine and human ones, — but only spirit:
Spirit is everywhere and always one.
The spirit, properly, is, all that is;
Force, love, and life, and clear self-consciousness.
And were there a creative will that could
Beget e'en spirits out of nothingness,
Then would the thing created be the germ
Of the creator, and the thing one willed
Were even higher than the one that willed;
The offspring of the will would give the will
Its first true being, *be* the will itself,
In its completed, its diviner shape!
In it the will would be first glorified.
Thou art the spirit's, thou art spirit: thou art
The *self* of all that lives and moves in thee,
Thy very frame is holy nature's self,
As man, thou livest nature's very life;

Thou holdest not the estate of love in fee,
Because thy love is love itself. As man,
Thou liv'st the beauteous life of God himself,
While he is yet God-man ; for to be man
No shadow, only God alone, has power.
Thou holdest God not only in short fee,
Not as a heavenly treasure hast thou him,
He did not let the fulness of his being
Sink into thee ; long hadst thou been thyself
Spirit and love itself ; thou wast before
Immortal, art immortal now as man ;
Man is immortal even on the earth, —
Immortal thou shalt still remain, when fades
The beauteous flower, whose form thy being took.

XXIV.

Contemplation of our loved Ones asleep.

To look upon our loved ones in their sleep,
How blissful ! and yet how disheartening, too !
By day they still are thine : they have no thought,
No wish, it ever could be otherwise ;
Then blooms their heart, as bloom the cups of flowers
— By day, — and close themselves at night in night,
As charmed away out of the lightsome realm
Of life and love ! Watching the sleepers now
Well dost thou see, and startling is the thought:
They are not wholly thine ! They half belong
To holy Nature, nay, are wholly hers,
Who only consecrates their thought to thee,
And takes them home to her at night in dream
Into her realm ne'er trod by human foot,

To which nor hate, nor earthly joy and woe,
Not even *love*, can ever follow them!
Where in the mother's arms alone they rest,
As little children for a single night
Go to sleep with and comfort "Grandmother!"
In sleep the loving one no longer loves,
The fairest is in sleep no longer fair,
The ugliest is no longer ugly then!
They are the hollow mask of man, — no more, —
A proof that 't is the soul makes beautiful,
Invests with charms and to itself wins love
By ever new transpiercings of bright flame,
Flashings and glowings, as of golden coals.
The child, with that unutterable mien,
As cool, as old, he looks, — as the full moon, —
And yet, at morning he will love thee so,
While now the rose-hue flushes cheek alone.
Now thou thyself wilt also sink to sleep,
Be lost to him, no longer be his stay,
His guard and guide! like one whose love has cooled,
Snatched off forever to a distant land, —
Yet with the sun love, too, comes back again
Just as to flowers come fragrance, heart and eyes!
— But thee the spectacle has not cast down,
It has uplifted thee, has made thee great,
For what belongs to God, thou callest thine
With right, for thou thyself art God's and *theirs!*

XXV.

Man hugs his selfish Wishes in Death.

A little naked child laid on its back
In ever so shallow water for a bath,
By its fond mother, all so carefully,
For fear of sinking into endless depth,
Holds fast so sweetly its own little hands !
So man clings to his wishes even then,
— Like the air-sailor to his light balloon, —
When earth, his mother, lays him in the grave
With her soft hand and holds him safely there !

XXVI.

Rest even in this fleeting Life.

One thing hold fast, and thinking on it, grow
More and more tender, tranquil and serene :
The earth is but the spirit's resting-place,
That hovers through the All with holy love ;
The constellations, — golden oases,
And all things, whatso'er, this earth brings forth
Are but its inn of rest, its tarrying-place ;
The *rose*, even *man*, is but its rest, the *heart*
Of man, so passionately though it beats.
And dost thou think, believe, see that, O Soul ?
Wilt thou not grant it, then, the peace of rest,
And be composed and calm in life and death ?
It were itself worse off thereby than thou,
Could it not find tranquillity and rest,
Content and love, in thee, as thou it !

For God's sake, therefore, live a godly life,
And lovingly repose in blessedness!

XXVII.

What is Death?

Man dies alive. Think upon that for once!
And does he die to death? or die to life?
Or is he born dead? does he at his birth
Begin to live? — thou askest? Know thou, then:
God is born with thee and within thee, — lives
In thee, with thee, loves and does good through thee!
And when thou diest, O man, God dies with thee,
In thee His spirit parts with human flesh:
Yet as God does not die, — dies not to death, —
Thou diest not, nor either of you dies,
Nor one of all who, living, die with Him.
For dying is itself His very life
Forevermore, as it is also thine:
'T is transformation, rest, and endless bliss;
Only the ending of a change is — Death.

XXVIII.

What can Man give God?

The child has taken flowers to bed with him,
To give them in the night to the dear God;
And gayly, too, has ready spotted cards,
To play with them with angels in the night;
And what wilt thou, then, take with thee to heaven?
Thy human virtue and thy human joy?

And what, O man, wilt thou then offer God
But what on earth He saw, created, was!
The universe is holy, one throughout,
No Solomon's temple, with its outer court
And inner, with its ark and sanctuary,
Man's life is rich as is his death itself,—
Its scenery full of pomp in every part;
Its "stream of death," clear as its fountain is,
Its fount immeasurable as its stream.

XXIX.

Love abideth forever.

What enters pure and changeless into heaven,
As morning dew from thousand cups of flowers,
As light of day into the evening sun,
As pure from cloudy as from pleasant days —
Is Love! While fear and sorrow and remorse
Are left behind as the precipitate
Of life, earth's portion. Even the great genii
Of man on earth: even Faith and Hope themselves
Have to wait out before the gates of Heaven,—
There they are nothing now, where in their place
Fulfilment comes and sight. There Love alone,
Abides the same, because it was from Heaven!
And as within, so too without, is she
The heavenly one; to men no less than spirits,
To all that lives in earth and Heaven is she,
The one great spirit of the universe,
And one felicity she grants to all!

XXX.

The great future Autumn of the Heavens.

Thou sawest the water-lilies in the pond,
Swimming with golden globules in their cups,
The star-like water-caltrops sawest thou
That rooted in the water swam and ripened,
And swimming passed away and were dissolved
Into their mother-water, just as here
The flowers sink back into their mother-earth.
Full of the sight and of the thoughts it wakes,
Thou liftest up thy eyes now to the stars;
And in the ocean of eternal blue
That fills the universe, from which proceeds
All that appears, and into which sink back
All things that pass away, and nourishes
All germs of things and all the things themselves,
Thou seest the constellations — golden flowers —
Bloom softly swimming in the great sea-pond —
Haply, — nay, certainly, so blooming *ripen*,
And meanwhile (like Libellas, and like bees)
Visit the creatures in their blossom-time,
Landing awhile upon their golden cups.
And as the water-lilies in the pond
Swim with the golden globules in their cups —
And as the star-like water-caltrops do,
So in the ether-ocean certainly,
Do they, too, fade and vanish like the flowers,
And to their children leave the germ, the seed.
Yea, as the flowers are in the pond dissolved,
As it thenceforth shows only its blue waves
And no flower more, so may one day, perchance,

The ether also be without a star,
Only still teeming with its ancient force,
And a *great autumn* reign in heaven's wide fields.
Now cast thy eyes down silently to earth,
And see, how through the dark twigs of the trees
Sparkle the golden stars! Look now thy fill,
Then lay thy hand upon thy beating heart,
And kiss thy children in their little beds,
That bloom as rosy as yon stars in heaven!
Not long, not always wilt thou love, dear heart,
Thine own, as now! Rare are the days and few,
And yet they are! And this is your *great day!*

THE LAYMAN'S BREVIARY.

DECEMBER.

DECEMBER.

I. Who shall write a Day's History?
II. Be at Home and at one with all Things.
III. The Realm of Light.
IV. Heaven the Cradle and Grave of Man.
V. Life the great Teacher.
VI. The Blessedness of being needed.
VII. Pity not the Sufferer, but the Sinner.
VIII. Servant of All, — free of All.
IX. Honor all Men
X. Beauty a Snare.
XI. Be Master of Fortune.
XII. Make the best of what is.
XIII. Enjoy simply the common Lot.
XIV. Live out a whole Life.
XV. Men are growing on into Man.
XVI. The poor rich Man.
XVII. It is Good to have been Good.
XVIII. Past Joys bitter, — past Woes sweet.
XIX. Reap daily the Harvest of Humanity.
XX. The Mirror of the Lake a Mirror of the Soul.
XXI. Man is what God yearned to be.
XXII. Moral Beauty surviving physical.
XXIII. Over-Anxiety.
XXIV. Nature's Lesson of Contentment.
XXV. The Ten Prohibitions and the One Commandment.
XXVI. Man's three Foes: Pain, Fate, and early Death.
XXVII. Life is more than the Means of Life.
XXVIII. Each Man can have unique Bliss.
XXIX. Stay at Home.
XXX. Live to Learn, and learn to Live.
XXXI. Man's Word the Porch; God's World, the Temple.

DECEMBER.

I.

Who shall write a Day's History?

OW full, how rapturously full, the hearts
Of men, of all men, all the days and nights!
Completely to express a single day,
The very commonest and least of all,
To give its full and faithful history,
That were a task which the whole human race,
All women and old people everywhere,
Could not accomplish in a thousand years!
So much has in that single earthly day
Transpired in every breast! In that one day
So much has come to pass for every man,
So many wonders happened, there has been
So much to gaze at, be astonished at,
So much to smile, weep or rejoice over,
So much to bear, and praise, so many things
Unutterable, to be silent of!
Yet, after all, what has one day brought forth?
What one unique, never recurring thing?
The sun rose in the morning, that was all,
It thundered, and the lightning killed a man,
A rainbow reared its many-colored arch,
The young wife o'er the way has borne a child,
And god-parents in festal, gay attire,
Have gone with him to church in the bright sun,

The wedding train has met a funeral;
The moon has risen in complete eclipse,
And yet the stars have sparkled bright o'erhead,
And that same wife has had a wondrous dream!
O, it has been the day of God's great works!
Yet verily, all poets that have lived,
All the old men and all the modern ones,
Have scooped out only a few handfuls, all,
From the great fountain of God's universe!
And all the painters, past and future ones,
Taken together, fail to represent
Completely so much as a moment's glimpse
Of earthly beauty and of earthly life,
As a mere image on their painting-ground!
And all the natural philosophers
May sit together till the day of doom,
To expound a wedding, a baptismal feast, —
With circumstance of mother, child, and flowers, —
Of earth below and of the heavens above,
With sinking of the sun and rise of moon,
Sweet drawings of the heart and gracious love,
Clear flow of life and peacefulness of dreams!
Yet are all living beings full of it,
And revel in it with unconscious bliss,
And all the dead were full of it and sank
Down into death sweetly forgetting it!
And holy knowledge must there be in death!

II.

Be at Home and at one with all Things.

Thy restless heart has never missed a throb,
Since first the ether filled thy little breast
So heavily, it overflowed in tears,
And put the work of secret nature, thus,
(Thy shape, God's cunning work,) upon the wing!
And stirs it still, feeding with every breath
The life and spirit, with a care so more
Than fatherly! Thy thinking, too, not once
Has stopped, in one continuance has the weft
Filled itself with new woof out of the All,
In waking hours by day, in sleep by night.
So evermore, then, to thyself be true!
Not one misstep will Heaven e'er let thee make
On this sharp, swaying, perilous bridge of life,
That leads through air across the grim abyss,
And suddenly hurls thee down, irrevocably!
Thou hast till now hit always the right track,
As if invisible spirits set thy foot,
And so thou pressest onward in the cloud,
The daylight, into spaces never dreamed,
That never *were*, to which the *seeing eye*
Gave their first shape, which the foot's tread stamped up
From earth, like fountains — for *thou bringest them.*
Thou liv'st and mov'st, and from within thyself
Picturest forth thy life in space and time.
Thou must go through with all, thyself alone;
Thou art alone within thy mother's womb;
Thou art alone upon thy mother's lap;
Thou art alone over against the Sun,

On the broad earth with human myriads ;
Thou art alone in all thy highest joy,
Thou art alone in all thy deepest woe,
Thou art alone, when thy last hour draws nigh,
When that old phantom death speaks low with thee,
Thou art alone within thy coffin ! But
Alone thou canst be, only *in thy home*,
As a blind child is in his father's house!
The spirit is always with thee, in its source ;
Thou feelst thyself at home, when once thou weepest,
Thou art at home, where Beauty beams on thee,
Thou art at home, where'er thou doest good,
Thou art at home, where rapture thrills thy breast
When death takes from thee some dear thing, some flower,
When gazing on the dead, when stark distress
Confronts thee, when some wrong that cries to heaven
Is done, when woe heart-rending seizes thee,
Then art thou speedily at home ! There stay !
When thou once lovest and art loved till death,
Then art thou in thy beauteous blessed home !
When, now, dear soul, art thou far off from it ?
Then be not, gentle spirit, *rent in twain*,
Beget thou not thy *double* in thy breast
By a bad deed ! When thou, no longer light,
Shalt cast a shadow ! When the universe
Shall be no more to thee a looking-glass !
Abide thou in thy lone simplicity,
One with all things and one in all thy powers !

III.

The Realm of Light.

There is a realm of light, — a million suns,
That in the world create a second world;
There is the power of vision, resident
Deep in the Spirit of the Universe,
Who frames himself the wonder-matching eye,
Calmly to feast on the fair realm of light;
The fish at ocean's dusky bottom sees,
The owl sees clearly in the gloom of night, —
The realm of light were there, were there no eye;
The seeing power were there without the light,
And only for each other both exist,
And jointly form a magic ring of life.
But softly ask'st thou: must one live, to see?
Or see, to live? or must one live to love?
Is then this realm of light the only realm?
O realm of light, realm of the wonderful,
Thou Universe within the Universe,
Thou from the rising to the setting sun
Of Time, illumined through unmeasured space,
Hall of the gods in this house of the gods,
In through thy gates there throng unceasingly
Troops of bright creatures turned to golden masks,
Each with two windows of the spirit and heaven,
One only has three eyes, the Sun but one, —
"The fair, blind maiden" in the golden world!
So these innumerable populations
Of beings come to the fair light of day,
That they, too, once may see the beauteous world,
All that their Master's hand mysteriously, —

He like one blind and with invisible hands, —
Has conjured up out of the deep of power, —
You, starry hosts above there! Thee, O Sun,
The moon, the clouds, the rainbow in the clouds,
The strength of mountains and repose of vales,
The gloss of green poured out upon the leaves,
The blue of heaven reposing on the sea,
The morning-redness lingering on the rose,
And myriad hues of all the myriad flowers,
The gleam of gold and silver's milder sheen
On clouds and shells, — all these they come to see,
Yet more than all the loving eye itself!
To see how love looks upon all and smiles,
Feasting itself with beauty, with the beauty
Of light's enchanting realm, than all the rest
Still greater wonder! Ah, and is this flight
Through the vast hall life's acme? Rather say,
The eyes of all are but a single eye,
Eye of the world, its morning light are they,
The still, immovable fly's-eye of God,
Which with its thousand mirrors searches all,
Sees into every day, each little nook,
With the bee's eye into each flower-cup sees,
And with the mouse pries through each dusky night!
See, then, the beautiful, O beauteous man!
And prize thy power to see, as all divine.
And now the blind man! O be kind to him
Who never saw the lovely realm of light!
O tell him much thereof, as thy best gift;
He understands thee well, the blind can see
Within himself, though painting with false hues;
And to the blind of spirit lend thine eye,
Who, seeing, in false colors paints the world.

Who makes one wise, bestows on him a world,
Who makes one good, bestows on him a God.

IV.

Heaven the Cradle and Grave of Man.

If thou shouldst see one, holding in his hand
A casket, shake therefrom a thousand pearls,
Thou wouldst think justly: "They were all therein!"
The house from which thou seest, day after day,
Children come trooping forth, thou call'st a school;
The place where hour by hour water runs
From the still rock, — thou callest it a spring,
And hence inferrest the great reservoir
Which shows so plainly all its richness here!
A child can tell, in Autumn, when his step
Rustles among the fallen leaves, how great,
How rich the tree was, that shook down such wealth!
And seest thou now in spring so many flowers
Strewed o'er the earth, seest thou on earth so many
Children of men, more than the ocean's pearls,
Thou thinkest justly: they were once therein,
In yonder visibly empty blue of heaven!
Calmly they live therein, there lives the power
That brought them forth. For thou canst clearly see,
Out of an empty cask there runs no drop,
Out of an empty casket trickles no pearl, —
And now thy wonder pierces holy heaven
That like a bee-hive infinitely swarms!
And this, too, clearly note — the grave of man
Is heavenly blue, not grassy-green; indeed
In yonder blue man really is buried, —

Ah no, not buried, only taken home
To his father, as the children are from school.
The blind man *hears* the barberry bushes bloom,
In the bee's humming! Pray, *see* thou my word!

V.

Life the great Teacher.

Man has full many a riddle here to solve,
And solves them not by highest science, no,
Nor yet by thought, by spirit, or by love.—
But easily he solves them all by life!
For what a child is,—that a child best solves;
And what a woman is man learns by marriage,
Treading the road of richly-gifted years.
Together easily they clear up life!
The joys and sorrows of a mortal lot
On earth! Send up and call a *new God* down,
And bid him suddenly declare to thee—
The nature of the joy that parents feel,
Who find again their lost, their only child,
After a year. Lo, you! there stands the God
Dumb as a very dunce! Not even as wise
As the house-dog who mingles in their joy!
The God must let himself be born on earth,
Become a child, grow up and take a wife,
Must have a child himself and lose the child,
Ere, with all heavenly wisdom, he can feel—
The joy of finding a lost child again.
And now, how many thousand finer joys,
And purer and mysterious ecstasies,
The human race has lived to know by heart

In all the ever new and changeful years!
And if, then, it demands a godlike heart,
A godlike mind, even to feel one's self
Born as a human being on the earth, —
Surely there dwells within the human race
No other being than the highest God.
And plain it is: Wherefore he lives therein!
And plain it is: How thou shouldst live therein:
As He, who 's thou; as thou, too, who art He.

VI.

The blessedness of being Needed.

'T is being needed makes the father's worth;
'T is being needed makes the mother's bliss;
'T is being needed makes up woman's life;
And just the best resisteth not the call,
The inner calling — to be needed! Hence
She bears both toil and trouble cheerfully.
Yet who more blessings gives than he men need!
Who more forlorn than he whom men need not!
How many would the human circle drop,
If all fell out of it whom men scarce need, —
Who need, themselves — God and the world and men,
And throne and cottage, water, bread, and salt.
Whatever a man truly needs, in haste
And without stint his neighbor offers him, —
The woman gives him her long hair to knit,
The miser gives him wine to put out fires,
The lame man gives his dog to guide the blind;
For what man truly *needs*, that verily
Belongs to him! and nothing but the doubt

Whether he truly needs a boon, holds back
In men the godlike impulse which cries "Give!"
To need is also, then, a human thing;
To need is for the poor a blessed lot.
It reaches bread to him from mercy's hand,
Necessity gives loves to loving ones,
Necessity discloses man to man.
Whoso needs not, lives far away from life:
He is a stupid fool who cheats himself,
Feeding with pride his void and craving soul; —
Nay, see, he 's dead, — one of the coffined dead!
And he there in the coffin, were he now
A really forlorn, unneeded one, —
Would he not, dead now first need everything?
Need a new life? Need a new world? Nay, more,
Would he not need a breath to draw, from heaven?
And how? does not God need *him* greatly, too,
As object for his love, for all his gifts?
He who needs all the world, — that one is God!
Therefore the world is! and we, needed ones!
And 't is because we need him, He loves us, —
And him, because he needs us, him we love!

VII.

Pity not the Sufferer but the Sinner.

"Fain would I live, as man shall one day live
On earth, when all that lay upon his mind,
And all that stirred him in his godlike heart,
Worked out, blooms round him gloriously now,
And he is happy, innocent, and free,
Free from the sight and knowledge of one woe!"

Such is thy prayer. Yet is 't quite right? For see:
That poor boy bears a basketful of wood;
He has purloined it from the hedge. But now
The small child sinks beneath his heavy load;
To his sick father he will carry it,
Who sits there freezing in the cold, dark hut.
He has his father's large, old jacket on,
The long sleeves cover well his little hands,—
He has no cap on in this biting cold.
But see, his good-will keeps him warm enough,
He hurries on. He stumbles. His foot bleeds,—
He has no time; helpfulness makes him brave.
He seeks no help,—himself must carry it.
He tells in passing how the darling child
Of his dead sister,—though she never had
A husband,—died last night, and father says
Now he has nothing more to love on earth!
And the boy weeps to think that all his toil
Is useless now, for it makes no one glad.
And now he enters. Soon the hut grows light,
I see the old man there, and the dead child
Which he, in the best place such close room yields,
Has laid upon his bed of straw, and now
He stands and muses: how from these old boards
And rusty nails, with nothing but his axe
Make a fit coffin for the darling child?
The forester meanwhile has tracked the boy,
Without a greeting enters, hales him off;
Feeling his guilt the boy goes willingly,
And silently the father suffers it;
Now in his loneliness he folds his hands
A little while, then, brightening, sets to work.
Yea, truly great, beyond conception grand

Must be the lot of good humanity
One day, an unknown life must dawn on it, —
Repaying it for all things it has missed,
All that oppress, depress and crush it now, —
Yea, and what *more than makes it whole* through patience,
Scorn, energy, exalted grief and love!
And hast thou pity, mountain-great, good soul,
Think well: to whom 't is due! and dedicate it
To them before all others who have none:
The hard, deceitful, and tyrannical.
For God once made this world — this very world
Which lives to-day — in tatters, gold, and love.
A thunder-clap might strike down every foe
Of human kind, the earth might easily
Yawn and devour them, legions of archangels
Might in one day bring wisdom, weal, and joy
To all earth's dwellers, — yet they come not down.
Humanity must choose all for itself,
Must do all, — but can ne'er retrace its steps,
Never entirely give up a good,
Nor miss one, — least of all: its childlike heart!

VIII.

Servant of all, — free of all.

The pious mind implies not slavery,
Neither to wear nor yet impose a yoke.
The pious man alone is free and strong;
The free man is the good man and the saint,
He wills that each should be as free as he;
And who, O who would rather men should lose,
All men, their reason, liberty of thought,

Courage and righteousness and truth and heart
And gladness and prosperity on earth,
And he himself rule o'er a race of slaves, —
Than that he might with wisdom rule like God,
Whom every servant faithfully helps rule,
And that the human race might keep unharmed
Reason and freedom, truth and righteousness
And heart and soul and joy and happiness!
Keep and increase! How many times would Christ
Still suffer willingly upon the cross,
Only to save one sinner, the last man,
The Prodigal son, in body and in soul!
Let none then ever speak the name of Christ,
Who will not try, himself too, so to live,
And so to each surrender everything.

IX.

Honor all Men.

When thou hast learned the world, thou knowest well:
Naught is so very diverse from all else,
Nothing is wholly to be reprobated,
Naught absolutely excellent; naught unique
So that that its equal, nay, a better still
May not be found. The handsomest of women
Is not removed wide as the poles of heaven
In all things from her ugly sister. Lo,
She is a wife, she is a mother still,
Still fair in person, even if not in face,
She meekly does her work, holds friendly speech!
The bad lives not so distant from the good:
He is not bad to all, still loves himself,

His wife and children; even the robber robs,
To carry home his booty to some one
Whom he loves more than all, loves even more
Than his own happiness and peace of mind.
An old dog will still watch, will still be true,
And make thee sad, he was so little while
Thy guest, thy friend. The feeble eyes still see
By mind and thought almost as well as sound ones;
A rich man *with* his gold still suffers want,
A king grows old and needs another's aid;
The poor man still has soul and body. He
Who must obey all others, he it is
Who like the greatest patriarch of old,
Is lord of children and his own strong frame,
The best of kingdoms! And the man who wants
A hut, a well to fill his pitcher at,
The very water-pitcher too, he turns
At length to his great Father, faithfully
Lifts up his tearful eyes to that high friend,
And thinks of all now, that the Father has,
Nay, rather thinks, what is there He has not?
The rich and poor, and him, too, with the rest, —
And comes into possession of Him now
And of himself more sweetly, utterly
Than he had e'er possessed himself before.
Humanity is knit so close in heart,
By virtues and by faults, by good and bad,
Possession, want, — made one by thousand ties.
And lives the shameless wretch, who would make his
Alone the blessings of humanity?
The good man yearns to have them shared by each!
The cool heart startled learns to love mankind;
The wise learns quietly: to be content
With each, and fairly honor each one's worth.

X.

Beauty a Snare.

Full many a one has beauty led astray,
The beauty that appeared before his eyes;
Yet there 's no devious path and no abyss,
Which beauty drives not its possessors to.
All human blessings ask the reins and yoke,
Fire does and fancy, soft compassion, too,
The best of hearts, even love and honor's self.
Hold others' beauty subject to thyself,
Thou conquerest them by nature's reverence.
Thou holdest sway o'er thine own beauty, too,
When thou hast once renounced the idle dream
Of blessing men with transient morning-red,
With the mere human image, here an hour
And gone the next. Beauty and Folly are
Brother and sister. But of Folly born
Are the twin-sisters: one's own misery
And mischief to one's neighbor. No good needs
More added ones than beauty, that it may
Not be ridiculously ruinous.
It needs grace, dignity, and modesty,
It needs repose and pride and worth and love;
— Which scarce the happiest one acquires late, —
Beauty, like every other image, needs
Life and a human heart. "For a rich man
How hard it is to enter into heaven!"
Still harder for the beautiful! and then
He enters, after all, no other one
Than every simple, good, and honest man!

XI.

Be Master of Fortune.

Much it concerns the world, nay, God himself:
The question in what mood, what inner frame,
Both good and evil fortune find their man,
That each, being properly received, may work,
Just as it should, — that which is good and right!
The tidings of a brother's death shall lay
The sick man on his death-bed; the poor wife
Swoons at a letter in the postman's hand,
When she expects her husband's punishment;
And yet the cry: "Thy house is all on fire!"
Awakes not the dead-drunk to put it out!
On the bad man ill-luck falls crushingly,
To the good man malice comes scarcely felt, —
Quenched as a torch that drops into the fount;
Good fortune comes quietly as a gift
From out the world of wonders to still hearts!
Then wilt thou take life rightly at all times,
Be clear in mind! steadfast and pure in heart!
The smallest ill have always, in thy soul,
Rightly disposed, the means of remedy, too,
Always at hand, have it appeased with hope,
Contentment, patience, if all else should fail!
Let every evening find thee to have mastered
Thy best good fortune, in that thou hast set
Thyself, thy soul, on high above it all.

XII.

Make the best of what is.

"How quietly thou bearest what is done!
Unmurmuring, pressing on to something new!"
Canst thou repair the crushed and ruined tower?
Drive back the ocean to its thousand springs?
Then let the ocean be, and sail it wisely!
The past event is now an element;
The words and deeds of man are in like wise
An ocean flowing from a thousand springs,
The works of man, too, become element, —
Let it be land, then, and drop in thy seed.
And should I wish my wife had borne to me
A son, instead of daughter; should I only
Wish that this leaf, just fallen from the tree
Had been so wafted as to lie one inch
From where it is, — lo! then I foolishly
Should wish a wholly different world had come!
Should wish the sounding, swift obedience
Of faithful elements not to have been,
And man's free art and soul not to exist, —
Should wish that God were not, who willed it so.
And were a piece of human littleness
— Such as a word is, and the greatest deed, —
In this *perpetually changing* world,
With man's perpetually changing heart,
Worth having God not be! Thou smil'st! But hear now:
What has been till to-day, how hinders it
That thou shouldst bring forth what is purely good
Out of thy heart! and bring it into life!

And propagate the good ! and extirpate
The evil utterly, and leave it dead!
In the good man 't is evil, properly,
First wakes the opposing good and beautiful, —
As the red rose blooms from the earth's black mould.
This thou canst always do resistlessly
With — man's *omnipotence* — *with all thy might.*

XIII.

Enjoy simply the common Lot.

Mistrust whatever is extraordinary !
For that which is uncommon is abortive,
Something that could not think greatly enough
To be as simply still as Nature is,
And counting itself higher, was more mean.
The world, in sooth, is always like a child !
The old, the holy immemorial old,
It leaves scarce noticed, like the sun ; as child,
Indeed, has many a one looked up at it, —
That is, forsooth, the commonplace ! 'T is naught
To what is new and strange. None looks at that,
None points it out. The peoples sweep along
In close and uniform ranks before our eyes
Like a long troop of horsemen richly dight,
But him, the one there with the wild, red beard,
Him and none else each child has seen ! A king
Was hunchbacked, — and on finest parchment now
Art shows the hunchback exquisitely drawn !
Thus the world's gallery holds strange things alone,
Wonders and wars and tragic histories,
Baffled designs and plots confused and wild, —

Yea, even poor insects in their amber coffin,
And poor sea-spiders that have turned to stone,
The gold-piece pilfered from the crumbling mouth
Of the dried mummy, and the humming-bird, —
That, miserably killed, sad beauty wears, —
This it sets up, and goes its way rejoicing,
While the fair palace of God's common things,
Of the old violets and the brave old stars, —
Only remains the house of heaven and earth,
For wholly common eyes to look upon!
I know no *happy* thing, this world has marked
With honorable name, and though it shows
Ever so great, so high, so beautiful.
What the world knows not, names not, *that* was good,
Was happy; for the commonplace, the old,
Primeval, like the flowers and like the moon,
That always look the same, is best and fairest!
Choose, rather, "to be one day quite forgot,"
Than to have one day a distinguished name, —
And live uncommonly — unhappy now!

XIV.

Live out a whole Life.

Life must be filled with meaning, pith, and worth!
The life of man thou must experience now,
For that, that only, wast thou made a man.
This note, then, clearly: Life itself consists
Of coming and of going, of losing, finding,
Being a sweet and tender child, a man,
Of growing old, being a gray old man,
Of seeing death and dying. Now be sure

Thou art not human, if thou dost not know
Thyself, thy heart, in sorrow and in joy,
In all the range and change of thine own mood
And of the fate that rules thy changeful days.
Whose eyes have never wept, has had no eyes,
He never learned to see as men do see!
Whose heart has never bled, has had no heart,
It never learned to beat as man's heart beats.
He who has never died — has never lived!
The always wretched all too little knows
Of human life, only the darker half, —
For he has no experience of its joy:
The always-happy knows too little of it, —
For he has no experience of its woe;
The sharp-eyed weighs the world, — himself weighs light!
The false is tested and outwitted, too:
The bad is just imprisoned in his heart,
Cut off from all the manifold of life;
The good man is assayed, but melted, too,
Is much misused, as faithful servants are,
And has no easy, pleasant life until
When many round about are also good.
We wait and watch and strive for even life,
Which, like the stream, no longer leaping down
From the steep rock, but sweeping broad and full,
Bear heaviest burdens lightly on its breast.
The most to be congratulated is
The wholly commonplace and simple man,
To whom there 's nothing wholly commonplace.
Who, godlike, and yet feeling as a man
Humanity's sweet limitations, now
Thinks humanly of man and of the earth.
The dream: of being man, is a god's dream

And more than heavenly ! For that dream hast cost
The greatest art, — even art's greatest work,
The greatest Artist's vast expense of toil,
The lustre of the round and azure dome,
The gorgeous decoration of the day,
Of all the sunsets and the sunrises,
The parting curtain of the starry night,
The pains of thousand tender genii :
To set a human child upon her lap, —
The thousand tears, the tender beings all
To sink in a delusion, — in the grave, —
It costs the very God almost his heart,
Just as it does his children, for their sake,
If they are not men ! feeling humanly !

XV.

Men are growing on into Man.

What grows will ripen yet. This, then, is truth :
Man will in holy nature ripen, too,
Just as the nut does, — in *his* heaven-blue shell,
Just as the cluster does, loaded with grapes,
Just as the child does in the mother's womb.
Out of all poets since the hoary eld, —
Out of the poems and the legends all, —
Out of all sages that have said their word,
Out of their words themselves and prophecies, —
Out of all painters, who have wrought their sketch,
Out of all pictures, even of those passed by, —
Out of all good men, who have done their work,
Out of all champions, who have fought the fight
With bodies, souls, dragons, and despotisms,

Down to this hour, and out of all the treasures
Which all shall still to the last day of earth
Conspire to swell with godlike energies, —
Out of all these comes man ! the only one
Among all beings, that forever grows,
While rock and cloud, lion and cypress-tree,
Are all alike, the latest and the first,
Just as one egg is like all other eggs.
Then trust not him who turns this growing shape,
Called man, to stone, who tears him into parts,
Reduces to its roots his sum of power,
Conjures away his soul and stretches him
Upon the rack of the dissecting-board, —
'T is a dead body he exhibits thee !
Not a live congress of harmonious
And gloriously co-operative powers !
No ! wisely thou believest him who says :
No one of all men was the highest man,
Nor will his teaching be the very last,
Nor will his work remain the loveliest ;
Him thou believest and thou lovest him,
Who in the spirit of greatness builds thee up
The great man, — though ideal only now, —
A sign and wonder to learn patience by,
The holy patience of humanity,
The mighty task of man ! and human hope !
The smile, the wrath of hollow spirits moves,
It is the sunny smile of the clear soul !
Look on more calmly now to see one build,
Another sail ; him in the temple there
Burn pious incense to his human gods ;
One praise ; another cavil ; this one climb ;
That other fall and sink ! Look on them all

As the rough metal for a mighty bell
That shall one day have the full ring of heaven,
Wherein each grain by the one tone divine
Is thrilled, which each contributes of itself
With the sweet silvery sound of the whole bell!

XVI.

The poor rich Man.

Naught, naught on earth is wretched to this day —
But man! nor ever was there being or thing
Wretched on earth but man, — alas, how long?
I prophesy fair days to come on earth,
But only then, when each shall clearly see:
The life of man upon the earth is not
A transitory, but a lasting one,
A festival to which from the blue heavens
Come millions, far and near; a standing feast,
A holiday of spirits and a Sabbath.
And now already these uncounted years
The palace has been standing gayly dight
With branches green and garlanded with flowers,
Which every spring God must replace with new,
Because not yet, not yet come other guests
Than cripples, beggars, sorrowing ones and lame,
Who in their sorry garments dare not sit
Before such golden tables, such a glow,
Such pomp and plenty, on the golden seats.
Only at times one hears this man and that
Say softly in his nearest neighbor's ear:
"We are the guests! The palace is our own,
The golden tables and the golden chairs;

Sit down, then! Eat and drink, nor merely break
A bit of bread for hunger from the board!
We none of us need aught but self-respect,
Self-consciousness: of what we are, can do
And must do, that we may not suffer more.
The sun there burns away his oil in vain,
Vainly the stars are lighted up in heaven,
Till light, till power is wakened in our soul.
Come on, ye brave musicians! All ye birds!
Sing me these gentlemen and ladies gay;
Ye fountains murmur, rivers swell their joy;
Thou beauteous earth, beam beauty into them!
Thou radiant, refulgent, rapturous heaven,
And Sun, thou Sun, O speak them holy, Thou
Great, godlike universe, O speak them godlike
And great! A godlike consciousness alone
Drives all exchangers, all who deal in doves
Out of the Temple; every son of God,
He preaches still his Sermon on the Mount,
And round him all the people sit and hear,
And, feasted with the Spirit, need few meats
Out of the baskets, satisfied with love;
And by the word made godly, strong, and great,
Endure no more earthly unworthiness,
Creating mightily a godlike world."
"I hunger!"—"To the table steal meanwhile,
And take a crumb for thee and one for me!"

XVII.

It is Good to have been Good.

'T is better, better far: to have been good,
Than now to be good. To have been good once
Shines back like red of evening on thy life;
It has spread out a solid ground for thee,
Has sowed the seed of a rich harvest there.
The having been good helps one be good now
And happy; while the having once been bad
Spoils also the new day, and the new soul
That yearns for better things, embarrasses
The good deed, hinders thee from being glad
And just! It holds of men and *peoples*, too!
Wicked men's works are like dead bodies all,
And come up ghastly on the sea of life!
O let no day be lost then, that might give
Thy life a bottom so that flowers shall come
Up from the sea! Not to be good and pure
And wise till late, can never make thee glad,
But only good and wise. A bitter grief
Is wisdom without joy. Folly itself,
That hits the right, is happier. *Early* then
In *life's day* to do good, will make a man
In life's most cloudy evening glad and blest.

XVIII.

Past Joys bitter,—past Woes sweet.

O tell me this, I pray thee, why past joys
Are bitter to me, and past sorrows sweet!

And has then memory other measurement
Than passing time? Does it transfigure all,
Conjuring away its old life for a *new?*
Why weeps Achilles o'er the deeds he did,
With his dear friend now buried in the earth?
Why does he now weep o'er the joyous days
Which by his side he fought through, lived, enjoyed?
Why does the youthful bridegroom fling himself
Upon the bridal bed of his dead spouse?
Each past delight now stings him to the heart,
And every rapture flown is now a pang,
So that he fain would flee the world himself!
(He has not lost it — for it had gone by
Already, and lives only in his heart;)
He stares upon the moon! in doubt and dread
Sits by the lonely sea, takes in his hand,
Full of amazement, like a child, the flowers,
Buries his senses in the fragrant cup,
Loses himself in thought before the old rocks,
Starts back, and now a star darts by o'erhead
And shoots down rays and sprinkles him therewith!
What now is memory then, — what doeth it?
Memory draws back the curtain that o'erhangs
Darkly our life, reveals to us the bright
Hall of the gods, wherein all things we did,
All things we ever suffered, came to pass —
And in this hall all is so magical,
So fair and charming, wonderful and godlike,
We stand ourselves therein so heavenly-young,
Our loves all seem therein so heavenly,
So fair, so dear, so deathless in their love, —
The *holiness of being* dawns on us!
What we have suffered with such godlike shapes,

That was no pain, it was felicity,
'T was life, this very, holy life itself.
And what enraptures us, is now first found
Wholly unutterable, and behold,
Where overfulness strikes the mortal dumb,
There the poor being finds relief in tears, —
This double being, that is like a glass
Of mountain crystal: crystal — and a glass!

XIX.

Reap daily the Harvest of Humanity.

Thou reapest bread from off thy field of wheat
Once every year. Come, I will show thee now
A harvest thou canst gather every day,
And where thou hast not sowed, but where the stalks
Come up to meet thee, shaking off their grains.
Go thou and reap now on the human field
That bread, for which thou livest on the earth.
'T is the true intercourse with human kind:
To gain from each life-wisdom studiously,
To learn from each one what he knows, can do,
Has done, and what has been his special lot.
He who must teach thee loves to be thy friend,
And grows by teaching better in his heart,
Pondering in silence faults, and what is right!
They all are many thousand times more wise,
Experienced, than one. Thou art but one!
No one man's course in life is like another's.
Musing on many a lot thou seest God's face!
Much slighted people, all respect for thee!
Because thou dwell'st in hovels, goest in rags, —

Because thy hands are black and grimed with earth, —
Because thy face is browned with noonday suns, —
Because thy maidens bear the scent of herbs
And flowers, they walked in, as they mowed the grain,
Therefore, forsooth, the God lives not in thee ?
Therefore come not the sons of God and all
Beauty and greatness out from thee alone ——

. . . .

My breath stops in me for astonishment,
My eyes run down with tears, my thoughts are gone,
I am imprisoned, stifled in the flowers,
Lost like a tone in thousand melodies !

XX.

The Mirror of the Lake a Mirror of the Soul.

In the clear lake the heavens are mirrored here,
O'erspreading with their blue the water's black
As if it were of crystal, yea of diamond,
So without chasm or alarming crack
It bears upon it such enormous load:
The rocks and heavy masses of the hills,
The huge old maples with their ponderous weight,
And such up-piled thick foliage, like light cloud
That softly glides o'er all the images.
Yonder green eminence with its green graves,
And with its open grave, inverted hangs,
In this enchanted picture, as in air;
And that dead man's sad burial, which o'erhead
Goes on with loud, sharp utterance, — it goes on
In tender, heavenly beauty down below ! —
That mirror be a mirror of thy soul !

So gently may it take the forms of earth!
So lightly let it bear the outward load,
So softly glorify the outward woe,
So purely hold the outer loveliness,
So peacefully preserve the open clear!

XXI.

Man is what God yearned to be.

Right well the universal spirit knows
What love is, what is death, what life, and power,
What moves the stars upon their silent course,
What wakes and clothes in beauty earth's fair flowers.
As if the best of mothers trained them up,
As if a God had painted them, who knew
Only to paint, so cunningly he paints,
Colors so beautiful beyond compare
He knows to mix. Thou, thou hast known all this
Long since as spirit, or wilt know it anew,
When thou art naught but spirit, — naught but love, —
Art nothing but Creator; for to love
Is only to create. So live thou now
In plenitude of love, and before all
Create as man things human: make thyself
Man all complete in spotless purity,
And so let God in thee be perfect man.
God cannot be a child now, cannot sleep, —
Too great to be a child, for sleep too wakeful;
God cannot, now, lift from the mother's lap
And kiss a child, as father, — say: I can;
God cannot share the house-rule with a wife,
He cannot bury a wife, — say thou: I can;

He cannot suffer sorrow, — say: I can;
God cannot die, now, say thou: but I can!
Yet do not *say* it only! Let thy "can"
Mean power to do divinely what thou say'st!
If now thou truly canst, canst master this,
How God will be a man, then canst thou do
And master what a human make implies;
And were it wholly mean and miserable
"To be a man," nothing so beautiful
So glorious and so holy as it is
In pure and unconstrained activity, —
If thou canst master that, to be a man,
Then canst thou master things diviner! Now then
Prove it! — The highest art, — a long life-long
In every fortune and in every change.

XXII.

Moral Beauty surviving physical.

The beauteous mother, plunging through the flames,
Has happily snatched her beauteous child from death,
For lo, unscathed, the fair girl lives to her;
Yet has the child's salvation cost the mother
Her charms, her beauty, and her loveliness,
And being herself still young, she must, henceforth,
Be ugly and disfigured for long years.
Yonder she sits now with her maiden, healed,
Hid in the woods, shunning the sight of men.
"Ah, mother dearest! how changed thy looks, alas!
Say, art thou then my own dear mother still?"
So asks the child and makes her glad to think
Of her good deed, and makes her sad to think

Not just of that most bitter loss of hers, —
(For beauty is not a good woman's all),
No, of the fire's rude violence to her,
For ugliness a woman ill can bear.
There then she sits, her lips severely closed,
And gazes on her child. Pure tenderness
And ardent love in which she wellnigh melts,
Break from her brimming eyes and overflow
Her face with radiance, while soft, heavenly meekness
And darkening bitterness and angels' wrath,
Pity, woe, envy, glad congratulation,
Serenity of patience, helplessness,
Rapture, and wretchedness, — all these by turns
Flit to and fro o'er beauty's faded lines,
And make the sad one seem a magic shape.
"Ah, had I perished in the flames," — she thinks, —
"Now were I wholly ashes! and if buried,
Then were I wholly dust! but living thus,
I am no woman more, — yet I am mother!
And is it enough, our children should grow up
To be what we are not, and never were?
Or ceased to be! Shall not each be himself?
May I be good and loving, but no more?"
Then softly I drew near to her and said
With serious tone: "They 've caught this very night
The man who fired your house: — none else than *he*,
The handsome man, who sought thy hand in vain.
Start not, good soul, with terror! rather say:
What shall the man do, who reaps misery
For his misdeed? For misdeeds, misery!
He whom misfortune meets upon the path
Of goodness, has a comfort left him still:
The flame must shine around him evermore

And brighten all his way, which urged him on
To his good deed. If once that fire goes down,
Then sinks his courage, as his life grows dark;
But if he stirs it up, God kindly gives him
A sense of heaven, that bides in every fate.
And to have done a good deed, shields a man
Like a divine hand softly leading him
Through all disaster peacefully to death.
The misery of the bad man is the chain
That draws him back to the ill-fated hour
Of his bad deed and holds him fast to it,
So that he cannot take a forward step,
Nor strive to do so, but with pain and blood;
And like a monstrous beast he wears a ring
Clamped through his soul, that burns him stingingly,
Yet soothingly — for 't is a heavenly fire.
Lo now, — they lead him off to prison there,
The *handsome* youth! Wilt thou exchange with him?

XXIII.

Over-anxiety.

What a small game, forsooth, does each man play
Daily, to win this little life of his,
To buy himself therewith the greater life!
And yet all men live on in cheerful trust
Despite the fact that each one's bread and salt,
His light, his water, and his very joy
Must fall out of the empty air from heaven!
And falls from the rich heaven day after day!
They none of them have aught, how rich, how great,
How honorable soever among men,

But what the old earth, what humanity
From need or pleasure grants to each of them!
And *that* they live with, that they live upon
As trustful, — as the child upon its mother!

XXIV.

Nature's Lesson of Contentment.

Contented Nature lives within herself
A life of blessedness. What she to-day
Is not, that was she yesterday, and what
She was not yesterday, that will she be
To-morrow and through all the coming time.
And this man sees! This should he ne'er forget;
An easy problem has he here to solve,
Things very near each other to unite:
Namely, that he is *man* and *nature* too,
That he is man in nature and that nature
Is man in him. Just this and nothing more.
And yet it seems to him a giant work, —
What even a goose, what even an ass can do:
She, gabbling, is a goose, — and nature, too,
He, singing, is glad nature and an ass,
And takes no thought about those holy powers,
Which, — as the earth blooms up in earthly heaps, —
Have now bloomed out into his own gray shape.
In man will Nature know not *this* alone,
That she is man; in man, too, will she know
That man is nature, that she is herself,
And yet, withal, will gladly be a man.
'T is nature's wisdom, human wisdom; thence
Proceeds what makes man good and prosperous.

If now the flowers should all begin to weep:
"Ah Heaven, we flowers are flowers, we are here,
And know not whence we come, or why we are,
Whither we go, what we shall one day be, —"
And if the leaves should all begin to moan,
And all the birds should cry up in the air,
And all the lions in the woods should roar,
And all the crocodiles howl frightfully:
Ah, heaven, good heavens, say to us what we are;
Tell us, what we shall one day be, O Heaven!
And if the clouds should weep now: we are clouds!
And if the stars should murmur: we are stars!
And even the sun should cry: "I am the sun, —
How terrible! who shall deliver us
From the body of this death!" Wouldst thou not laugh,
And rightfully, at all these fools, O man?
And yet art thou the greatest of all fools,
When thou as man complainest so of man.
How peaceful are the stars above there: stars!
How peaceful are the clouds above there: clouds!
And their blest murmur is the thunder's voice!
Only a deathless being Nature has.
She has not even a second life. Therewith
Be man contented. And whoever only
Hopes for a second life, no third, no fourth,
No thousandth and no hundred-thousandth life,
No such immortal life as Nature has,
Such man would gladly fall away from life
And cannot! Nay, — 't is what he never shall;
And each must be immortal, as she is!
With her, part of her, in her golden halls.

XXV.

The Ten Prohibitions, and the One Commandment.

The ten commandments we from Moses have
Are only prohibitions, not commands,
What Law *forbids* they tell, not what Love *bids*,
Yet high as heaven above us still they stand!
The first and second and third are answered for;
The fourth we are immersed in to the heart.
Before the fifth: "Man! thou shalt not kill man!"
We stand confounded as before a wall
Of rock that barricades our further course.
And not one step humanity can take
Till this, "Thou shalt not kill!" is done away,
And murder — war — and menace, — laid aside.
Three thousand years it took humanity
Only to set its face 'gainst death by man!
Three thousand years ere that is laid away
In the old rubbish-chamber of the earth!
Three thousand years seem needed three times over
The sixth of these *forbiddings* to shake off,
Beauty from love clearly distinguishing:
No more to say, "Who pleases me is mine!"
Nor yet to think, "Whom *I* please, he is mine!"
The seventh, eighth, ninth, and tenth, are all of them
Essentially uprooted with the sixth.
Then, and not till then, ope the gates of love!
A mount appears far distant, far ahead,
Where Jesus stands and still doth preach, preach, preach.
Then from the mountain to each separate home, —
To every heart, — to each pure bridal bed, —
To every word, — again is far, far, far!

Then first begin the holy depths of love
Ineffable, and after the creation
Of Love, — *and not till then, comes Life itself*, —
Pure — beautiful — worthy humanity,
And heavenly glad, — upon the ancient earth!
Because God, by his power of vision, saw
One man, *one* pair alone, by this 't was made
A Paradise. 'T is Paradise again,
When only *man*, one pair, is on the earth.
And when again *one* man is on the earth,
Woman and man, as once in Paradise,
The many will have risen into one!
Into a hand all strength will then have fused,
And what he will, *that* the one man can do.
I pray beforehand, then, good people all,
To leave unvexed the preacher on his mount.
Yet this I swear to, surely as the old,
Old men and times, shall live again no more:
Soon, soon will God be all! Soon God will live!
And now when he comes down to you, into you,
And hid in twofold, threefold, million-fold
Guises, as man, as all men, lives with you;
He will not wear the triple crown of gold,
Nor thrust an order in his button-hole,
Will not be called the Lord of Bethlehem,
Nor sing in cloisters, by no woman blest;
He will not know the art of shooting guns,
To hang a man, or break him on the wheel;
He will not chisel you the naked Venus,
He will not paint for you the Fornarina,
He knows her not, knows only woman, child;
The unalloyed delight of the pure soul,
And what this life of beauty brings with it,

That shall you freely, fearlessly enjoy.
He will not poison in the bridal bed
The bridegroom's lovely bride, he will not strip
The spring-time of its flowers, nor blot from heaven
The morning red, nor scare the lark away
Out of its nest, nor lay, with sudden rage,
The hatchet to the roots of the old vines
On all the mountains, will not crush the worm
That spins the golden silk, nor yet will he
Shatter to pieces all the flutes and harps,
Nor from the lips of any child will he
Snatch the sweet strawberry, nor wrench the ball
From the boy's hand, — see God already live!
Man, live already thou with God's glad heart!
Behold how near and real and kind he is, —
The *Father of the flowers* is childhood's friend!
A children's-friend is friend to all glad things!

XXVI.

Man's three Foes: Pain, Fate, and early Death.

Three things alone still bring distress on man:
Sorrow and destiny and early death.
All woes are in this trefoil gathered up,
Even tyranny and fawning fear of priests.
One time I saw a man of eighty years,
As lively as a youth, and always well,
And he had never known what sorrow was.
Thus had he travelled on in the right way, —
By wisdom, or hap-hazard, travelled on, —
So then there was at that time a right way!
That which has ever prospered to one man,

Shall the more prosper to humanity.
Then strike out sorrow from the lot of men,
And strike out from their lot untimely death, —
Sure in advance that they will find *the* way.
But Fate, *that* is the fear of liberty,
Of man himself and other beings all,
Of the departed, as of living ones,
And even of Nature. What all these have done,
Becomes to each a chain of adamant,
Which only the death-daring spirit rends.
Freedom from fault and error, that alone
Absolves from fate; errors and faults of thine, —
Errors and faults as well of other men!
But who, now, errs and sins? Ah, love alone,
In anxious tremulous precipitancy.
For man must understand even how to love!
Who is it errs then? Holy reason does,
In the eclipse of dark humanity!
And erring is transgression against reason, —
The godlike power resembling love of good, —
And failing is transgression 'gainst the soul.
Naught then but knowledge saves humanity!
The holy science, the complete acquaintance
Of open nature, of the open man;
Even the knowing this: that holy love
Can master lesser arts upon the earth:
"To rescue man from death and banish fate!"
The highest science teaches how to live,
And for an end to live none learns but man.

XXVII.

Life is more than the Means of Life.

A hall alone is not a festival,
Nor are flute, organ, trumpet, viol, harp,
As yet a tone; the noble human voice
Itself no music is, no stirring song!
A camphor-wood, a hill of golden brimstone,
Are yet no fireworks, whole nations are
Not yet a battle; and sun, moon, and stars
Together with this earth, are not the life
So much as of a mole or of a bee, —
Or of a mouse happily lying-in, —
Although their life sounds from the universe,
As from an organ sounds a gentle tone.
Nor yet is wisdom life; wisdom is only
Life's eye and doctrine. Even love itself, —
That is not life, only the spirit of life.
And therefore, as the music from a flute
Is worth far more than the whole flute itself,
While it is wood as yet and called a flute, —
So is thy life better than all the world!
The elements better than the great world-clock
Which from its holy works strikes out and plays
Thy life! And therefore highly prize thy life,
O man, both in thyself and every man!
Tread not the violet willingly to death!
Help every being nobly live its life;
Thou honorest not the living after all
So much as does that sense-endowed God's-work,
Which is and moves for them, and stirs and roars.

XXVIII.

Each Man can have unique Bliss.

His best gifts God bestows on every one,
And leaves to worried sense by multitudes
Of the same kind to vex and craze itself
Out of its life and soul! Well, *in thy sphere*
Thou canst possess whate'er the greatest has.
Well, — thou canst have one cat, like the famed cat
Of Mahomet; and one as faithful dog
As that Ulysses had. But keep ten dogs,
And all the ten are not so true to thee
As one, for even the very dog too knows
What faithful means: grateful for special love;
But thy ten dogs are not a darling dog.
Thou canst have roses too, more beautiful
Than which the Shah of Persia never saw;
One great, bright, silver-beaming star in heaven
Shining more gloriously than the sun
E'er shone on Crœsus; and one wife so fair,
So dear, so true, so blessed in her children,
No Pasha ever bought so beautiful
For heavy gold; and water cystal-clear, —
More sparkling, pure, refreshing, never gushed
In Chios from old Homer's chosen spring;
And daughters, blooming maidens canst thou have,
Dearer than ever proudest empress rocked;
And boys than whom not Moses to his breast
Clasped fairer ones. A frame can gladden thee
With health and lightness, buoyant and unfelt,
Better than ever an Achilles knew;
And thou canst sleep a light, sweet, strengthening sleep,

And thou canst dream deep, sweet, and tender dreams,
Such as ne'er Plato had, nor Adam, when
The Lord of Heaven took woman from his soul;
And thou canst have a cottage, still and cool
And friendly, as Caserta cannot boast, —
And merriment and love and joy therein,
As ever ear in Zarskoisielo hears;
Thou in thy house canst be a patriarch,
As never people yet obeyed a king,
Loved and was loved, and eyed him hourly, gladly!
A fresh eye can array the world for thee
In colors bright as childhood ever saw;
And life-long ecstasy, day after day,
A soul can give thee to experience
In this enchanted, beauteous universe,
In its inhabitants and changing scenes,
Divine, as God himself doth feel in man!
And if the great and simple goods of life
Content thee not, nor the fair life itself
That comes to thee with them and out of them,
As fragrance, grace and garlands come from flowers, —
O man, then this is what thy mood declares:
Thou hast perhaps spoiled for thyself the goods
By idle folly, by thy own heart's fault, —
Thou hast them not! Yet, yet, thou still hast time,
O go, go, earn these blessings for thyself, —
Yet needst thou not go far: into thyself
Come home and make thee ready, fit for them!

XXIX.

Stay at Home.

Leave not thy home! Not to be gone for years!
Else were it better for thee, thou should'st die,
And find a new one that is dear to thee.
Man can have nothing better than a home:
A place which is to him, from childhood's hour,
No new one, but a sweet, familiar friend,
Life's Eden, the old Paradise *un*-lost,
Wherein the earliest trees still stand and bloom,
Where the old fountains gurgle, and the same
First holy sun, the sun of childhood, beams
Down through the very same clear blue of heaven,—
Where earth became to him a Father's house.
If thou should'st leave thy home, why then expect
It will, meanwhile, be buried from thy sight,
That the whole world will become strange to thee.
In thy home only knowest thou the men,
Because thou know'st the children, in thy house
Alone thy mood is mild, and hardness there
Is but its name, because all know thee there.
Thou hast no dignity there which hinders thee.
There, meritless, envy assails thee not,
Only at home learn'st thou the lot of man,
And ways of Providence; for human works
And thoughts and fortunes here are plain to thee.
Abroad thou hardly findest God himself,
Save as the sculptor, painter, millionnaire!
Wilt see the ruined homes of ancient men,
Wilt look upon the home of all mankind,
Then visit what, for thee, are barren lands!
Wilt thou be learnéd, then search cities through!

Wilt thou get gold, islands and seas explore!
Wilt thou an office, follow where it leads!
Yet say, is office, gold, or knowledge, life?
Seek'st thou thy life, the highest: to be man,—
Stay in thy home! Not even stir thy foot
From out thy birthplace, stay, if possible,
In the paternal house, and on the spot
Where thou wast born, there also one day die.
O blest, to whom parental industry
And virtue one day leaves a happy home!
Whose life springs forth out of a sire's good name,
As a new fruit grows on the same old tree!
And fortunate the daughter, who, not far
From home and mother by her husband led,
Can secretly slip home to her at eve
To the old hearth whereon the fire still burns,
As if it never had been quenched; who can
With few swift steps bear every little grief
And each great pleasure, thereby lightening both,
To mother's heart, and so enjoy, herself,
The greatest joy, and give the greatest joy
To the dear ones! who so mysteriously
And strangely altered, now, in silver locks,
Love her more tenderly and touchingly!
Who, at the selfsame table where she sat,
And on the selfsame chair, now sets her child,—
Where once her mother, too, sat opposite;
While the old holy form still looks on both,
And notices with rapture,—how they live!
And grow! How grows the holy thing called life!
And blessed is it, if the old sire, too, is
Himself the son, the child, of the old house,
Fresh as a well-spring in the same old spot!

XXX.

Live to Learn, and learn to Live.

Whoso lives wisely, he alone is wise.
But live thou must, must mingle in the throng
Of men with all thy heart and soul and strength,
And bravely help them win the fight of life!
Looking out idly down from a watch-tower,
Thou feelest wounds and conflict, pain, and foe,
But friend and helper, joy and victory not.
Lo, wisdom is enough in this wide world!
Beneath this veil of Nature round about,
Glows love unwearied, power defiant swells,
The artistic Spirit works in all and thee,
The wind has skill thou comprehendest not,
And truth and freedom are the source of things;
And have thou firm faith! On the universe
Light is enough! The sun is not a lamp
Hung up for dead men in a sepulchre,
No, but to light the living to their work.
And what is living?—With the powers of heaven
And energies of earth, while these endure,
Nobly enshrined in human form to appear;—
Light, truth, right, freedom, and pure happiness,
On earth creating, to possess on earth.
Man has no object but to be just man,
The strength *it* tasks is in itself all else!
And long has been so! Now, were he a God,
Who could, throughout all heaven extend himself,
And always say: "I, I have everything,
Therefore am all things; I have hands and feet,
And heart and mind and strength, as none besides;
Yet having hands, I therefore nothing do,

And, having feet, I therefore do not walk,
Because I have a heart, I do not feel,
Because I have a mind, I do not think,
I am a God!" And justly from the depths,
The spirits should cry to him: "Thou art a fool!"
Man, be it not told thee: "Thou art a fool!"
Not worse be thou than one of these field flowers,
That feels at least the sunshine and the spring.
Not duller be thou than the very stone
That mutely feels the weather on the earth,
Freezes and sweats and is dissolved at last.
Feel thou the changes of earth's atmosphere!
Swell thou the life of the great Universe
By thine own fate, by thine own joy and grief,
And thine own death. — One man more in the world
Is a new world more, is forever worth
There having been a God, who should create,
Create the earth and crowd the heaven with stars, —
A soul has prayed within this temple here;
And even though God should vanish, though the temple
Should fall to ruins, — it stood not in vain.
But now whole hosts of spirits pray therein,
Nay, whole processions of whole spirit-hosts:
And thou, O man, art of these spirits one,
As good as they in past and future too,
In worth and dignity, — only be as good,
Then shalt thou equal all in deed and life!

XXXI.

Man's Word the Porch: God's World the Temple.

Mere prefaces to human life's great book,
True words of introduction to the feast,

The text of the great preacher in the temple,
I modestly have given thee, like the boy
Who waits upon the porch of the Lord's house;
Now go thyself in through the temple door,
The very Holy of Holies enter thou,
Tread thou the old oft-thronged and trodden floor,
Feel in the spirit all the heavenly shapes
That ever knelt upon the well-worn steps,
And all that in succession have gone down
Into the holy crypt, stir round thee still!
Look reverently round thee on the long
Procession of the "saints of life," their works
Borne in their hands in sign of gratitude.
Listen in silence to the Preacher's voice,
The invisible, mighty one, who, not with words,
No, but with stars, with sunshine, and with spring,
Autumn and death, with dead men and with graves,
With myriad new-born children, — preaches truth;
Most manifestly, most intelligibly
With men, with generations, — even with Thee.
Thou hear'st him not at all, if not in Thee, —
Then hear, O hear thyself, and so hear Him!
And learn thou the one sentence in thy heart,
Which runs in large, bright letters round the dome,
And ceaseless teaches and proclaims itself:
"Be godly, — thou art in the House of God!
Be good, — else art thou vile and miserable!
Each thing rejoices to be what it is:
O man, rejoice thou, too, to be a man!"

Cambridge: Stereotyped and Printed by Welch, Bigelow, & Co.

www.ingramcontent.com/pod-product-compliance
Lightning Source LLC
LaVergne TN
LVHW021125110826
845150LV00005B/949

9781425550684